The
Core Knowledge™
Series

$e^{i\pi} + 1 = 0$

Resource Books for Children
from Year 1 to Year 6

PRAISE FOR THE CORE KNOWLEDGE UK SERIES

'A strong foundation of knowledge gained in the earliest years of education is such an important asset for children, sparking their imagination and providing the cornerstone for their future learning. I welcome the aim of the Core Knowledge books to do just that and I am sure that they will be valued by many parents wishing to help their children do well at school.'

– Munira Mirza
Deputy Mayor for Education and Culture for London

'Creativity, the arts and design are crucial to the environment and life of every citizen. They should occupy a central place in the curriculum at both primary and secondary levels. The new series published by Civitas, giving examples of how the arts and creativity can play a part in the education of every child, is a real contribution to the teaching of these subjects in all our schools.'

– Sir Nicholas Serota, Director of Tate

'As a parent, I was always interested to know what my child had been learning at school. As a teacher, I was able to share my knowledge with the children in my class. The ideas and information provided by Core Knowledge UK do both. With clear explanations, examples and illustrations, it can help any parent with their child's education. It has helped me ensure that the children in my class have access to old and new ideas, stories and philosophies. I look forward to introducing it further to the pupils at my school and their parents.'

– Sonia Gomez
Primary Teacher and Parent, Greater London, UK

'The book is full of stories, poems, explanations, activities, games and experiments, together with recommendations for outings and further reading. It is attractively produced with many illustrations, diagrams and photos. Each section is written in a style suitable to be read aloud by a parent to a child. The book is not intended to be a complete curriculum nor a textbook or workbook, but is designed to be used by parents wishing to complement and reinforce their child's school education. It will also serve as a practical help and confidence-builder for parents considering or embarking on home education. Civitas has provided a valuable service in publishing a UK edition.'

– *Family Bulletin*,
Published by the Family Education Trust

What Your Year 4 Child Needs to Know

PREPARING YOUR CHILD
FOR A LIFETIME OF LEARNING

Edited by E. D. HIRSCH, JR

General Editors for the Civitas UK edition:
ROBERT WHELAN & TANYA LUBICZ-NAWROCKA

Original illustrations for this edition by MARK BEECH AND GAIL McINTOSH

 Core Knowledge®

Published by

Civitas
55 Tufton Street
London SW1P 3QL

First edition published in the USA in 2002 as *What Your Third Grader Needs to Know*

UK edition published June 2013

ISBN: 978-1-906837-26-6

Book design and layout by Luke Jefford (www.lukejefford.com)

Printed in Great Britain by Berforts Group Ltd, Stevenage, SG1 2BH

Acknowledgements: US edition

Editor-in-Chief of the Core Knowledge Series: E. D. Hirsch, Jr

Text Editors: John Holdren, Susan Tyler Hitchcock

Art Editor: Tricia Emlet

Writers: John Hirsch (Mathematics); Michele Josselyn (Visual Arts); Mary Beth Klee (American History); Barbara Lachman (Music); Deborah Mazotta Prum (World History); Christiana Whittington (Music)

Artists and Photographers: Jonathan Fuqua, Dave Garbot, Steve Henry, Sara Holdren, Phillip Jones, Bob Kirchman, Gail Mcintosh, Mary Michaela Murray, Meg West

Art Research and Permissions: Tricia Emlet

Text Permissions: Jeanne Nicholson Siler

This series has depended on the help, advice and encouragement of two thousand people. Some of those singled out here already know the depth of our gratitude; others may be surprised to find themselves thanked publicly for help they gave quietly and freely for the sake of the enterprise alone. To helpers named and unnamed we are deeply grateful.

Advisers on Multiculturalism: Minerva Allen, Barbara Carey, Frank de Varona, Mick Fedullo, Dorothy Fields, Elizabeth Fox-Genovese, Marcia Galli, Dan Garner, Henry Louis Gates, Cheryl Kulas, Joseph C. Miller, Gerry Raining Bird, Connie Rocha, Dorothy Small, Sharon Stewart-Peregoy, Sterling Stuckey, Marlene Walking Bear, Lucille Watahomigie, Ramona Wilson

Advisers on Elementary Education: Joseph Adelson, Isobel Beck, Paul Bell, Carl Bereiter, David Bjorklund, Constance Jones, Elizabeth LaFuze, J. P. Lutz, Sandra Scarr, Nancy Stein, Phyllis Wilkin

Advisers on Subject Matter: Marilyn Jager Adams, Diane Alavi, Richard Anderson, Judith Birsh, Cheryl Cannard, Paul Gagnon, David Geary, Andrew Gleason, Blair Jones, Connie Juel, Eric Karell, Joseph Kerr, Mary Beth Klee, Michael Lynch, Joseph C. Miller, Jean Osborne, Margaret Redd, Nancy Royal, Mark Rush, Janet Smith, Ralph Smith, Nancy Strother, Nancy Summers, James Trefil, Nancy Wayne, Linda Williams, Lois Williams

Writers and Editors: This revised edition involved a careful reconsideration of material in the first edition of this book and others in the series. In that spirit, we acknowledge previous writers and current editorial staff at the Core Knowledge Foundation: Linda Bevilacqua, Nancy Bryson, Matthew Davis, Marie Hawthorne, Pamela C. Johnson, Blair Logwood Jones, Michael Marshall, James Miller, Eleaine Moran, Kristen Moses, A. Brooke Russell, Peter Ryan, Lindley Shutz, Helen Storey, Souzanne Wright

Conferees, March 1990: Nola Bacci, Joan Baratz-Snowden, Thomasyne Beverley, Thomas Blackton, Angela Burkhalter, Monty Caldwell, Thomas M. Carroll, Laura Chapman, Carol Anne Collins, Lou Corsaro, Henry Cotton, Anne Coughlin, Arletta Dimberg, Debra P. Douglas, Patricia Edwards, Janet Elenbogen, Mick Fedullo, Michele Fomalont, Mamon Gibson, Jean Haines, Barbara Hayes, Stephen Herzog, Helen Kelley, Brenda King, John King, Elizabeth LaFuze, Diana Lam, Nancy Lambert, Doris Langaster, Richard LaPointe, Lloyd Leverton, Madeline Long, Allen Luster, Joseph McGeehan, Janet McLin, Gloria McPhee, Marcia Mallard, William J. Maloney, Judith Matz, John Morabito, Robert Morrill, Roberta Morse, Karen Nathan, Dawn Nichols, Valeta Paige, Mary Perrin, Joseph Piazza, Jeanne Price, Marilyn Rauth, Judith Raybern, Mary Reese, Richard Rice, Wallace Saval, John Saxon, Jan Schwab, Ted Sharp, Diana Smith, Richard Smith, Trevanian Smith, Carol Stevens, Nancy Summers, Michael Terry, Robert Todd, Elois Veltman, Sharon Walker, Mary Ann Ward, Penny Williams, Charles Whiten, Clarke Worthington, Jane York

Schools: Special thanks to Three Oaks Elementary for piloting the original Core Knowledge Sequence in 1990. And thanks to the schools that have offered their advice and suggestions for improving the Core Knowledge Sequence, including (in alphabetical order): Academy Charter School (CO); Coleman Elementary (TX); Coral Reef Elementary (FL); Coronado Village Elementary (TX); Crooksville Elementary (OH); Crossroads Academy (NH); Gesher Jewish Day School (VA); Hawthorne Elementary (TX); Highland Heights Elementary (IN); Joella Good Elementary (FL); Mohegan School-CS 67 (NY); The Morse School (MA); Nichols Hills Elementary (OK); Ridge View Elementary (WA); R. N. Harris Elementary (NC); Southside Elementary (FL); Three Oaks Elementary (FL); Washington Core Knowledge School (CO). And to the many other schools teaching Core Knowledge – too many to name here, and some of whom we have yet to discover – our heartfelt thanks for 'sharing the knowledge'!

Benefactors: The Brown Foundation, The Challenge Foundation, Mrs. E. D. Hirsch, Sr, The Walton Family Foundation.

Our grateful acknowledgment to these persons does not imply that we have taken their (sometimes conflicting) advice in every case, or that each of them endorses all aspects of this project. Responsibility for final decisions must rest with the editors alone. Suggestions for improvements are very welcome, and we wish to thank in advance those who send advice for revising and improving this series.

Acknowledgements: UK edition

General Editors of the UK edition: Robert Whelan & Tanya Lubicz-Nawrocka

Contributing Editor of the UK edition: Nigel Williams

Editor of the Mathematics chapter of the UK edition: Nick Cowen

Editorial Assistant: Catherine Green

Author of British and European Geography and British History: Andrew Phemister

Design and typesetting of the UK edition: Luke Jefford

Original illustrations for the UK edition: Mark Beech

Maps: Jo Moore, Ed Dovey and Mark Otton

Owl illustrations: Mark Otton

Compiling the UK edition of a book that has already become an established classic in the United States has been both a privilege and a challenge. Our first thanks must go to E.D. Hirsch, Jr, Linda Bevilacqua and the team at the Core Knowledge Foundation for sharing with us the fruits of their labours over so many years. We fully share their view that all children deserve access to a first-class education, and we hope that the Civitas edition of the Core Knowledge texts will do as much for children in the UK as the US edition has done for thousands of children in the US and abroad.

Many people have helped us. We are especially grateful for the assistance given to the project by Anne Anderson in Visual Arts; Andrew Phemister in British and European History and Geography; Sean Lang, Chris Gray and Margaret Lenton in History; Chris Cull in Music; Peter Clarke in Mathematics; and Matthew Robinson in Language and Literature. Marilyn Brocklehurst of the Norfolk Children's Book Centre shared her passion for children's books and helped us to find titles for the suggested resources sections.

We are grateful to Gail McIntosh for permission to reproduce her excellent original illustrations from the US edition and for creating new illustrations for us; to Paul Collicutt for adding the dimension of colour to illustrations that were originally black and white; and to all those generous authors, illustrators and copyright owners who have allowed us to reproduce material for this book because they share our passion for bringing to children the very best in words and images.

Thanks to our colleagues past and present at Civitas for their help, especially Emma Lennard, Curriculum Project Director; Annaliese Briggs for help with the UK Sequence; and Janet Russell for help with the text. Special thanks are due to Anastasia de Waal, Head of Family and Education at Civitas, for her help and guidance.

A Note to Teachers

Throughout the book, we have addressed the suggested activities and explanations to 'parents', since you as teachers know your students and will have ideas about how to use the content of this book in relation to the lessons and activities you plan. To discuss using Core Knowledge UK materials in your school, please contact Civitas at 55 Tufton Street, London SW1P 3QL, 020 7799 6677.

Email: coreknowledge@civitas.org.uk

Companion Website

There is a wealth of additional activities, readings and resources to supplement this book available on the Core Knowledge UK website. This includes a Teacher's Portal with teaching ideas and resources, curriculum planning documents and images from the book that are available for use by teachers and home educators. Please visit our website at:

www.coreknowledge.org.uk

About the Editor

E.D. Hirsch, Jr is a professor at the University of Virginia and the author of *The Schools We Need* and the bestselling *Cultural Literacy* and *The Dictionary of Cultural Literacy*. He and his wife, Polly, live in Charlottesville, Virginia, where they raised their three children.

E. D. Hirsch, Jr receives no renumeration for editing the series nor any other renumeration from the Core Knowledge Foundation.

Contents

Language and Literature

History and Geography

Visual Arts

Music

Mathematics

Science

Foreword to the UK Edition of the Core Knowledge Series

This is the fourth in a series of books for parents who want to help their children do well at school. It describes what every child should aim to have learnt by the end of the school year. It is not a description of everything that could be known but rather a guide to the knowledge that children will need to advance to the next stage of their education. Nor is it primarily a textbook, although it could be used as such – along with other teaching resources – if schools wish.

The Core Knowledge series gives parents the tools to judge how effectively their children are being taught. And it provides teachers with clear aims that can be shared with parents, thereby enlisting them in the common cause of getting the best from every child.

Why publish a British version of a book originally designed for American children? For the last 50 years in both Britain and America there has been no consensus about how and what children should be taught. Sometimes knowledge was dismissed as mere 'rote learning', which was contrasted unfavourably with 'critical thinking skills'. Others argued that education should be 'child centred' not 'subject centred'. Professor Hirsch, who inspired the Core Knowledge series, was among the first to see that the retreat from knowledge was misguided. Above all, he showed that to compare 'knowledge' with 'thinking skills' was to make a false contrast. They are not mutually exclusive alternatives. Thinking skills can be 'knowledge-rich' or 'knowledge-lite'. The purpose of a good education is to teach children how to think clearly – to see through dubious reasoning, to avoid being conned, to learn how to question their own assumptions, to discover how to be objective or to argue a case with clarity. Knowledge does not get in the way of reasoning: it's what we reason with.

The Core Knowledge approach has six main strengths.

- It helps parents to bring out the best in their children. It provides a guide to what young people should be learning and helps parents decide on the school best suited to their child.

- It helps teachers. By providing clear expectations that are shared with parents, teachers are better able to benefit every child. Schools are always at their best when parents and teachers work together.

- It helps children to learn on their own initiative. The books are written in language suitable for each year group, so that children can read alone or with their parents.

- It provides more equal opportunities for everyone. Some children do not receive effective support at home, perhaps because some of us did not ourselves get the best education. A good school can do much to make up for lost ground and the Core Knowledge series is designed for this very task. The books describe what every child can learn if given the chance. What's more, many parents find that they learn as much as their children!

- It encourages social cohesion. Britain today has more cultures, ethnic groups and religions than 50 years ago. If we all share in a common stock of knowledge, social solidarity based on mutual respect for our legitimate differences is more likely.

- It strengthens democracy. A free and democratic society depends on the mass of people being well-informed. We often say that modern societies are 'knowledge based'. It's true. People who do not share in the knowledge that is regularly used by television news programmes or in our newspapers are at risk of being misled.

We are keen to work with teachers who share our ideals and who hope to play a leading part in developing this new curriculum in Britain. In co-operation with teachers, we have been evolving lesson plans and teacher resource guides, which are available on our website at www.coreknowledge.org.uk. If any teachers would like their school to be one of the pioneers, please contact Civitas at *coreknowledge@civitas.org.uk*.

David G. Green
Director of Civitas

Introduction to the UK Edition of the Core Knowledge Series for Year 4

The concerns that led Professor Hirsch and others to set up the Core Knowledge Foundation in the USA in 1986 are shared by many in Britain. Civitas has acquired direct experience of the problem through its network of supplementary schools. Beginning with a group of children in the East End of London in 2005, Civitas now runs 22 supplementary schools for over 600 children in different parts of the UK. The children attend once a week, either on Saturdays or after school, for help with English and maths. The children are, for the most part, attending full-time schools in areas with higher-than-average indicators of social deprivation, where academic outcomes are not the best in the country. Some children join supplementary schools at the age of seven, eight or even older, unable to read properly and unable to handle simple addition and subtraction. Our approach in the Civitas Schools has been to employ dedicated teachers with high expectations and a commitment to providing solid learning foundations. Children are assessed annually and it has become quite usual to see them make two or three years of progress in their reading and maths ages over the course of one calendar year.

The concepts that Professor Hirsch mentions in his General Introduction such as 'critical thinking' and 'learning to learn' have been just as prevalent in the UK's schools, where the curriculum has become less knowledge-based and more focused on attaining 'skills', as if the two things can be separated. The acquisition of skills requires knowledge, and a knowledge-poor curriculum is one that condemns pupils – especially children from less advantaged backgrounds – to remain outside the mainstream of attainment and fulfilment. The Core Knowledge Foundation believes that all children should be able to unlock the library of the world's literature; to comprehend the world around them; to know where they stand (literally) on the globe; and to realise the heritage that the history of their country has bestowed on them.

Making a reality of this ideal has been the outstanding achievement of the Core Knowledge Foundation in the hundreds of schools across the USA where its curriculum is being taught, and it is why we so admire the work of Professor Hirsch and his colleagues at the Core Knowledge Foundation.

As Professor Hirsch explains in his General Introduction, the project operates within the overarching framework of the Core Knowledge Sequence, produced by dozens of educators over a gestational period of several years. To bring this sequence into the classroom or the home, the Sequence is fleshed out by a book for each year group. We at Civitas were honoured and delighted to be entrusted by the Core Knowledge Foundation with the task of adapting the books for teachers, parents and pupils in the UK. This has entailed some changes to reflect differences between our cultures, for example, Visual Arts describes pictures in the National Gallery, tapestries in great houses around Britain and needlework prepared for royalty. Our songs come from Wales, Scotland, Ireland and Yorkshire. Elgar and Holst appear in our music chapter and Richard of York helps us to remember the colours of the rainbow. We illustrate the speed of sound with Concorde; British musical nomenclature has been used in the Music chapter and metric rather than imperial measures in Science. We have revised the lists of resources to include books and educational materials readily available in the UK. However, for the most part, the US text has been left intact – because knowledge is universal!

We have adapted the Core Knowledge Sequence for the UK and it is freely available online at http://www.coreknowledge.org.uk/sequence.php. This will enable parents and teachers to understand how the grammar of each subject is unrolled over six years of primary school education. The UK Sequence follows the US Sequence very closely, with a few obvious changes. Maths has been slightly revised to reflect the demands of the National Curriculum; and British history and geography replace American. (American history and geography will be covered under World History and Geography.)

We share the view of the Core Knowledge Foundation that knowledge is best conveyed through subjects, and so we have followed their division of each book into chapters covering Language and Literature, History and Geography, Visual Arts, Music, Mathematics and Science. We will be producing volumes for each year group up to Year 6, and these will tie in with the UK version of the Core Knowledge Sequence.

In most states of the USA, children start their full-time education in Kindergarten when they are five rising six, whereas in the UK children of that age would be starting Year 1, having already spent a year in Reception. For this reason, the first book in Civitas UK Core Knowledge series, *What Your Year 1 Child Needs to Know*, represented, with small alterations, the text of *What Your Kindergartner Needs to Know*. The second book, *What Your Year 2 Child Needs to Know*, followed the text of the next book in the US series, *What Your First Grader Needs to Know*. This volume follows the text of *What Your Third Grader Needs To Know*, published in the USA in 2002.

Robert Whelan
General Editor, Civitas Core Knowledge UK Project

General Introduction to the Core Knowledge Series

I. WHAT IS YOUR CHILD LEARNING IN SCHOOL?

A parent of identical twins sent me a letter in which she expressed concern that her children, who are in the same grade in the same school, are being taught completely different things. How can this be? Because they are in different classrooms; because the teachers in these classrooms have only the vaguest guidelines to follow; in short, because the school, like many in the United States, lacks a definite, specific curriculum.

Many parents would be surprised if they were to examine the curriculum of their child's elementary school. Ask to see your school's curriculum. Does it spell out, in clear and concrete terms, a core of specific content and skills all children at a particular grade level are expected to learn by the end of the school year?

Many curricula speak in general terms of vaguely defined skills, processes and attitudes, often in an abstract, pseudo-technical language that calls, for example, for children to 'analyse patterns and data', or 'investigate the structure and dynamics of living systems', or 'work cooperatively in a group'. Such vagueness evades the central question: what is your child learning in school? It places unreasonable demands upon teachers, and often results in years of schooling marred by repetitions and gaps. Yet another unit on dinosaurs or 'pioneer days'. *Charlotte's Web* for the third time. 'You've never heard of the Bill of Rights?' 'You've never been taught how to add two fractions with unlike denominators?'

When identical twins in two classrooms of the same school have few academic experiences in common, that is cause for concern. When teachers in that school do not know what children in other classrooms are learning in the same grade level, much less in earlier and later grades, they cannot reliably predict that children will come prepared with a shared core of knowledge and skills. For an elementary school to be successful, teachers need a common vision of what they want their students to know and be able to do. They need to have *clear, specific learning goals*, as well as the sense of mutual accountability that comes from shared commitment to helping all children achieve those goals. Lacking both specific goals and mutual accountability, too many schools exist in a state of curricular incoherence, one result of which is that they fall far short of developing the full potential of our children. To address this problem, I started the non-profit Core Knowledge Foundation in 1986. This book and its companion volumes in the Core Knowledge Series are designed to give parents, teachers – and through them, children – a guide to clearly defined learning goals in the form of a carefully sequenced body of knowledge, based upon the specific content guidelines developed by the Core Knowledge Foundation (see below, 'The Consensus Behind the Core Knowledge Sequence').

Core Knowledge is an attempt to define, in a coherent and sequential way, a body of widely used knowledge taken for granted by competent writers and speakers in the United States. Because this knowledge is taken for granted rather than being explained when it is used, it forms a necessary foundation for the higher-order reading, writing and thinking skills that children need for academic and vocational success. The universal attainment of such knowledge should be a central aim of curricula in our elementary schools, just as it is currently the aim in all world-class educational systems.

For reasons explained in the next section, making sure that all young children in the United States possess a core of shared knowledge is a necessary step in developing a first-rate educational system.

II. WHY CORE KNOWLEDGE IS NEEDED

Learning builds on learning: children (and adults) gain new knowledge only by building on what they already know. It is essential to begin building solid foundations of knowledge in the early grades when children are most receptive because, for the vast majority of children, academic deficiencies from the first six grades can *permanently* impair the success of later learning. Poor performance of American students in middle and high school can be traced to shortcomings inherited from elementary schools that have not imparted to children the knowledge and skills they need for further learning.

All of the highest-achieving and most egalitarian elementary school systems in the world (such as those in Sweden, France and Japan) teach their children a specific core of knowledge in each of the first six grades, thus enabling all children to enter each new grade with a secure foundation for further learning. It is time American schools did so as well, for the following reasons:

(1) Commonly shared knowledge makes schooling more effective.

We know that the one-on-one tutorial is the most effective form of schooling, in part because a parent or teacher can provide tailor-made instruction for the individual child. But in a non-tutorial situation – in, for example, a typical classroom with twenty-five or more students – the instructor cannot effectively impart new knowledge to all the students unless each one shares the background knowledge that the lesson is being built upon.

Consider this scenario: in third grade, Ms Franklin is about to begin a unit on early explorers – Columbus, Magellan and others. In her class she has some students who were in Mr Washington's second-grade class last year and some students who were in Ms Johnson's second-grade class. She also has a few students who have moved in from other towns. As Ms Franklin begins the unit on explorers, she asks the children to look at a globe and use their fingers to trace a route across the Atlantic Ocean from Europe to North America. The students who had Mr Washington look blankly at her: they didn't learn that last year. The students who had Ms Johnson, however, eagerly point to the proper places on the globe, while two of the students who came from other towns pipe up and say, 'Columbus and Magellan again? We did that last year.'

When all the students in a class *do* share the relevant background knowledge, a classroom can begin to approach the effectiveness of a tutorial. Even when some children in a class do not have elements of the knowledge they were supposed to acquire in previous grades, the existence of a specifically defined core makes it possible for the teacher or parent to identify and fill the gaps, thus giving all students a chance to fulfill their potential in later grades.

(2) Commonly shared knowledge makes schooling more fair and democratic.

When all the children who enter a grade can be assumed to share some of the same building blocks of knowledge, and when the teacher knows exactly what those building blocks are, then all the students are empowered to learn. In our current system, children from disadvantaged backgrounds too often suffer from unmerited low expectations that translate into watered-down curricula. But if we specify the core of knowledge that all children should share, then we can guarantee equal access to that knowledge and compensate for the academic advantages some students are offered at home. In a Core Knowledge school, *all* children enjoy the benefits of important, challenging knowledge that will provide the foundation for successful later learning.

(3) Commonly shared knowledge helps create cooperation and solidarity in our schools and nation.

Diversity is a hallmark and strength of our nation. American classrooms are usually made up of students from a variety of cultural backgrounds, and those different cultures should be honoured by all students. At the same time, education should create a school-based culture that is common and welcoming to all because it includes knowledge of many cultures and gives all students, no matter what their background, a common foundation for understanding our cultural diversity.

In the next section, I will describe the steps taken by the Core Knowledge Foundation to develop a model of the commonly shared knowledge our children need (which forms the basis for this series of books).

III. THE CONSENSUS BEHIND THE CORE KNOWLEDGE SEQUENCE

The content in this and other volumes in the Core Knowledge Series is based on a document called the *Core Knowledge Sequence*, a grade-by-grade sequence of specific content guidelines in history, geography, mathematics, science, language arts and fine arts. The *Sequence* is not meant to outline the whole of the school curriculum; rather, it offers specific guidelines to knowledge that can reasonably be expected to make up about *half* of any school's curriculum, thus leaving ample room for local requirements and emphases. Teaching a common core of knowledge, such as that articulated in the *Core Knowledge Sequence*, is compatible with a variety of instructional methods and additional subject matters.

The *Core Knowledge Sequence* is the result of a long process of research and consensus building undertaken by the Core Knowledge Foundation. Here is how we achieved the consensus behind the *Core Knowledge Sequence*.

First we analysed the many reports issued by state departments of education and by professional organisations – such as the National Council of Teachers of Mathematics and the American Association for the Advancement of Science – that recommend general outcomes for elementary and secondary education. We also tabulated the knowledge and skills through grade six specified in the successful educational systems of several other countries, including France, Japan, Sweden and West Germany.

In addition, we formed an advisory board on multiculturalism that proposed a specific knowledge of diverse cultural traditions that American children should all share as part of their school-based common culture. We sent the resulting materials to three independent groups of teachers, scholars and scientists around the country, asking them to create a master list of the knowledge children should have by the end of grade six. About 150 teachers (including college professors, scientists and administrators) were involved in this initial step.

These items were amalgamated into a master plan, and further groups of teachers and specialists were asked to agree on a grade-by-grade sequence of the items. That sequence was then sent to some one hundred educators and specialists who participated in a national conference that was called to hammer out a working agreement on an appropriate core of knowledge for the first six grades.

This important meeting took place in March 1990. The conferees were elementary school teachers, curriculum specialists, scientists, science writers, officers of national organisations, representatives of ethnic groups, district superintendents and school principals from across the country. A total of twenty-four working groups decided on revisions in the *Core Knowledge Sequence*. The resulting provisional *Sequence* was further fine-tuned during a year of implementation at a pioneering school, Three Oaks Elementary in Lee County, Florida.

In only a few years, many more schools – urban and rural, rich and poor, public and private – joined in the effort to teach Core Knowledge. Based largely on suggestions from these schools, the *Core Knowledge Sequence* was revised in 1995: separate guidelines were added for kindergarten, and a few topics in other grades were added, omitted or moved from one grade to another, in order to create an even more coherent sequence for learning. Revised editions of the books in the Core Knowledge Series reflect the revisions in the *Sequence*. Based on the principle of learning from experience, the Core Knowledge Foundation continues to work with schools and advisors to 'fine-tune' the *Sequence*, and is also conducting research that will lead to the publication of guidelines for grades seven and eight, as well as for preschool. (*The Core Knowledge Sequence UK* can be downloaded from the Civitas Core Knowledge UK website www.coreknowledge.org.uk/sequence.php)

IV. THE NATURE OF THIS SERIES

The books in this series are designed to give a convenient and engaging introduction to the knowledge specified in the *Core Knowledge Sequence*. These are resource books, addressed primarily to parents, but which we hope will be useful tools for both parents and teachers. These books are not intended to replace the local curriculum or school textbooks, but rather to serve as aids to help children gain some of the important knowledge they will need to make progress in school and be effective in society.

Although we have made these books as accessible and useful as we can, parents and teachers should understand that they are not the only means by which the *Core Knowledge Sequence* can be imparted. The books represent a single version of the possibilities inherent in the *Sequence*, and a first step in the Core Knowledge reform effort. We hope that publishers will be stimulated to offer educational software, games, alternative books and other imaginative vehicles based on the *Core Knowledge Sequence*.

These books are not textbooks or workbooks, though when appropriate they do suggest a variety of activities you can do with your child. In these books, we address your child directly, and occasionally ask questions for him or her to think about. The earliest books in the series are intended to be read aloud to children. Even as children become able to read the books on their own, we encourage parents to help their children read more actively by reading along with them and talking about what they are reading. You and your child can read the sections of this book in any order, depending on your child's interests or depending on the topics your child is studying in school, which this book may complement or reinforce. You can skip from section to section and re-read as much as your child likes.

We encourage you to think of this book as a guidebook that opens the way to many paths you and your child can explore. These paths may lead to the library, to many other good books and, if possible, to plays, museums, concerts and other opportunities for knowledge and enrichment. In short, this guidebook recommends places to visit and describes what is important in those places, but only you and your child can make the actual visit, travel the streets and climb the steps.

V. WHAT YOU CAN DO TO HELP IMPROVE EDUCATION

The first step for parents and teachers who are committed to reform is to be sceptical about oversimplified slogans like 'critical thinking' and 'learning to learn'. Such slogans are everywhere and, unfortunately for our schools, their partial insights have been elevated to the level of universal truths. For example: 'What students learn is not important; rather, we must teach students to learn *how* to learn.' 'The child, not the academic subject, is the true focus of education.' 'Do not impose knowledge on children before they are developmentally ready to receive it.' 'Do not bog children down in mere facts, but rather, teach critical-thinking skills.' Who has not heard these sentiments, so admirable and humane, and – up to a point – so true? But these positive sentiments in favour of 'thinking skills' and 'higher understanding' have been turned into negative sentiments against the teaching of important knowledge. Those who have entered the teaching profession over the past 40 years have been taught to scorn important knowledge as 'mere facts', and to see the imparting of this knowledge as somehow injurious to children. Thus it has come about that many educators, armed with partially true slogans, have seemingly taken leave of common sense.

Many parents and teachers have come to the conclusion that elementary education must strike a better balance between the development of the 'whole child' and the more limited but fundamental duty of the school to ensure that all children master a core of knowledge and skills essential to their competence as learners in later grades. But these parents and teachers cannot act on their convictions without access to an agreed upon, concrete sequence of knowledge. Our main motivation in developing the *Core Knowledge Sequence* and this book series has been to give parents and teachers something concrete to work with.

It has been encouraging to see how many teachers, since the first volume in this series was published, have responded to the Core Knowledge reform effort.

Parents and teachers are urged to join in a grassroots effort to strengthen our elementary schools. The place to start is in your own school and district. Insist that your school clearly state the core of *specific* knowledge and skills that each child in a grade must learn. Whether your school's core corresponds exactly to the Core Knowledge model is less important than the existence of some core – which, we hope, will be as solid, coherent, and challenging as the *Core Knowledge Sequence* has proven to be. Inform members of your community about the need for such a specific curriculum, and help make sure that the people who are elected or appointed to your local school board are independent-minded people who will insist that our children have the benefit of a solid, specific, world-class curriculum in each grade.

Share the knowledge!

E. D. Hirsch, Jr
Charlottesville, Virginia

Language and Literature

Reading, Writing and Your Year 4 Child

The best way to nurture your child's reading and writing abilities is to provide rich literary experiences, as well as frequent and varied opportunities to work and play with language.

By the end of Year 3, children should have developed a reading vocabulary of familiar words and should be able to decode the letter-sound patterns of many unfamiliar one- and two-syllable words. During Year 4, as they increase their knowledge about words (including the concepts of syllables, prefixes and suffixes), they put that knowledge to work, decoding unfamiliar multi-syllabic words. If a child has not mastered the skill of decoding simple words, that practice should continue.

By Year 4, the mental process of turning letters into sounds should be nearly automatic. This year, children focus more on meaning as they read. Their reading vocabulary expands tremendously, as does their ability to read longer and more complex literature. They read for information and begin to use non-fiction reference books like children's dictionaries and encyclopaedias. They continue to read a range of both fiction and non-fiction texts, and enjoy longer and more complicated 'chapter books'.

In Year 4, children continue to learn about language as they write it: identifying parts of speech, properly using punctuation and recognising sentence types. They begin to shape their own writing, understanding how paragraphs relate to a larger whole and exerting more control over vocabulary and structure. The teaching of grammar is an important part of any literacy programme, and the topics covered here are not intended to represent an all-encompassing literacy resource. Rather, they point students, teachers and parents towards further work that can be supported by available resources such as Irina Tyk's *Butterfly Grammar* and others included in the list of further resources on page 87.

Parents can do many things to help their children reach these new levels of understanding language:

● **Read aloud to your child.** While Year 4 children are beginning to read on their own, they also still enjoy listening. Continue reading aloud, both fiction and nonfiction, even as your child becomes an independent reader.

- **Have your child read aloud to you.**

- **Visit your local library with your child.**

- **Encourage your child to write letters and/or keep a diary or journal.**

- **Play word games with your child.** Scrabble, Hangman, Boggle and other popular games that involve spelling, word recognition and vocabulary development, combine fun with language facility.

- **Find language wherever you go.** Use road signs, advertising, magazines – the written word all around you – to keep your child thinking and talking about language.

- **Support your child's interests through reading.** When your child shows an interest in something special – insects or tennis, great explorers like Francis Drake or jazz music – go together to your local library to find more to read on that subject.

The more a child reads and writes, the more fluent in language that child becomes. By using these strategies, you communicate the enjoyment of reading and writing and you help build the foundation for learning that will last a lifetime.

Literature

Introduction

This selection of poetry, stories and myths can be read aloud or, in many cases, read independently by Year 4 children. We hope you'll take it as a starting point in your search for more literature for your child to read and enjoy.

We have included both traditional and modern poetry. Poems can be silly – written for the sheer enjoyment of rhythm and rhyme – or they can be serious. Rhythm and rhyme make poetry the perfect literature for a Year 4 child to memorise a few of their favourites.

The stories selected here include classic folktales from many cultures and excerpts from great works of children's literature. Some of them have been chosen as literary links to topics elsewhere in the book. In the case of book-length works, we can provide only short excerpts, hoping that you and your child will read the rest on your own.

This book continues the effort, begun in *What Your Year 3 Child Needs to Know*, to share the wealth of classical mythology. Since Year 4 children learn about ancient Rome, several myths were chosen to convey a sense of Roman history. Likewise we offer some Norse mythology. Therefore, parents can coordinate readings about literature and history. Age-old myths also give parents the opportunity to discuss traditional virtues such as friendship, courage and honesty.

Poetry

For Want of a Nail

(traditional Mother Goose rhyme)

For want of a nail, the shoe was lost,

For want of a shoe, the horse was lost,

For want of a horse, the rider was lost,

For want of a rider, the battle was lost,

For want of a battle, the kingdom was lost,

And all for the want of a horseshoe nail.

Colonel Fazackerley Butterworth-Toast
by Charles Causley

Colonel Fazackerley Butterworth-Toast
Bought an old castle complete with a ghost,
But someone or other forgot to declare
To Colonel Fazak that the spectre was there.

On the very first evening, while waiting to dine,
The Colonel was taking a fine sherry wine,
When the ghost, with a furious flash and a flare,
Shot out of the chimney and shivered, 'Beware!'

Colonel Fazackerley put down his glass
And said, 'My dear fellow, that's really first class!
I just can't conceive how you do it at all.
I imagine you're going to a Fancy Dress Ball?'

At this, the dread ghost made a withering cry.
Said the Colonel (his monocle firm in his eye),
'Now just how you do it, I wish I could think.
Do sit down and tell me, and please have a drink.'

The ghost in his phosphorous cloak gave a roar
And floated about between ceiling and floor.
He walked through a wall and returned through a pane
And backed up the chimney and came down again.

Said the Colonel, 'With laughter I'm feeling quite weak!'
(As trickles of merriment ran down his cheek).
'My house-warming party I hope you won't spurn.
You MUST say you'll come and you'll give us a turn!'

At this, the poor spectre – quite out of his wits –
Proceeded to shake himself almost to bits.
He rattled his chains and he clattered his bones
And he filled the whole castle with mumbles and moans.

But Colonel Fazackerley, just as before,
Was simply delighted and called out, 'Encore!'
At which the ghost vanished, his efforts in vain,
And never was seen at the castle again.

'Oh dear, what a pity!' said Colonel Fazak.
'I don't know his name, so I can't call him back.'
And then with a smile that was hard to define,
Colonel Fazackerley went in to dine.

Eletelephony

by Laura Richards

Once there was an elephant,
Who tried to use the telephant –
No! No! I mean an elephone
Who tried to use the telephone –
(Dear me! I am not certain quite
That even now I've got it right.)

Howe'er it was, he got his trunk
Entangled in the telephunk;
The more he tried to get it free,
The louder buzzed the telephee –
(I fear I'd better drop the song
Of elephop and telephong!)

Dream Variations
by Langston Hughes

To fling my arms wide
In some place of the sun,
To whirl and to dance
Till the white day is done.
Then rest at cool evening
Beneath a tall tree
While night comes on gently,
Dark like me –
That is my dream!

To fling my arms wide
In the face of the sun,
Dance! Whirl! Whirl!
Till the quick day is done.
Rest at pale evening…
A tall, slim tree…
Night coming tenderly
Black like me.

By Myself
by Eloise Greenfield

When I'm by myself
And I close my eyes
I'm a twin
I'm a dimple in a chin
I'm a room full of toys
I'm a squeaky noise
I'm a gospel song
I'm a gong
I'm a leaf turning red
I'm a loaf of brown bread
I'm a whatever I want to be
An anything I care to be
And when I open my eyes
What I care to be
Is me

Do you remember reading other poems by
Eloise Greenfield and Langston Hughes in Year 2?

Ducks' Ditty

by Kenneth Grahame

All along the backwater,
Through the rushes tall,
Ducks are a-dabbling,
Up tails all!

Ducks' tails, drakes' tails,
Yellow feet a-quiver,
Yellow bills all out of sight
Busy in the river!

Slushy green undergrowth
Where the roach swim –
Here we keep our larder,
Cool and full and dim.

Everyone for what he likes!
WE like to be
Heads down, tails up,
Dabbling free!

High in the blue above
Swifts whirl and call –
WE are down a-dabbling
Up tails all!

> This poem comes from *The Wind in the Willows*, which we will be reading on page 32.

Stories

Alice's Adventures in Wonderland

(adapted from the book by Lewis Carroll)

In 1865, Lewis Carroll – whose real name was Charles Dodgson – introduced the world to a girl named Alice and the strange and funny world of Wonderland. Alice's Adventures in Wonderland *was so popular that Carroll wrote another book, called* Through the Looking-Glass and What Alice Found There.

Alice was beginning to get very tired of sitting by her sister on the riverbank and of having nothing to do: once or twice she had peeped into the book her sister was reading, but it had no pictures or conversations in it, 'and what is the use of a book,' thought Alice, 'without pictures or conversations?'

So she was considering, in her own mind (as well as she could, for the hot day made her feel very sleepy and stupid), whether the pleasure of making a daisy-chain would be worth the trouble of getting up and picking the daisies, when suddenly a White Rabbit with pink eyes ran close by her.

There was nothing so very remarkable in that; nor did Alice think it so very much out of the way to hear the Rabbit say to itself, 'Oh dear! Oh dear! I shall be too late!' But when the Rabbit actually *took a watch out of its waistcoat-pocket*, and looked at it, and then hurried on, Alice started to her feet, and burning with curiosity, she ran across the field after it, and was just in time to see it pop down a large rabbithole under the hedge.

In another moment down went Alice after it, never once considering how in the world she was to get out again.

The rabbit-hole dipped suddenly down, so suddenly that Alice found herself falling down what seemed to be a very deep well.

Either the well was very deep, or she fell very slowly, for she had plenty of time as she went down to look about her, and to wonder what was going to happen next. She looked at the sides of the well, and noticed that they were filled with cupboards and bookshelves.

'Well!' thought Alice to herself. 'After such a fall as this, I shall think nothing of tumbling down stairs!' Down, down, down. Would the fall never come to an end? 'I wonder how many miles I've fallen by this time?' she said aloud. 'I must be getting somewhere near the centre of the earth. Let me see: that would be four thousand miles down, I think. I wonder if I shall fall right *through* the earth! How funny it'll seem to come out among the people that walk with their heads downwards! I shall have to ask them what the name of the country is. 'Please, Ma'am, is this New Zealand? Or Australia?'

She felt that she was dozing off when suddenly, thump! thump! down she came upon a heap of sticks and dry leaves.

Alice was not a bit hurt. She looked up: before her was another long passage, and the White Rabbit was hurrying down it. Away Alice went like the wind, and was just in time to hear the Rabbit say, as it turned a corner, 'Oh my ears and whiskers, how late it's getting!' She was close behind it when she turned the corner, but the Rabbit was no longer to be seen. She found herself in a long, low hall.

There were doors all around the hall, but they were all locked. Alice sadly wondered how she was ever to get out again. Suddenly she came upon a little three-legged table, all made of solid glass; there was nothing on it but a tiny golden key. But alas! It would not open any of the doors. However, Alice then came upon a low curtain she had not noticed before, and behind it was a little door about 15 inches high. She tried the little golden key in the lock, and it fitted!

The door led into a small passage, not much larger than a rat-hole. Alice knelt down and looked along the passage into the loveliest garden you ever saw. How she longed to get out of that dark hall, and wander about among those beds of bright flowers and those cool fountains, but she could not even get her head through the doorway.

There seemed to be no use in waiting by the little door, so she went back to the table. This time she found a little bottle on it ('which certainly was not here before,' said Alice), and tied round the neck of the bottle was a paper label with the words 'DRINK ME' printed in large letters.

It was all very well to say 'Drink me', but the wise little Alice was not going to do that in a hurry: 'No, I'll look first,' she said, 'and see whether it's marked "*poison*", or not.' However, this bottle was not marked 'poison', so Alice ventured to taste it, and finding it very nice (it had, in fact, a sort of mixed flavour of cherry-tart, custard, pineapple, roast turkey, toffee, and hot buttered toast), she very soon finished it off.

'What a curious feeling!' said Alice, 'I must be shutting up like a telescope.'

She was now only ten inches high, the right size for going through the little door into that lovely garden. But alas for poor Alice! When she got to the door, she found she had forgotten the little golden key, and when she went back to the table for it, she found she could not possibly reach it. The poor little thing sat down and cried, but soon her eye fell on a little glass box that was under the table: she opened it, and found in it a very small cake, on which the words 'EAT ME' were beautifully marked in currants. 'Well, I'll eat it,' said Alice, and very soon finished off the cake.

We started learning in Year 3 about how to use inches and feet for measuring length.

$$e^{i\pi} + 1 = 0$$

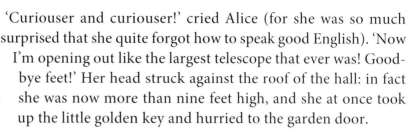

'Curiouser and curiouser!' cried Alice (for she was so much surprised that she quite forgot how to speak good English). 'Now I'm opening out like the largest telescope that ever was! Good-bye feet!' Her head struck against the roof of the hall: in fact she was now more than nine feet high, and she at once took up the little golden key and hurried to the garden door.

Poor Alice! It was as much as she could do, lying down on one side, to look through into the garden with one eye; but to get through was more hopeless than ever: she sat down and began to cry again. She went on, shedding gallons of tears, until there was a large pool around her, about four inches deep and reaching half down the hall.

After a time she heard a pattering of feet in the distance, and she hastily dried her eyes to see what was coming. It was the White Rabbit returning, splendidly dressed, with a pair of white kid gloves in one hand and a large fan in the other. He was muttering to himself, 'Oh! The Duchess! Oh! *Won't* she be a savage if I've kept her waiting!'

Alice felt so desperate that she was ready to ask help of anyone; so when the Rabbit came near her, she began, in a low, timid voice: 'If you please, sir–' The Rabbit started violently, dropped the white kid gloves and the fan, and scurried away into the darkness as fast as he could go.

'Dear, dear!' said Alice. 'How queer everything is today!' As she said this, she looked down at her hands, and was surprised to see that she had put on one of the Rabbit's little white kid gloves. 'How can I have done that?' she thought. 'I must be growing small again.' She was shrinking rapidly, and in another moment, splash! She was up to her chin in salt water. She was in the pool of tears which she had wept when she was nine feet high.

The Crocodile by Lewis Carroll

As Alice becomes small, then large, then small again, she begins to wonder who she is. She decides to recite a poem, to make sure she is still herself, but unfortunately the words come out all wrong!

How doth the little crocodile
Improve his shining tail,
And pour the waters of the Nile
On every golden scale!

How cheerfully he seems to grin!
How neatly spreads his claws,
And welcomes little fishes in
With gently smiling jaws!

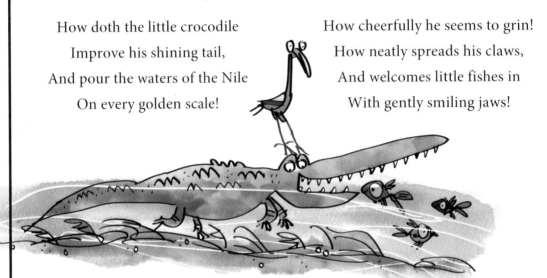

The poem that Alice was trying to remember was a very serious one called 'Against Idleness and Mischief' by Isaac Watts. Here it is:

How doth the little busy bee
Improve each shining hour,
And gather honey all the day,
From every opening flower!

And labours hard to store it well
With the sweet food she makes.

How skilfully she builds her cell!
How neat she spreads the wax!

In books, or work, or healthful play
Let my first years be passed,
That I may give for every day
Some good account at last.

Lewis Carroll has used the same rhythm and rhyme for Alice's nonsense version, perhaps because he was feeling mischievous!

Alice soon makes her way to dry ground and once again encounters the White Rabbit. But the Rabbit disappears, leaving Alice – who has shrunk again – to wander until she comes upon a caterpillar, sitting upon a mushroom and smoking a kind of pipe called a hookah.

Alice stretched herself up on tiptoe and peeped over the edge of the mushroom, and her eyes immediately met those of a large blue caterpillar. The Caterpillar and Alice looked at each other for some time in silence. At last the Caterpillar took the hookah out of its mouth, and addressed her in a languid, sleepy voice.

'Who are *you*?' said the Caterpillar.

Alice replied, rather shyly: 'I – I hardly know, sir, just at present – at least I know who I was when I got up this morning, but I think I must have been changed several times since then.'

'What do you mean by that?' said the Caterpillar sternly. 'Explain yourself!'

'I can't explain myself, I'm afraid, sir,' said Alice, 'because I'm not myself, you see.'

'I don't see,' said the Caterpillar.

'I'm afraid I can't put it more clearly,' Alice replied, 'for being so many different sizes in one day is very confusing.'

'It isn't,' said the Caterpillar.

Alice felt a little irritated at the Caterpillar's making such *very* short remarks. As the Caterpillar seemed to be in a very unpleasant state of mind, she turned away.

'Come back!' the Caterpillar called after her. 'I've something important to say!'

This sounded promising, so Alice turned and came back again.

'Keep your temper,' said the Caterpillar.

'Is that all?' said Alice, swallowing down her anger as well as she could.

'No,' said the Caterpillar.

Alice thought she might as well wait, as she had nothing else to do, and perhaps after all it might tell her something worth hearing. For some minutes it puffed away without speaking, but at last it unfolded its arms, took the hookah out of its mouth again, and said: 'So you think you're changed, do you?'

'I'm afraid I am, sir,' said Alice; 'I can't remember things as I used – and I don't keep the same size for ten minutes together!'

'Can't remember *what* things?' said the Caterpillar.

'Well, I've tried to say "*How Doth the Little Busy Bee*", but it all came different!' Alice replied in a very melancholy voice.

'Repeat, "*You are Old, Father William*",' said the Caterpillar.

Alice folded her hands, and began:

'You are old, Father William,' the young man said,
  'And your hair has become very white;
And yet you incessantly stand on your head –
  Do you think, at your age, it is right?'

'In my youth,' Father William replied to his son,
  'I feared it might injure the brain;
But now that I'm perfectly sure I have none,
  Why, I do it again and again.'

'You are old,' said the youth, 'as I mentioned before,
  And have grown most uncommonly fat;
Yet you turned a back somersault in at the door –
  Pray, what is the reason of that?'

'In my youth,' said the sage, as he shook his grey locks,
  'I kept all my limbs very supple
By the use of this ointment – one shilling the box –
  Allow me to sell you a couple?'

'You are old,' said the youth, 'and your jaws are too weak
For anything tougher than suet;
Yet you finished the goose, with the bones and the beak –
Pray how did you manage to do it?'

'In my youth,' said his father, 'I took to the law,
And argued each case with my wife;
And the muscular strength which it gave to my jaw
Has lasted the rest of my life.'

'You are old,' said the youth, 'one would hardly suppose
That your eye was as steady as ever;
Yet you balanced an eel on the end of your nose –
What made you so awfully clever?'

'I have answered three questions, and that is enough,'
Said his father. 'Don't give yourself airs!
Do you think I can listen all day to such stuff?
Be off, or I'll kick you downstairs!'

'That is not said right,' said the Caterpillar.

'Not *quite* right, I'm afraid,' said Alice, timidly; 'some of the words have got altered.'

'It is wrong from beginning to end,' said the Caterpillar decidedly, and there was silence for some minutes.

The Caterpillar was the first to speak.

'What size do you want to be?' it asked. 'Well, I should like to be a *little* larger, sir, if you wouldn't mind,' said Alice: 'three inches is such a wretched height to be.'

'It is a very good height indeed!' said the Caterpillar, rearing itself up angrily as it spoke (it was exactly three inches high). 'You'll get used to it in time,' he said, and began smoking again.

In a minute or two the Caterpillar took the hookah out of its mouth, and yawned once or twice, and shook itself. Then it got down off the mushroom and crawled away into the grass, remarking as it went, 'One side will make you grow taller, and the other side will make you grow shorter.'

'One side of *what*? The other side of *what*?' thought Alice to herself.

'Of the mushroom,' said the Caterpillar, just as if she had asked it aloud; and in another moment it was out of sight.

Alice stretched her arms around the mushroom and broke off a bit of the edge with each hand. Very carefully, she nibbled first at one and then at the other, and after some violent rising and shrinking, managed to bring herself back to her usual height.

Alice wandered until she came upon a cat – the Cheshire Cat – sitting on a bough of a tree and grinning from ear to ear.

'Cheshire Puss,' she began, rather timidly, 'would you tell me, please, which way I ought to walk from here?'

'That depends a good deal on where you want to get to,' said the Cat.

'I don't care much where,' said Alice.

'Then it doesn't matter which way you go,' said the Cat.

'– so long as I get *somewhere*,' Alice added.

'Oh, you're sure to do that,' said the Cat, 'if you only walk long enough.'

Alice tried another question. 'What sort of people live about here?'

'In *that* direction,' said the Cat, waving its right paw round, 'lives a Hatter, and in *that* direction,' waving the other paw, 'lives a March Hare. Visit either you like: they're both mad.'

'But I don't want to go among mad people,' Alice remarked.

'Oh, you can't help that,' said the Cat. 'We're all mad here.' Then it vanished slowly, beginning with the end of the tail, and ending with the grin, which remained some time after the rest of it had gone.

'Well! I've often seen a cat without a grin,' thought Alice, 'but a grin without a cat! It's the most curious thing I ever saw in my life!'

She had not gone far before she came upon a house, with a table set out under a tree in front of the house. The March Hare and the Mad Hatter were having tea at it; a Dormouse was sitting between them, fast asleep. The table was a large one, but the three were all crowded together at one corner of it. 'No room! No room!' they cried out when they saw Alice coming.

'There's *plenty* of room!' said Alice indignantly, and she sat down in a large arm chair at one end of the table.

'Have some wine,' said the March Hare.

Alice looked all round the table. 'I don't see any wine,' she remarked.

'There isn't any,' said the March Hare.

'Then it wasn't very civil of you to offer it,' said Alice angrily.

'It wasn't very civil of you to sit down without being invited,' said the March Hare.

The Hatter had been looking at Alice for some time and said, 'Why is a raven like a writing desk?'

'Riddles! We shall have some fun now!' thought Alice. 'I believe I can guess that,' she added aloud.

'Do you mean that you think you can find out the answer to it?' said the March Hare.

'Exactly so,' said Alice.

'Then you should say what you mean,' the March Hare went on.

'I do,' Alice replied. 'At least – at least I mean what I say – that's the same thing, you know.'

'Not the same thing a bit!' said the Hatter. 'Why, you might just as well say that "I see what I eat" is the same thing as "I eat what I see"!'

'You might just as well say,' added the March Hare, 'that "I like what I get" is the same thing as "I get what I like"!'

'You might just as well say,' added the Dormouse, which seemed to be talking in its sleep, 'that "I breathe when I sleep" is the same thing as "I sleep when I breathe"!'

'It *is* the same thing with you,' said the Hatter. Then he turned to Alice again and asked, 'Have you guessed the riddle yet?'

'No, I give it up,' Alice replied. 'What's the answer?'

'I haven't the slightest idea,' said the Hatter.

'Nor I,' said the March Hare.

'This,' thought Alice, 'is the stupidest tea-party I ever was at in all my life!' She got up in great disgust, and walked off; the Dormouse fell asleep instantly, and neither of the

others took the least notice of her going, though she looked back once or twice, half hoping that they would call after her: the last time she saw them, they were trying to put the Dormouse into the teapot.

Alice wanders into many more adventures in Wonderland. She meets a walking, talking deck of cards, ruled by a furious Queen of Hearts, who responds to everyone – including Alice – by shouting, 'Off with your head!' You'll enjoy reading about the Queen and Alice in the full book of Alice's Adventures in Wonderland.

Aladdin and the Wonderful Lamp

This story and the next one, 'Ali Baba and the Forty Thieves', come from a book called A Thousand and One Nights. *This book begins with the story of a cruel sultan in Persia who chose a new wife every day and killed her before the next morning. However, one of his wives, a clever young woman called Scheherazade [shuh-HAIR-uh-zahd], outwitted him. When it came to her turn to be the wife of the sultan, she told him a story on their wedding night that was so fascinating that he could not wait to hear the end. But the crafty Scheherazade would not finish her story! She said she was so tired, she would tell the sultan the rest the next day. So, the next morning, the sultan did not kill Scheherazade, because he wanted to hear the end of the story. His wife finished the story she had begun the night before, then started another one. Once again, she refused to tell him the end of the story until the next day so, once again, he did not kill her in the morning. This went on until Scheherazade had told 1,001 stories, by which time the sultan had fallen in love with her and spared her life. 'Aladdin and the Wonderful Lamp' and 'Ali Baba and the Forty Thieves' were two of the stories Scheherazade told. The Russian composer Rimsky-Korsakov wrote musical pieces about Scheherazade and her stories. You can learn more about them in the music chapter of this book, on page 209.*

There was once an idle, good-for-nothing boy called Aladdin. When his father, the tailor, died, Aladdin's mother took up spinning to earn their living.

One day a stranger approached Aladdin.

'Tell me, my son,' said the stranger. 'Are you not the son of the tailor?'

Aladdin answered yes, and the stranger threw his arms around him. 'My dear nephew!' he cried. 'Your father was my brother! And now I learn he is dead!'

Aladdin introduced the man to his mother, who had never in her life heard that her husband had a brother. She received him kindly, though, and when the man promised to set Aladdin up in business as a merchant, she believed him.

But the stranger was really a magician from faraway Africa. He had come to China in search of a magic lamp, known to give all the riches anyone could imagine. To find the lamp, the magician needed someone who would help without asking any questions. He thought Aladdin was just the right person. The next day, the magician came to fetch Aladdin. 'Come with me,' he said. 'I will introduce you to the other merchants.' Then he led the boy out into the country.

They climbed a steep mountain to a spot where no flowers grew. 'Fetch me a pile of sticks to make a fire, and I will show you a wonderful thing,' the magician ordered. Aladdin did as he was told. The magician lit the fire, threw perfumes into it and uttered magical words. The sky darkened and the earth opened at their feet. There before them was a large stone with a brass ring attached.

'Under this stone is a treasure to make you richer than a king,' said the magician. 'Lift the stone by the ring. Go down the stairs. You will pass many riches, but you must touch nothing. You will go into a garden, where you will see a lamp hanging from a fruit tree. Bring that lamp to me. Once you have it, you may gather any of the fruits that you see.'

Aladdin could not believe what he was being asked to do, but he agreed. 'Take this ring,' said the magician, removing it from his finger. 'It will keep you safe from harm.'

Aladdin lifted the stone, stepped down the stairs, and found his way through a hallway of glittering objects, which he took care not to touch. When he found the lamp, he tucked it inside his shirt. Then he couldn't resist filling his pockets with all the glittering things he saw. He didn't know they were precious jewels. He just kept thinking, 'I will gather these glass fruits to play with at home.'

All those jewels weighed Aladdin down, so when he came to the top of the staircase, he could not climb out. 'Give me a hand, Uncle,' he cried.

'First give me the lamp,' the magician answered.

But the lamp was buried deep beneath all the jewels that Aladdin was carrying. 'I cannot reach it now,' he said.

'Hand it up to me,' said the magician.

'But I can't,' Aladdin said.

The magician's anger was growing. 'The lamp!' he cried, for that was all he cared about.

But Aladdin did not want to drop any jewels. 'I will give it to you when I get out,' he said.

The impatient magician uttered a magic chant. The stone rolled back, trapping Aladdin in the cave's black darkness. He called a thousand times for his uncle to help him, but the magician had whisked himself back to Africa. All he wanted was the lamp, and if Aladdin would not help him get that, he cared nothing for Aladdin.

For three days, Aladdin stayed in the pitch-black cave. He wept and shouted. Finally, he put his hands together to pray. As he did so, he happened to rub the ring that the magician had placed on his finger. Instantly, a genie rose before him and said, 'I am the slave of him who wears the ring. What do you wish?'

Aladdin found the genie frightening, but he said, 'Bring me out of this cave!' Hardly had he finished speaking when he found himself outside again. He ran home to tell his mother all that had happened. He showed her the jewels, which she thought were coloured fruit as well. Then he showed her the lamp.

'It is so dirty,' said Aladdin's mother. 'If I clean it, perhaps I could sell it and bring home some food.' She took a cloth and started rubbing it. Suddenly, there appeared a monstrous genie, far bigger than the one who had appeared when Aladdin rubbed the ring.

'I am the slave of her who holds the lamp,' thundered the genie. 'What do you wish?' The poor woman almost fainted with fear. Aladdin commanded, 'We are hungry! Fetch us something to eat.'

In the twinkling of an eye, the genie returned with 12 silver platters piled high with food. Aladdin and his mother ate their fill. Then they sold the silver platters and bought more food.

One day at the market, Aladdin caught a glimpse of the sultan's daughter. She was so beautiful that he fell in love at once. He told his mother that he wanted the princess for his wife.

'Have you lost your senses?' his mother said. 'Your father was a poor tailor!'

'Take the beautiful glass fruit as a gift to the sultan,' Aladdin answered.

His mother agreed. 'O lord sultan,' she said, 'my son, named Aladdin, wishes to marry your daughter.'

The sultan burst out laughing. 'Your son and my daughter?' he boomed. Aladdin's mother opened her handkerchief and displayed the jewels, which lit up the room. 'Never have I seen jewels of such size and radiance,' the sultan thought to himself. 'Your son may

marry my daughter,' he said to the woman, 'but only after he sends 40 slaves, each carrying a golden basin full of jewels like these.'

Hearing the sultan's request, Aladdin rubbed his lamp. The genie reappeared. Aladdin repeated the sultan's wish. Almost instantly, the genie returned with 40 slaves, each carrying on his head a large golden basin filled with pearls and diamonds, rubies and emeralds.

At that, the sultan agreed to let Aladdin marry his daughter.

Aladdin was delighted. He rubbed the lamp and commanded the genie to prepare a wedding in princely style. Slaves brought him rich clothes, sweet perfumes and a splendid horse, which he rode to the wedding. Slaves threw gold pieces into the hands of all the people who lined the streets to see him. He commanded the genie to build a palace right next to the home of the sultan, with kitchens full of golden dishes and stables full of handsome horses. Finally, at Aladdin's request, the genie spread a thick carpet from the sultan's home to Aladdin's palace so his bride's feet would not have to touch the earth.

When the sultan saw such magnificence, he was sure that Aladdin was the right husband for his daughter. They celebrated their wedding with a feast and music that lasted all day and all night. Aladdin thought that his life could not be more perfect.

But danger lurked afar. The magician caught wind of Aladdin's good fortune. 'That lazy boy? Surely this must be the magic of the lamp,' he said, and he whisked himself back to China. He dressed himself as a poor peddler and carried a few shiny lamps in a basket. As he walked by Aladdin's palace, he shouted, 'New lamps for old!'

It just so happened that on that morning, Aladdin had gone out hunting. His wife, the princess, heard the voice from the street. 'We have that ugly old lamp,' she thought. 'I would gladly trade it for a shiny new one.' With that, she handed over Aladdin's lamp to the disguised magician.

Immediately, the magician rubbed the lamp and the genie appeared.

'Take Aladdin's palace and all that it contains,' commanded the magician. 'Set it down in my country in Africa.'

'I hear and I obey,' said the genie.

The next morning, when the sultan looked out the window, both the palace and his daughter had disappeared. He sent his soldiers out, and they dragged Aladdin before the sultan. 'Find my daughter!' he stormed. 'If you fail, you die!'

Poor Aladdin wandered far from the city. He walked beside a river and rubbed his hands, wondering what to do. The genie of the ring appeared once more, asking, 'What do you wish?'

'Bring my palace and my beloved wife home to me,' asked Aladdin.

'Alas,' said the genie, 'that duty belongs only to the genie of the lamp.'

'Then take me to be with my wife.'

Instantly, Aladdin found himself in Africa. His wife greeted him joyfully. When Aladdin heard her story, he knew that the magician had used the lamp to work his evil deed. They hit on a plan to get back the lamp.

While Aladdin kept out of sight, the princess treated the magician to a fine supper. Into his cup of wine, she slipped a poison powder. No sooner had the magician swallowed one gulp of wine than he fell on the floor, dead.

Aladdin ran in and discovered the lamp, hidden inside the magician's sleeve. He rubbed it and the monstrous genie appeared. 'What do you wish?' the genie thundered.

'Take this building with all it contains,' commanded Aladdin, pointing to the palace. 'Carry it to China and set it down beside the sultan's home.'

'I hear and I obey,' replied the genie, and the palace was lifted up into the air.

The next morning, when the sultan arose and looked out the window, he was overjoyed to see his daughter and her palace once again. He ordered a month of celebrations. From then on, Aladdin lived with the princess in peace and pleasure and safety. When the old sultan died, Aladdin took his throne and ruled justly over all people, rich and poor.

Ali Baba and the Forty Thieves

Here is another story from A Thousand and One Nights, *told by Scheherazade to the Persian sultan to save her life.*

Many years ago there lived two brothers in Persia, Cassim and Ali Baba. The elder brother had married the daughter of a rich merchant and lived very well. But Ali Baba had married a poor woman and barely had enough to get by.

One day, as Ali Baba was coming home from cutting wood, a troop of horsemen came riding at full speed towards him. Hiding in the bushes, he watched as the horsemen, who numbered 40, climbed off their horses. Each heaved onto the ground a heavy saddlebag, and Ali Baba began to understand that these were thieves hiding their treasure.

One stood in front of a steep rock. 'Open, sesame!' he cried, and a doorway appeared in the rock. The robbers entered and the door shut behind them. Ali Baba waited quietly. Then the door opened again. The leader of the thieves counted all the men as they passed by him, then cried, 'Shut, sesame!' The door in the rock closed.

When the robbers were out of sight, Ali Baba tried the magic trick for himself. 'Open, sesame!' he called, and the door opened.

Inside was a huge room, filled with bags of treasure and heaps of coins. Ali Baba picked up a few bags of coins – just a few – then he said the magic words that opened the door again. 'Open, sesame!' Once out of the cave, he said, 'Shut, sesame!' The door in the rock closed.

Ali Baba hurried home. To his poor wife, a few bags of coins were a treasure. 'Let me weigh the money, to know how much we have,' she said.

'Just be sure to keep our secret,' Ali Baba said.

His wife ran to Cassim's house to borrow a scale with which to weigh the coins.

'What would my poor sister-in-law need to weigh?' wondered Cassim's wife. She secretly rubbed some wax on the bottom of the scale. When Ali Baba's wife returned it, a shiny gold coin stayed stuck to the wax. 'Do they have so much gold that they must weigh it?' Cassim exclaimed when he heard what had happened.

Now, Cassim was rich, but he was also jealous. Early the next morning he went to his brother and demanded to know where the gold coin came from. Ali Baba told him. 'I will go and fetch some treasure for myself,' said Cassim.

Cassim remembered to say, 'Open, sesame!' To his joy, the door opened wide, showing bags of treasure and heaps of coins. He filled ten bags as full as he could. He was so excited he forgot the magic words. 'Open, barley!' he cried. 'Open, oats!' But nothing he said opened the door. He was locked inside the cave of treasure.

At noon, the robbers returned to their cave. They spoke the magic words and the door in the rock opened. Cassim tried to hide, but he could not escape from 40 thieves. They cut Cassim's body into four quarters and hung them inside the cave.

By night-time, Cassim's wife was worried. Ali Baba knew where to find his brother. He went to the rock and spoke the magic words: 'Open, sesame!' Then he found his worst fears to be true. He wrapped what was left of his brother's body in cloth, laid the bundle on the back of his mule, covered it with branches, and carried it back to his brother's house.

A clever young slave girl named Morgiana worked for Cassim and his wife. When she heard what Ali Baba had brought home, she agreed to help him keep it secret. She ran to the chemist, asking for strong medicine. 'My master is sick unto death,' she said. 'He cannot eat or speak.' Having heard that, no one was surprised to hear the next day that Cassim had died and that his brother, Ali Baba, had moved into his house to console the widow and take care of unfinished business.

Now Morgiana considered Ali Baba her master, and she willingly helped him carry out his plan. She ran to the cobbler's and put two gold pieces into his hand. 'I have a task for you, but it must be kept a secret,' she said. She led him blindfolded to Cassim's house. She asked him to sew Cassim's body back together, so that he might be buried without anyone knowing what had happened to him. She gave the cobbler a third piece of gold for his trouble and led him blindfolded back home again.

When the 40 thieves found Cassim's body missing, they knew that someone still knew the secret of how to get into their cave. They went from person to person throughout the town, trying to discover who it was. One thief happened on the cobbler, who was working at the crack of dawn.

'How can you see your work?' asked the thief. 'It is scarcely light.'

'I have very good eyes,' said the cobbler. 'Yesterday I sewed together a dead body in a room much darker than this.'

'Aha!' thought the thief. To the cobbler he said, 'You must be joking. Show me the house where you did such a strange job.'

'I was blindfolded,' said the cobbler, 'but I think I can remember the way.' He walked down the street, counting his steps as he went, and stopped at Cassim's doorstep.

The thief gave the cobbler a gold piece, thanked him, and sent him on his way. When he asked the neighbours, the thief learnt that Ali Baba had recently lost his brother yet come into great riches. The thief was sure that Ali Baba was the man who had discovered the way into the cave. He marked Ali Baba's door with chalk.

But clever Morgiana noticed the chalk marks on the door. 'Either an enemy plans to do my master wrong or a boy has been playing tricks,' she thought. 'Either way, it is best to guard against all possible evil.' She fetched a piece of chalk and marked three other doors near her master's.

When the thief returned, he was confused by all the chalk marks. He returned to his leader and said he couldn't remember which house the cobbler had shown him. In a rage, his leader killed him on the spot. He sent another thief to find the cobbler, who pointed out Ali Baba's house, which this thief marked with red chalk.

But Morgiana was watching. She marked all the doors up and down the street with red chalk, too. Again, the thief didn't know which house was the right one, and again the leader killed the thief when he found out.

The leader decided to follow the cobbler himself. He made no marks on Ali Baba's door. He just looked at it very carefully, so he would remember it. He went back to his fellow thieves and told them his new plan.

'Bring 19 mules,' he said. 'To each mule, attach two earthen jars, big enough for a man to fit in. Put oil in only one of those jars.' And do you know what he did with the other 37 jars? He made the thieves crawl into them!

$$e^{i\pi} + 1 = 0$$

> How many jars did the leader have? What is 19 mules × 2 jars each? It is 20 + 20 − 1 − 1, since 19 is one less than 20, or 40 − 2 = 38.

The leader of the thieves led the 19 mules carrying 38 jars right up to Ali Baba's door. 'Sir, I have some oil to sell at market tomorrow,' he told Ali Baba. 'Might I stay the night with you?' Ali Baba told Morgiana to show the man to a room and feed him. As the man left the mules behind, he whispered to the thieves in hiding: 'I'll be back at midnight. Come out when you hear my voice.'

As Morgiana was making soup for the stranger, her lamp went out. 'All I need is a little oil for the lamp, just enough to finish cooking,' she said to herself. 'I can borrow a bit from those jars belonging to the stranger.'

So she went outside and cautiously opened the first jar. As she did so, a voice whispered: 'Is it time?'

'No, not yet, be patient,' she answered, wondering. She went from jar to jar, hearing a voice from each and always answering the same way, until she finally came to the jar of oil. The clever girl went back to her kitchen, lit the lamp, then built a great fire of wood, upon which she set a huge black kettle and filled it with oil from the jar outside. She heated that oil until it was boiling, then poured some into each of the jars, killing the thieves inside the jars, one by one. When the leader found out, he ran away into the night, afraid for his own life.

When Morgiana told Ali Baba what had happened, he was so grateful that he offered his slave her freedom. She thanked him, asking that she be allowed to continue living with him and his family.

But that is still not the end of the story! The leader of the 40 thieves came back to town many weeks later, hoping for revenge. He learnt that the son of Cassim owned a shop. He brought treasures from his secret cave and pretended to be a merchant, too. In that way he became friends with the nephew of Ali Baba.

One night, not knowing who this new merchant really was, Ali Baba invited him to dinner. The man came to Ali Baba's house, but refused to eat anything. 'Thank you, no,' the man answered, when he was offered food. 'My doctor says I must eat no salt.'

'Who is this difficult man who eats no salt?' asked Morgiana.

'He is our new friend,' Ali Baba answered.

But Morgiana looked closely and recognised him. Looking even more closely, she saw a dagger hidden in his robe.

Knowing that danger might befall her master, Morgiana dressed like a dancing girl and offered to entertain the visitor after dinner. She danced with grace and spirit. She swept a jewelled dagger through the air as part of the art of her dance. As the leader of the thieves reached to give the dancer a coin of gold, Morgiana plunged the dagger into his heart.

'What have you done?' cried Ali Baba. 'You have murdered my new friend!'

'Nay, master, I have saved your life,' answered Morgiana. She drew back the guest's robe and revealed his hidden dagger.

Again Morgiana had saved the life of Ali Baba. Since she already had her freedom, he found something even more wonderful to give her in thanks. He said that she could marry his nephew, who truly loved her. So Morgiana joined the family of Ali Baba and shared the fortunes of his house.

The Little Match Girl

This is one of many well-known fairy tales written by Hans Christian Andersen, who lived in Denmark. We read his stories 'The Princess and the Pea' in Year 2 and 'The Emperor's New Clothes' in Year 3.

It was terribly cold and nearly dark on the last evening of the old year. Snow was falling fast, and yet a poor little girl, with a bare head and naked feet, roamed through the streets.

It is true she had had on a pair of slippers when she left home, but they were not of much use. They had belonged to her mother, and were so large that she had lost them in running across the street to escape the carriages. She found one, but a boy seized the other and ran away with it. So the little girl went on, her little naked feet blue with the cold.

In an old apron she carried matches. She held a bundle of them in her hands. No one had bought any matches from her the whole day. Shivering with cold and hunger, she crept along. The snowflakes fell on her hair, which hung in lovely curls on her shoulders.

Lights were shining from every window, and there was a fine smell of roast goose in the air. The little girl remembered that it was New Year's Eve. Between two houses, she huddled herself together, but she could not keep out of the cold. She dared not go home, for she had sold no matches and could not take home even a penny of money. Her father would certainly be angry with her. Besides, it was almost as cold at home as here, for the wind howled through the house, even though the holes in the walls and windows which had been stopped up with straw and rags.

Her little hands were almost frozen. Perhaps a burning match might warm her fingers. She drew one out. Scratch! How it sputtered as it burned! It gave a warm, bright light, like a little candle, as she held her hand over it. It was really a wonderful light. It seemed to the little girl that she was sitting by a large iron stove, with polished brass feet and pretty brass ornaments. It seemed so beautifully warm that she stretched out her feet as if to warm them. But then the flame of the match went out, the stove vanished and she had only the half-burned match in her hand.

She rubbed another match on the wall. It burst into flame. Where its light fell, the little girl could see through the wall to a table, covered with a snowy-white tablecloth, with splendid dishes and a steaming roast goose, stuffed with apples and plums. What was still more wonderful, the goose jumped down from the dish with a knife and fork stuck into its breast and waddled across the floor to the little girl. Then the match went out, and there remained nothing but the cold wall before her.

She lit another match, and she found herself sitting under a beautiful Christmas tree, with thousands of candles and twinkling decorations. The little girl stretched her hand out. Then the match went out.

At that, the Christmas lights began to rise up into the sky. They rose higher and higher, until they looked to the little girl like the stars in the sky. Then she saw a star fall, leaving behind it a bright streak of fire.

'Someone is dying,' thought the little girl, for her grandmother, the only person who had ever loved her and who was now dead, had told her that when a star falls, a soul is on its way to heaven. The little girl struck a match and light shone all around her. In the brightness stood her grandmother, clear and shining, kind and loving.

'Grandmother,' cried the girl. 'I know you will vanish like the warm stove, the roast goose and the Christmas tree. Take me with you.' She made haste to light the whole bundle of matches. They glowed with a light that was brighter than the noonday sun, and her grandmother appeared more beautiful than ever. She took the little girl in her arms, and they both flew upward in brightness and joy, far above the earth, where there was no cold or hunger or pain.

As the next day dawned, the poor little girl with pale cheeks and smiling mouth was still there, leaning against the wall. She had been frozen to death on the last evening of the old year. Now the new year's sun rose and shone upon her. The child still sat, in the stiffness of death, holding the bundle of burned matches.

'She tried to warm herself,' said some. No one imagined what beautiful things she had seen, nor into what glory she had entered with her grandmother on New Year's Day.

William Tell

The people of Switzerland have told this legend for a long time. No one knows if William Tell was a real man. His story may be a way of telling about an actual rebellion that took place around 1300.

Many years ago a cruel governor named Gessler ruled over the people of Switzerland. He taxed them heavily, so nothing could be bought or sold unless the governor received some of the money. Many people who did nothing wrong were put into prison for a long time. The Swiss people had much to suffer.

One day Gessler set up a tall pole in the public square of the town called Altdorf. Atop that pole he put his own cap, announcing that all citizens must uncover their heads as they passed by the cap, or else they would be put to death. Guards stood in the square day and night to see that the order was obeyed.

Now, in a small village not far away, there lived a famous hunter by the name of William Tell. No one in all the land could shoot with a bow and arrow as well as he could.

One morning Tell took his little son, Walter, with him into Altdorf on business. He heard the news about Gessler's order, but he could not bring himself to bare his head to a cap atop a pole.

'Take off your hat and bow!' a guard commanded.

'Why should I bow to a cap on a pole?' asked William Tell.

'This man will not uncover his head as he passes by your cap,' the guards reported to Gessler.

'You are said to be the best shot in the mountains,' said Gessler to William Tell. 'I will design a punishment just for you.' He sent a soldier to an orchard for an apple. 'Place this fruit upon the head of your son,' said Gessler. 'Then walk a hundred yards away and shoot that apple with your bow and arrow.'

Tell begged the tyrant to come up with another punishment. 'Obey my order!' roared Gessler. Walter took his place, with the apple on top of his head. Tell drew an arrow from his quiver. He slowly fitted the arrow to the bow and raised them to his shoulder.

'Shoot, Father,' said young Walter firmly. 'I am not afraid. I am staying still.' Tell pulled back his bowstring. Ping! The arrow flew through the air. It pierced the apple, which dropped in two pieces onto the ground. The people watching shouted for joy. As William Tell rushed to embrace his son, a second arrow fell from under his coat.

'Why did you bring a second arrow?' asked Gessler angrily.

'That arrow was for your heart, you tyrant!' William Tell responded. 'If I had hurt my beloved son, you can be sure I would not have missed the mark a second time.'

Legend has it that, in the years to come, William Tell did send an arrow through the heart of Gessler – and set the people of Switzerland free.

The River Bank

adapted from *The Wind in the Willows* by Kenneth Grahame

This episode from The Wind in the Willows *will give you a taste of the wonderful book by Kenneth Grahame, published in 1908. Grahame was born in Scotland in 1859. He worked as a banker and lived in England most of his life. If you enjoy this story, you will like the whole book, full of the adventures of little animals in the English countryside, including Toad, who loves his speedy motorcar.*

The Mole had been working very hard all the morning, spring-cleaning his little home. First with brooms, then with dusters; then on ladders and steps and chairs, with a brush and a pail of whitewash; till he had dust in his throat and eyes, and splashes of whitewash all over his black fur, and an aching back and weary arms. Spring was moving in the air above and in the earth below and around him, penetrating even his dark and lowly little house. It was small wonder, then, that he suddenly flung down his brush on the floor, said 'Bother!' and 'O blow!' and also 'Hang spring-cleaning!' as he bolted out of the house and found himself rolling in the warm grass of a great meadow.

'This is better than whitewashing!' he said to himself. The sunshine struck hot on his fur, soft breezes caressed his heated brow as he pursued his way across the meadow till he reached the hedge on the further side.

He thought his happiness was complete when, as he meandered aimlessly along, suddenly he stood by the edge of a river. Never in his life had he seen a river before. The Mole was bewitched, entranced, fascinated.

As he sat on the grass and looked across the river, a dark hole in the bank opposite, just above the water's edge, caught his eye. As he gazed, something bright and small seemed to twinkle down in the heart of it, vanished, then twinkled once more like a tiny star. Then, as he looked, it winked at him, and so declared itself to be an eye. A small face began gradually to grow up round it, like a frame round a picture.

A brown little face, with whiskers.

Small neat ears and thick silky hair.

It was the Water Rat!

Then the two animals stood and regarded each other cautiously.

'Hullo, Mole!' said the Water Rat.

'Hullo, Rat!' said the Mole.

'Would you like to come over?' enquired the Rat presently.

'Oh, it's all very well to *talk*,' said the Mole, rather pettishly, he being new to a river and riverside life and its ways.

The Rat said nothing, but stooped and unfastened a rope and hauled on it; then lightly stepped into a little boat which the Mole had not observed. It was painted blue outside and white within, and was just the size for two animals.

The Rat sculled smartly across and made fast. Then he held up his forepaw as the Mole stepped gingerly down. 'Now then, step lively!' he said, and the Mole found himself actually seated in the stern of a real boat.

'Do you know, I've never been in a boat before in all my life.'

'What?' cried the Rat, open-mouthed: 'Never been in a – you never – well I – what have you been doing, then?'

'Is it so nice as all that?' asked the Mole shyly, though he was quite prepared to believe it as he leant back in his seat and surveyed the cushions, the oars, the rowlocks and all the fascinating fittings. Then he felt the boat sway lightly under him.

'Nice? It's the *only* thing,' said the Water Rat solemnly, as he leant forward for his stroke. 'Believe me, my young friend, there is *nothing* – absolutely nothing – half so much worth doing as simply messing about in boats.'

'Look ahead, Rat!' cried the Mole suddenly.

It was too late. The boat struck the bank full tilt. The dreamer, the joyous oarsman, lay on his back at the bottom of the boat, his heels in the air.

'– about in boats – or *with* boats,' the Rat went on composedly, picking himself up with a pleasant laugh. 'In or out of 'em, it doesn't matter. Look here! If you've really nothing else on hand this morning, supposing we drop down the river together, and have a long day of it?'

The Mole waggled his toes from sheer happiness, spread his chest with a sigh of full contentment, and leaned back blissfully into the soft cushions. '*What* a day I'm having!' he said. 'Let us start at once!'

'Hold hard a minute, then!' said the Rat. He climbed up into his hole above and, after a short interval, reappeared staggering under a fat, wicker luncheon-basket.

'Shove that under your feet,' he observed to the Mole, as he passed it down into the boat. Then he untied the painter and took the sculls again.

'What's inside it?' asked the Mole, wriggling with curiosity.

'There's cold chicken inside it,' replied the Rat briefly; 'coldtonguecoldhamcoldbeefpickled gherkinssaladfrenchrollscresssandwichespottedmeatgingerbeerlemonadesodawater –'

'O stop, stop,' cried the Mole in ecstasies: 'This is too much!'

'Do you really think so?' enquired the Rat seriously. 'It's only what I always take on these little excursions.'

The Mole never heard a word he was saying. Absorbed in the new life he was entering upon, intoxicated with the sparkle, the ripple, the scents and the sounds and the sunlight, he trailed a paw in the water and dreamed long waking dreams. 'I beg your pardon,' said the Mole, pulling himself together with an effort. 'You must think me very rude; but all this is so new to me. So – this – is – a – river!'

'*The* river,' corrected the Rat.

'And you really live by the river? What a jolly life!'

'By it and with it and on it and in it,' said the Rat. It's my world, and I don't want any other. What it hasn't got is not worth having, and what it doesn't know is not worth knowing.'

'What lies over *there?*' asked the Mole, waving a paw towards a background of woodland that darkly framed the water-meadows on one side of the river.

'That? O, that's just the Wild Wood,' said the Rat shortly. 'We don't go there very much, we river-bankers.'

'Aren't they – aren't they very *nice* people in there?' said the Mole, a trifle nervously.

'Well…' replied the Rat, 'let me see. The squirrels are all right. *And* the rabbits – some of 'em, but rabbits are a mixed lot. And then there's Badger, of course. He lives right in the heart of it; wouldn't live anywhere else, either, if you paid him to do it. Dear old Badger! Nobody interferes with *him*. They'd better not,' he added significantly.

'Why, who *should* interfere with him?' asked the Mole.

'Well, of course – there – are others,' explained the Rat in a hesitating sort of way. 'Weasels – and stoats – and foxes – and so on. They're all right in a way – I'm very good friends with them – pass the time of day when we meet, and all that – but they break out sometimes, there's no denying it, and then – well, you can't really trust them, and that's the fact.'

'And beyond the Wild Wood again?' he asked.

'Beyond the Wild Wood comes the Wide World,' said the Rat. 'And that's something that doesn't matter, either to you or me. I've never been there, and I'm never going, nor you either, if you've got any sense at all. Don't ever refer to it again, please. Now then! Here's our backwater at last, where we're going to lunch.'

The Rat brought the boat alongside the bank and made her fast. The Mole begged as a favour to be allowed to unpack it all by himself; and the Rat was very pleased to indulge him, and to sprawl at full length on the grass and rest, while his excited friend shook out the tablecloth and spread it, took out all the mysterious packets one by one and arranged their contents in due order, still gasping, 'O my! O my!' at each fresh revelation. When all was ready, the Rat said, 'Now, pitch in, old fellow!' and the Mole was indeed very glad to obey, for he had started his spring-cleaning at a very early hour that morning and had not paused for bite or sup.

'Well, well,' said the Rat, when they had finished eating, 'I suppose we ought to be moving. I wonder which of us had better pack the luncheon-basket?' He did not speak as if he was frightfully eager for the treat.

'O, please let me,' said the Mole. So, of course, the Rat let him.

The afternoon sun was getting low as the Rat sculled gently homewards in a dreamy mood, murmuring poetry-things over to himself, and not paying much attention to Mole. But the Mole was very full of lunch, and self-satisfaction and pride, and already quite at home in a boat (so he thought): and presently he said, 'Ratty! Please, *I* want to row, now!'

The Rat shook his head with a smile. 'Not yet, my young friend,' he said, 'wait till you've had a few lessons. It's not so easy as it looks.'

The Mole was quiet for a minute or two. But he began to feel more and more jealous of Rat, sculling so strongly and so easily along, and his pride began to whisper that he could do it every bit as well. He jumped up and seized the sculls, so suddenly, that the Rat, who was gazing out over the water, was taken by surprise and fell backwards off his seat with his legs in the air for the second time, while the triumphant Mole took his place and grabbed the sculls with entire confidence.

'Stop it, you *silly* thing!' cried the Rat, from the bottom of the boat. 'You can't do it! You'll have us over!'

The Mole flung his sculls back with a flourish, and made a great dig at the water. He missed the surface altogether, his legs flew up above his head, and he found himself lying on the top of the prostrate Rat. Greatly alarmed, he made a grab at the side of the boat, and the next moment – *Sploosh*!

Over went the boat, and he found himself struggling in the river.

O my, how cold the water was, and O, how *very* wet it felt. How it sang in his ears as he went down, down, down! How bright and welcome the sun looked as he rose to the surface coughing and spluttering! How black was his despair when he felt himself sinking again! Then a firm paw gripped him by the back of his neck. The Rat propelled the helpless animal to shore, hauled him out, and set him down on the bank, a squashy, pulpy lump of misery.

When the Rat had rubbed him down a bit, and wrung some of the wet out of him, he said, 'Now, then, old fellow! Trot up and down the towing-path as hard as you can, till you're warm and dry again, while I dive for the luncheon-basket.'

So the dismal Mole, wet without and ashamed within, trotted about till he was fairly dry, while the Rat plunged into the water again and dived successfully for the luncheon-basket.

When all was ready for a start once more, the Mole, limp and dejected, took his seat in the stern of the boat. As they set off, he said in a low voice, broken with emotion, 'Ratty, my generous friend! I am very sorry indeed for my foolish and ungrateful conduct. Will you overlook it this once and forgive me, and let things go on as before?'

'That's all right, bless you!' responded the Rat cheerily. 'What's a little wet to a Water Rat? I'm more in the water than out of it most days. Don't you think any more about it; and, look here! I really think you had better come and stop with me for a little time. It's very plain and rough, you know; still, I can make you comfortable. And I'll teach you to row, and to swim, and you'll soon be as handy on the water as any of us.'

The Mole was so touched by his kind manner of speaking that he could find no voice to answer him; and he had to brush away a tear or two with the back of his paw.

When they got home, the Rat made a bright fire in the parlour. He planted the Mole in an arm-chair in front of it, having fetched down a dressing-gown and slippers for him, and told him river stories till supper-time. Supper was a most cheerful meal; but very

shortly afterwards a terribly sleepy Mole had to be escorted upstairs by his considerate host, to the best bedroom, where he soon laid his head on his pillow in great peace and contentment, knowing that his new-found friend the River was lapping the sill of his window.

This day was only the first of many similar ones for the emancipated Mole, each of them longer and full of interest as the ripening summer moved onward. He learnt to swim and to row, and entered into the joy of running water; and with his ear to the reed stems he caught, at intervals, something of what the wind went whispering so constantly among them.

Bertie and the Lion

by Michael Morpurgo

This is an extract from Michael Morpurgo's novel for young readers called The Butterfly Lion. *It is about Bertie, a six-year-old boy who has grown up on a farm in South Africa where his father raises cattle. Bertie has been told that he must never leave the compound – the fenced-in area around the farmhouse – as lions and other dangerous animals might harm him. He sits in a tree watching the animals, especially the lions, as they come to the waterhole. One day he sees a mother lion with a cub that is completely white, which is very rare. Shortly afterwards, he learns that his father has shot the lioness, as she was attacking his cattle, so Bertie knows that the white lion cub must be an orphan.*

One morning, a week or so later, Bertie was woken by a chorus of urgent neighing. He jumped out of his bed and ran to the window. A herd of zebras was scattering away from the waterhole, chased by a couple of hyenas. Then he saw more hyenas, three of them, standing stock still, noses pointing, eyes fixed on the waterhole. It was only now that Bertie saw the lion cub. But this one wasn't white at all. He was covered in mud, with his back to the waterhole, and he was waving a pathetic paw at the hyenas who were beginning to circle. The lion cub had nowhere to run to, and the hyenas were sidling ever closer.

Bertie was downstairs in a flash, leaping off the veranda and racing barefoot across the compound, shouting at the top of his voice. He threw open the gate and charged down the hill towards the waterhole, yelling and screaming and waving his arms like a wild thing. Startled at this sudden intrusion, the hyenas turned tail and ran, but not far. Once within range Bertie hurled a broadside of pebbles at them, and they ran off again, but again not far. Then he was at the waterhole and between the lion cub and the hyenas, shouting at them to go away. They didn't. They stood and watched, uncertain for a while. Then they began to circle again, closer, closer…

That was when the shot rang out. The hyenas bolted into the long grass, and were gone. When Bertie turned round he saw his mother in her nightgown, rifle in hand, running towards him down the hill. He had never seen her run before. Between them they gathered up the mud-matted cub and brought him home. He was too weak to struggle, though he tried. As soon as they had given him some warm milk, they dunked him in the bath to wash him. As the first of the mud came off, Bertie saw he was white underneath.

'You see!' he cried triumphantly. 'He *is* white! He is. I told you, didn't I? He's my white lion!' His mother still could not bring herself to believe it. Five baths later, she had to.

They sat him down by the stove in a washing basket and fed him again, all the milk he could drink, and he drank the lot. Then he lay down and slept. He was still asleep when Bertie's father got back at lunch time. They told him how it had all happened.

'Please, Father. I want to keep him,' Bertie said.

'And so do I,' said his mother. 'We both do.' And she spoke as Bertie had never heard her speak before, her voice strong, determined.

Bertie's father didn't seem to know quite how to reply. He just said: 'We'll talk about it later,' and then he walked out.

They did talk about it later when Bertie was supposed to be in bed. He wasn't, though. He heard them arguing. He was outside the sitting-room door, watching, listening. His father was pacing up and down.

'He'll grow up, you know,' he was saying. 'You can't keep a grown lion, you know that.'

'And you know we can't just throw him to the hyenas,' replied his mother. 'He needs us, and maybe we need him. He'll be someone for Bertie to play with for a while.' And then she added sadly: 'After all, it's not as if he's going to have any brothers and sisters, is it?'

At this, Bertie's father went over to her and kissed her gently on the forehead. It was the only time Bertie had ever seen him kiss her.

'All right then,' he said. 'All right. You can keep your lion.'

So the white lion cub came to live amongst them in the farmhouse. He slept at the end of Bertie's bed. Wherever Bertie went, the lion cub went too – even to the bathroom, where he would watch Bertie have his bath and lick his legs dry afterwards. They were never apart. It was Bertie who saw to the feeding – milk four times a day from one of his father's beer bottles – until later on when the lion cub lapped from a soup bowl. There was impala meat whenever he wanted it, and as he grew – and he grew fast – he wanted more and more of it.

For the first time in his life Bertie was totally happy. The lion cub was all the brothers and sisters he could ever want, all the friends he could ever need. The two of them would sit side by side on the sofa out on the veranda and watch the great red sun go down over Africa, and Bertie would read him *Peter and the Wolf*, and at the end he would always promise him that he would never let him go off to a zoo and live behind bars like the wolf in the story. And the lion cub would look up at Bertie with his trusting amber eyes.

'Why don't you give him a name?' his mother asked one day.

'Because he doesn't need one,' replied Bertie. 'He's a lion, not a person. Lions don't need names.'

Bertie's mother was always wonderfully patient with the lion, no matter how much mess he made, how many cushions he pounced on and ripped apart, no matter how much crockery he smashed. None of it seemed to upset her. And strangely, she was hardly ever ill these days. There was a spring to her step, and her laughter pealed around the house. His father was less happy about it. 'Lions,' he'd mutter on, 'should not live in houses. You should keep him outside in the compound.' But they never did. For both mother and son, the lion had brought new life to their days, life and laughter.

Running Free

It was the best year of Bertie's young life. But when it ended, it ended more painfully than he could ever have imagined. He'd always known that one day when he was older he would have to go away to school, but he had thought and hoped it would not be for a long time yet. He'd simply put it out of his mind.

His father had just returned home from Johannesburg after his yearly business trip. He broke the news at supper that first evening. Bertie knew there was something in the wind. His mother had been sad again in recent days, not sick, just strangely sad. She wouldn't look him in the eye and she winced whenever she tried to smile at him. The lion had just lain down beside him, his head warm on Bertie's feet, when his father cleared his throat and began. It was going to be a lecture. Bertie had had them before often enough, about manners, about being truthful, about the dangers of leaving the compound.

'You'll soon be eight, Bertie,' he said. 'And your mother and I have been doing some thinking. A boy needs a proper education, a good school. Well, we've found just the right place for you, a school near Salisbury in England. Your Uncle George and Aunt Melanie live nearby and have promised to look after you in the holidays, and to visit you from time to time. They'll be father and mother to you for a while. You'll get on with them well enough, I'm sure you will. They are fine, good people. So you'll be off on the ship to

England in July. Your mother will accompany you. She will spend the summer with you in Salisbury, and after she has taken you to your school in September, she'll then return here to the farm. It's all arranged.'

As his heart filled with a terrible dread, all Bertie could think of was his white lion. 'But the lion,' he cried, 'what about the lion?'

'I'm afraid there's something else I have to tell you,' his father said. Looking across at Bertie's mother, he took a deep breath. And then he told him. He told him he had met a man whilst he was in Johannesburg, a Frenchman, a circus owner from France. He was over in Africa looking for lions and elephants to buy for his circus. He liked them young, very young, a year or less, so that he could train them up without too much trouble. Besides, they were easier and cheaper to transport when they were young. He would be coming out to the farm in a few days' time to see the white lion for himself. If he liked what he saw, he would pay good money and take him away.

It was the only time in his life Bertie had ever shouted at his father. 'No! No, you can't!' It was rage that wrung the hot tears from him, but they soon gave way to silent tears of sadness and loss. There was no comforting him, but his mother tried all the same.

'We can't keep him here for ever, Bertie,' she said. 'We always knew that, didn't we? And you've seen how he stands by the fence gazing out into the veld. You've seen him pacing up and down. But we can't just let him out. He'd be all on his own, no mother to protect him. He couldn't cope. He'd be dead in weeks. You know he would.'

'But you can't send him to a circus! You can't!' said Bertie. 'He'll be shut up behind bars. I promised him he never would be. And they'll point at him. They'll laugh at him. He'd rather die. Any animal would.' But he knew as he looked across the table at them that it was hopeless, that their minds were quite made up.

For Bertie the betrayal was total. That night he made up his mind what had to be done. He waited until he heard his father's deep breathing next door. Then, with his white lion at his heels, he crept downstairs in his pyjamas, took down his father's rifle from the rack and stepped out into the night. The compound gate yawned open noisily when he pushed it, but then they were out, out and running free. Bertie had no thought of the dangers around him, only that he must get as far from home as he could before he did it.

The lion padded along beside him, stopping every now and again to sniff the air. A clump of trees became a herd of elephants wandering towards them out of the dawn. Bertie ran for it. He knew how elephants hated lions. He ran and ran till his legs could run no more. As the sun came up over the veld he climbed to the top of a kopje and sat down, his arm round the lion's neck. The time had come.

'Be wild now,' he whispered. 'You've got to be wild. Don't come home. Don't ever come home. They'll put you behind bars. You hear what I'm saying? All my life I'll think of you,

I promise I will. I won't ever forget you.' And he buried his head in the lion's neck and heard the greeting groan from deep inside him. He stood up. 'I'm going now,' he said. 'Don't follow me. Please don't follow me.' And Bertie clambered down off the kopje and walked away.

When he looked back, the lion was still sitting there watching him; but then he stood up, yawned, stretched, licked his lips and sprang down after him. Bertie shouted at him, but he kept coming. He threw sticks. He threw stones. Nothing worked. The lion would stop, but then as soon as Bertie walked on, he simply followed at a safe distance.

'Go back!' Bertie yelled, 'you stupid, stupid lion! I hate you! I hate you! Go back!' But the lion kept loping after him whatever he did, whatever he said.

There was only one thing for it. He didn't want to do it, but he had to. With tears filling his eyes and his mouth, he lifted the rifle to his shoulder and fired over the lion's head. At once the lion turned tail and scampered away through the veld. Bertie fired again. He watched till he could see him no more, and then turned for home. He knew he'd have to face what was coming to him. Maybe his father would strap him – he'd threatened it often enough – but Bertie didn't mind. His lion would have his chance for freedom, maybe not much of one. Anything was better than the bars and whips of a circus.

Would you like to read the rest of The Butterfly Lion? *Michael Morpurgo has written many more books for children, and some of them have animal characters who play an important part in the story, like* Running Wild, Why the Whales Came *and* Kaspar the Prince of Cats. *Joey the horse in* War Horse *actually tells the whole story himself!*

Legends

We study science to learn about the way in which this great universe we live in works. Science tells us about the stars in the sky and the boiling lava under the earth. It explains why continents and oceans are where they are, what makes some countries hot and others cold. However, for thousands of years people had no way of understanding the science behind the wonderful things they saw around them, so they made up stories, passed down from generation to generation, to explain them in another way. These stories are called legends.

Finn MacCool and the Giant's Causeway

Ulster is the most northern of Ireland's ancient kingdoms. Its landscape is fabulously beautiful – it has towering cliffs and rocky hills, winding rivers and scooped-out lakes that look like they could have been made by the hands of slightly crazy giants.

There are many stone tombs here, five thousand years old, made of enormous boulders that could not possibly be lifted by one man, or even a whole family of ordinary men and women. For many years the local people have named them 'Giants' Graves'.

Learn more about Northern Ireland and the Giant's Causeway on page 117.

Stories are told of one great Irish Giant, Finn MacCool, whose most fearsome enemies were the Scottish giants. Finn was so angry, and so determined to get his hands on them, that he built a whole causeway from Ulster across the sea to Scotland. He built it of unusual six-sided cobblestones, so they would fit neatly together like a honeycomb, and they made a very pretty pavement indeed!

One day he shouted a challenge to the Scottish giant Benandonner, 'the Red Man', to cross the causeway and fight him. But as soon as he saw the Scot getting closer and closer on the causeway, he realised Benandonner was much, much bigger than he had imagined! Finn skidaddled back home to the Fort-of-Allen in County Kildare, and he told his wife he'd picked a fight but had thought better of it now.

Finn heard the stamping feet of Benandonner from Kilcock, and when those feet got to Robertstown, Finn had to stuff five pounds of moss into each ear to block out the booming sound. The Red Man's spear was as tall and thick as a Round-Tower, and he used it to knock on the door of the Fort-of-Allen. Finn would not answer the door, so his wife shoved him in the great bath with a couple of sheets over him.

Finn's wife, Oonagh, thought quickly. She opened the door to Benandonner saying: 'Sure 'tis a pity, but Finn is away hunting deer in County Kerry. Would you like to come in anyway and wait? I'll show you into the Great Hall where you can sit down after your journey.'

Oonagh invited the Red Man to look around the room, and showed him what she said were some of Finn's possessions.

'Would you like to put your spear down? Just there next to Finn's.' It was a huge fir tree with a pointed stone at the top.

'Over there is Finn's shield.' It was a block of building-oak as big as four chariot wheels.

'Finn's late for his meal. Will you eat it if I cook his favourite?'

Oonagh cooked a cake of griddle-bread – baked with the iron griddle pressed inside it. The Red Man bit it hungrily, and broke three front teeth. The meat was a strip of hard fat nailed to a block of red timber; two back teeth cracked. He was given a five-gallon bucket of honey-beer to drink.

'Would you like to say hello to the baby? Wait! I'll have to feed her first!'

Oonagh threw a loaf of bread to the huge baby in the bath-cradle and, peeping out from a huge sheet-like dress and bonnet was Finn MacCool himself, contentedly sucking his thumb. Benandonner said he wasn't much good with babies. The honey-beer made him feel woozy, and he asked to go outside to clear his head.

Oonagh showed the Red Man out, where the gardens were scattered about with boulders as tall as the giant.

'Finn and his friends play catch with these rocks. Finn practises by throwing one over the Fort, then running round to catch it before it falls.'

Of course the Red Man tried, but it was so heavy he could only just lift it above his head before dropping it. The blow only ricked his neck – luckily the Scotsman's head was very hard. But it was also full of good sense. He thanked Oonagh for her hospitality and said he would wait no longer, but return to Scotland before the tide came in.

Finn leapt from the cradle, thanked Oonagh for her shrewdness, and chased Benandonner out of Ireland. Passing Portadown, County Antrim, Finn scooped a huge clod of earth out of the ground to fling at the retreating Scot. The hole filled up with water and became the biggest lough in Ireland – Lough Neagh! The clod he flung missed its target and landed in the middle of the Irish Sea – it became The Isle of Man.

Both giants tore up the Giant's Causeway, just leaving the ragged ends at the two shores. And if you go to the north coast of Ulster, or to Staffa, the nearest isle of Scotland, you may visit them today – the ends of the beautiful causeway that was built for giants. But don't worry, those giants are long since in their graves!

The Hunting of the Great Bear

This legend comes from the Iroquois people, a Native American tribe from the eastern part of the United States.

There were four hunters who were brothers. No hunters were as good as they were at following a trail. Once they began tracking their quarry, they never gave up.

One day, in the time when the cold nights return, an urgent message came to the four hunters. A great bear had appeared at a village nearby, so large and powerful that many of the villagers thought it must be some kind of monster. The people of the village were afraid.

Picking up their spears and calling to their small dog, the four hunters set forth for that village. As they came closer, they noticed how quiet the woods were. There were no signs of rabbits or deer. Even the birds were silent. They found where the great bear had reared up on its hind legs and made deep scratches on a pine tree to mark its territory. The tallest of the brothers tried to touch the highest scratch mark with the tip of his spear.

'It is as the people feared,' the first brother said. 'This one we are to hunt is Nyah-gwaheh [NY-ah-GWA-ha], a monster bear.'

'The Nyah-gwaheh has special magic, but that magic will do the bear no good if we find its track,' said the second brother.

'I have always heard that from the old people,' said the third brother. 'The Nyah-gwaheh can only chase a hunter who has not yet found its trail. When you find its trail and begin to chase it, then it must run from you.'

'Brothers,' said the fourth and laziest, 'did we bring along enough food to eat? It may take a long time to catch this big bear. I'm feeling hungry.'

Before long, the four hunters and their small dog reached the village. It was a sad sight to see. There was no fire burning in the centre of the village, and the doors of all the long-houses were closed. No game hung from the racks; no skins were stretched for tanning. All the people looked hungry.

The elder of the village appeared.

'Uncle,' said the tallest brother, 'we have come to help you get rid of the monster.'

Then the laziest brother spoke. 'Uncle, is there some food we can eat? Can we find a place to rest before we start chasing this big bear?'

The second hunter shook his head and smiled. 'My brother is only joking, Uncle,' he said. 'We are going now to pick up the monster bear's trail.'

'I am not sure you can do that, nephews,' the elder said. 'Though we find tracks closer and closer to the doors of our lodges each morning, whenever we try to follow those tracks they disappear.'

The third hunter knelt down and patted the head of their small dog. 'Uncle,' he said, 'that is because they do not have a dog such as ours.' He pointed to the two black spots above the eyes of the small dog. 'Four-Eyes can see any tracks, even those many days old.'

'May Creator's protection be with you,' said the elder.

'I think we should have something to eat first,' said the fourth hunter, but his brothers did not listen. The four hunters walked, following their little dog, who kept lifting up its head, as if to look around with its four eyes.

'Brothers,' the laziest hunter complained, 'don't you think we should rest? We've been walking a long time.' But his brothers paid no attention to him. Though they could see no tracks, they could feel the presence of the Nyah-gwaheh. They knew that if they did not soon find its trail, the monster bear would circle around them, and then they would be the hunted ones.

The laziest brother decided to eat while they walked. He opened his pemmican pouch, and shook out the strips of meat and berries that he had pounded with maple sugar and dried in the sun. Pale, squirming things fell out instead! The magic of the Nyah-gwaheh had changed the food into worms.

> Pemmican is a high-energy food created by Native Americans. Explorers such as Robert Scott and Roald Amundsen, whom we learnt about in Year 2, ate pemmican on their journeys.

'Look what that bear did to my pemmican!' the laziest brother shouted. 'Now I'm getting angry.'

Meanwhile, like a giant shadow, the Nyah-gwaheh was moving through the trees. Its huge teeth shone; its eyes flashed red. Soon it would be behind them, on their trail.

Just then, though, the little dog lifted its head and yelped.

'Eh-heh!' the first brother called.

'Four-Eyes has found the trail,' shouted the second brother.

'We have the track of the Nyah-gwaheh,' said the third brother.

'Big Bear,' the laziest one yelled, 'we are after you now!'

Fear filled the heart of the great bear for the first time, and it began to run. As it broke from the cover of the pines, the four hunters saw it: a gigantic shape, so white as to appear

almost naked. The great bear's strides were long and swifter than a deer's. The four hunters and their little dog were swift as well. The trail led through swamps and thickets. It was easy for the hunters to follow, for the bear pushed everything aside as it ran, even knocking down big trees. They came to a mountain and followed the trail higher and higher, every now and then catching a glimpse of their quarry over the next rise.

But the lazy hunter was getting tired of running. He pretended to fall and twist his ankle. 'Brothers,' he called, 'I have sprained my ankle. You must carry me.'

His brothers did as he asked, two of them carrying him while the third carried his spear. They ran more slowly now, but they were not falling any farther behind. The day turned into night, yet they could still see the white shape ahead of them. They were at the top of the mountain now. The bear was tiring, but so were they. Four-Eyes, the little dog, was close behind the great bear, nipping at its tail as it ran.

The laziest brother asked to be put down. 'I think my leg has got better,' he said. Fresh and rested, he dashed ahead of the others. Just as the great bear turned to bite at the little dog, the laziest brother thrust his spear into the heart of the Nyah-gwaheh. The monster bear fell dead.

By the time the other brothers caught up, the laziest one had built a fire and was cutting up the bear. 'Come on, brothers,' he said. 'Let's eat. All this running has made me hungry!'

So they cooked the meat of the great bear, and its fat sizzled as it dripped into their fire. They ate until even the laziest brother leaned back in contentment. Just then, though, the first brother looked down. 'Brothers,' the second brother exclaimed, 'look below us!'

'We aren't on a mountaintop at all,' said the third brother. 'We are up in the sky.' Below them, thousands of lights sparkled in the darkness. The great bear had indeed been magical, and they had followed it up into the heavens.

Just then their little dog yelped twice. There, where they had piled the bones of their feast, the bear was coming back to life. It rose to its feet and began to run again, Four-Eyes close on its heels. Grabbing up their spears, the four hunters again began to chase the great bear across the skies.

So it was, as the old people say, and so it still is. Each autumn the hunters chase the Great Bear across the skies and kill it. As they cut it up for meat, the blood of the bear falls from the sky and colours the leaves of the maple trees scarlet. As they cook the meat, the dripping fat bleaches the grass white.

If you look in the night-time skies as the seasons change, you can read this story. The Great Bear is the shape some call the Plough (or the Big Dipper), which rotates around the North Star. During the summer, you can see the hunters and their small dog (just barely) in the Plough's handle, running close behind the Great Bear. When autumn comes, the constellation seems to turn upside down. Then, the old people say, the lazy hunter has killed the bear. As more moons pass (which is how the old people talk about months going by), the constellations revolve. The bear slowly rises back on its feet, and the chase begins again.

You can read about constellations, including the Great Bear or Plough, on page 351.

Mythology

Gods, Heroes and Tricksters from Scandinavia

Like the ancient Greeks and Romans, the Vikings told stories to explain things like how the world began, or why we have different seasons, or what happens to people after they die. We call these stories myths.

Norse Gods and Goddesses

The Norse gods lived in a land called Asgard, ruled by the chief god, **Odin** (also called **Woden**). The Vikings believed that the world began when Odin and his brothers fought and killed a terrible frost giant. The earth was made out of the giant's body, the oceans out of his blood, the mountains out of his bones and the trees out of his hair.

In Year 2, we read about the Vikings. The Vikings were also called Norsemen, from a word meaning 'north'. They came from the part of northwest Europe called Scandinavia, which includes the countries of Norway, Sweden, Finland, Denmark and Iceland. Can you find these countries on a map?

We first started reading myths from ancient Greece and Rome in Year 3

Odin was very wise, but he wanted to be wiser. He once went to the Well of Wisdom and sacrificed one of his eyes to drink of its water. That is why many pictures of Odin show him with one empty eye socket. Maidens called the **Valkyries** [VAL-keer-eez] waited on Odin. When a Viking warrior was killed in battle, one of the Valkyries picked up the dead warrior and carried him on her swift warhorse to Valhalla, a great palace in Asgard. In Valhalla, the honoured warriors lived forever, fighting by day and feasting by night.

Odin, the greatest of all the gods in Norse mythology

Odin's oldest son, **Thor**, was the god of thunder. Two goats pulled his chariot through the sky. When he swung his mighty hammer, thunderbolts flew and rain fell onto the earth.

While the Norse gods lived above the clouds, dwarfs and trolls lived in dark, secret caves. A hag named Hel ruled the underworld – also called Hel – where spirits went after death. Our word for the underworld, 'hell', is similar.

Four of the days of the week are named after Norse gods. The day we call Wednesday comes from 'Woden's Day'. From **Tyr**, the Norse god of war, comes 'Tyr's Day', which is our Tuesday. Friday comes from '**Freya**'s Day', after the Norse goddess of love and beauty. Which day of the week do you think might be 'Thor's Day'?

Thor, son of Odin,
the Norse god of thunder

The German composer Richard Wagner [RICK-kart VAHG-ner] wrote a series of operas based on Norse myths called *The Ring of the Nibelung* [NEE-beh-loong]. Wagner set up a theatre in the German town of Bayreuth where his operas are still performed. The theatre is run by his descendants.

The World Tree and the End of the World

The Vikings believed that a giant 'world tree' called **Yggdrasill** [IG-druh-sil] held up the universe. Yggdrasill had three roots. One root stretched to the land of ice. One root reached to Asgard, the land of the gods. And one root stretched to the land of the giants. Three sisters who lived beside the tree controlled everyone's past, present and future. A giant serpent chewed at the roots of the tree. One day the tree would fall and bring down the world, causing a second great battle between the gods and the giants. The Vikings predicted that the giants would win this battle. The world would be destroyed, then begin again – but this time, everything would be perfect.

Loki and the Gifts for the Gods

*Here is a Norse myth about a god named **Loki**, the son of a giant and a god, who loved to cause mischief. Odin invited him to the great feasts of the gods, even though he was always playing tricks on them.*

Thor's wife, **Sif**, had long, golden hair that shimmered like a field of ripe barley grain. Loki knew how much Thor admired his wife's hair. Still, one night as she was sleeping, Loki crept into her room and cut off all of Sif's golden hair!

Loki cuts off Sif's golden hair while she is fast asleep.

Imagine Thor's surprise when he awakened the next morning to find his beautiful wife with nothing but fuzz on her head! Thor knew instantly who had played this trick on him. Thunderbolts seemed to shoot out of his angry eyes at Loki.

'Spare me, Thor!' cried Loki. 'I know just where to go to ask for long locks of golden hair, even more beautiful than those Sif had before.'

Loki travelled beneath the earth, where dwarfs lived in secret caves and hideaways. The dwarfs were so ugly Loki did not even want to look at them, but they were the best craftsmen in all the world.

'What do you want with us?' the dwarfs grumbled. They were never friendly to anyone.

'Dear dwarfs, I have come with a mission from the gods in Asgard,' Loki said. 'Only you can work this magic.'

The only thing that could turn a dwarf even half-friendly was flattery. Loki wondered how much the dwarfs would give him. 'First, Odin needs a spear that will never miss its mark,' he said. 'Second, the gods need a ship that can sail both land and sea.' The dwarfs grunted and grumbled, but Loki kept on. 'And third, beautiful Sif, wife of Thor, needs hair spun of the finest gold, and magic, so that it comes alive as soon as it touches her head.'

The dwarfs could not resist the challenge. They worked all night and day and the next night, too. They made all three of the things that Loki asked for. He tucked the spear under his arm. He folded the ship up and put it in his pocket. He took the hair of pure gold, more beautiful than any human hair could ever be, and draped it across his shoulder. He winked at the dwarfs – that was the only thank-you he gave them – and in a flash he was gone.

On his way back to Asgard, Loki met two more dwarfs, the brothers Brokk and Sindri. 'See these gifts?' he said, showing off. 'I'll bet you can't make anything better, and you can cut off my head if I'm wrong!'

To answer Loki's challenge, Brokk and Sindri created three more gifts fit for the gods. They made a fierce boar with golden bristles. They made a shining golden ring. Then Brokk worked the bellows and Sindri hammered iron on the anvil and together they made a massive hammer. 'We'll put magic into it,' one brother told the other, 'so it will always hit its mark and return to the one who threw it.'

Loki, in the shape of a gadfly, pesters Brokk as he works the bellows.

Loki worried that he would lose the bet. He turned himself into a gadfly and buzzed around their faces. Brokk swatted the fly away from his eyes as he made the hammer's handle, and it came out a bit too short. Loki grabbed the gifts and fled to Asgard, with an angry dwarf close after him.

When Sif received the golden hair, she was overjoyed. Magically, it attached to her head, just as if it had grown there. Odin, greatest of all the gods and father to Thor, took the spear for his own. Odin also claimed the ring, which had the magic power to make eight more rings every ninth night. Another god claimed the golden boar, believing it better than a horse for riding through the darkness. All the gods of Asgard marvelled over the ship, seeing that the wind would fill its sails whenever they wished to travel.

Then Thor picked up the hammer and swung it high above his head. All the gods said it was the best gift of all, because it could defeat the giants. Brokk grinned at Loki, sure now that he had won the bet and ready to cut off Loki's head.

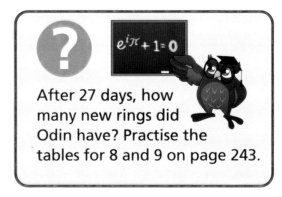

After 27 days, how many new rings did Odin have? Practise the tables for 8 and 9 on page 243.

'But only my head!' cried Loki. 'Not one inch of my neck shall you have!' It was a silly argument, but the gods agreed with Loki.

Enraged, Brokk sewed Loki's lips shut. The gods laughed a deep, thunderous laugh. They were thankful for all Loki had brought them, but they were also happy to have his mouth shut for a little while. As Loki scampered away, struggling to open his lips, Thor forgave him for the mischief that had started this whole adventure.

Myths from Ancient Greece and Rome

Jason and the Golden Fleece

*Here is an ancient Greek myth about the hero named **Jason**. Jason was raised by a centaur, half man and half horse. His adventures fill a whole book, called* The Golden Fleece.

One day long ago, a centaur sat on the bank of a river, speaking to a handsome young man. 'You are now twenty years old,' said the centaur, who had raised this man from childhood. 'The time has come for you to reclaim the kingdom that your step-uncle, **Pelias**, stole from your father. Go, and may the gods be with you.'

Wearing a leopard's skin and sandals tied with golden strings, Jason set out for the kingdom of his step-uncle. He waded across a river, and one of his sandals came loose. When Jason arrived wearing only one sandal, it worried Pelias. A wise man had long ago predicted that he would lose his kingdom to a man with one shoe.

Pelias kept his worries secret, though. He said that Jason should rule the country. 'First there is something that you must do,' said Pelias. 'Bring me the golden fleece, and I will make you king.'

Pelias believed he had given Jason an impossible assignment. Many years before, **Hermes**, the messenger of the gods, had saved a boy from drowning by sending a large golden ram to carry him across the sea. In thanks, the boy had sacrificed the ram to the gods and nailed its golden fleece high upon an oak tree.

Jason and the centaur who raised him

Jason gathered the bravest heroes of the land and set sail in quest of the golden fleece. He named his ship **Argo** and his crew the **Argonauts**. At every island they passed, they met with danger and adventure. They sailed safely through a narrow strait where two huge rocks moved back and forth in the water and crushed anything between them. They finally arrived at the island where the golden fleece hung.

When the island's king heard what Jason and the Argonauts were after, he said: 'I will give you the fleece after you prove your powers. In my fields, you will find two brass bulls. Hitch those bulls to a plough and use them to sow the teeth of a dragon in my fields.'

This king, like Pelias before him, felt certain that he had given Jason an impossible assignment. He knew that the brass bulls were wild and strong and difficult to handle. He also knew that when a dragon's teeth are planted, iron men spring up out of the earth ready to attack.

The king's beautiful daughter, **Medea**, had already fallen in love with Jason. She was ready to do anything – even use her magic spells – to help him. 'Here is some magic

Medea helps Jason just as Ariadne helped Theseus in 'Theseus and the Minotaur', which we read in Year 3.

ointment,' she said to Jason. 'Rub it on your body, your sword and your shield. Then nothing can harm you. And remember: when you have sown the dragon's teeth, throw a great stone among the warriors. Then they will destroy each other.'

Strengthened through Medea's magic, Jason wrestled the bulls to the ground, yoked them to a plough and drove them through the field. The plough cut a deep furrow in the soil. Into that furrow, Jason sowed the dragon's teeth. When the army of iron men sprang up out of the earth, he threw a stone among them. The men turned upon each other, and when the battle was over, Jason was the only man left alive.

The king was furious. 'The golden fleece hangs high on a tree, guarded by a giant dragon,' he said. 'Go and get it for yourself.'

Again the king believed he had given Jason an impossible task, but again Medea helped Jason. They approached the massive dragon, coiled at the foot of the tree. Medea began to sing. At the sound of her voice, the dragon's eyes grew heavy. Slowly, the creature lowered its head and fell asleep.

'Hurry,' Medea whispered. Jason reached up and took hold of the precious treasure. As he and Medea fled, they heard a horrible roar as the dragon awoke and found its treasure stolen.

Their ship, the Argo, awaited them. With a wild leap, Jason and Medea were on board. The Argonauts rowed the ship swiftly, leaving the monster spitting fire behind them. Jason's step-uncle had never expected to see him

Medea charms the serpent that guards the golden fleece.

again, but the young hero sailed back victorious. Through bravery and magic, he had won the golden fleece.

Perseus and Medusa

*This ancient myth describes the **Gorgons**, frightening female monsters with snakes for hair.*

There was once a lovely young woman, so lovely that **Zeus** himself, the king of the gods, fell in love with her. Together they had a son, named **Perseus**. The father of the young woman was horrified, because it had been predicted that he would be killed by his own grandson. So he put his daughter and her baby boy into a chest and threw them into the sea.

They floated for many days and finally washed up on an island shore, where they made a home. Perseus grew up to be a strong and handsome young man.

Now, the king of the island was also cruel. He wanted Perseus's mother all to himself. He assigned Perseus to a great adventure, but he really intended a task so difficult that Perseus would not survive.

'Bring me the head of **Medusa**,' said the king.

'Medusa?' asked Perseus in wonder. Medusa was a Gorgon, a hideous monster with a head full of snakes. Any man who looked into her face would be instantly turned to stone. No one could approach Medusa, let alone cut her head off! But Perseus accepted the challenge.

Zeus sent his messenger, **Hermes**, with gifts for Perseus.

'Your father has sent me from Mount Olympus, home of the gods, with three things,' said Hermes. 'From **Athena**, the goddess of wisdom, here is a bright brass shield. From **Hades**, the god of the underworld, here is a helmet to make you invisible. And from me, here is a sword that cuts through anything with one stroke.'

Then Hermes took the winged sandals off his feet and gave them to Perseus.

With gifts from the gods, Perseus felt even braver. He thanked Hermes, and through him all the gods, including great Zeus. 'But where will I find this monster Medusa?' he asked.

'You must put that question to the **Three Grey Sisters**,' said Hermes. 'These three women share a single eye. They live together in a deep, dark cave at the western edge of the world.'

Perseus travelled for days and nights until he came to a twilight land. There he stood at the opening of a deep, dark cave and listened as the Three Grey Sisters mumbled amongst themselves.

'Someone is coming,' said the first sister. 'I can feel him.'

'Someone is coming,' said the second sister. 'I can hear him.'

'Someone is coming,' said the third sister. 'I can see him with my eye.'

Perseus bargains with the Three Grey Sisters

'Give me the eye,' said the first.

'No, me,' said the second, 'so that I can see, too!'

As they struggled over the one eye they shared, Perseus grabbed it. A howl shot up from all three sisters when they realised that not one of them had the precious eye anymore.

'Never fear, good women,' said Perseus. 'I will return your eye as long as you tell me where I will find the Gorgon Medusa.'

The sisters told Perseus how to find Medusa. With Hermes's sandals on his feet, he flew over land and sea to the land of the Gorgons. There they were, three massive monsters, lying asleep. The biggest and most horrible one was Medusa.

Perseus put on the helmet of invisibility so that Medusa would not see him coming. He held up the bright shield so that his gaze would not meet hers and yet he could see her face, reflected as in a mirror. Aided by Hermes's winged sandals, he approached the Gorgon, raised the sword and, with one swing, cut the head off the horrible Medusa. The snakes on her head hissed in pain. Perseus shoved her head into a goatskin pouch and instantly flew away.

Returning to the island where the cruel king kept his mother, Perseus approached the throne. 'Just as I suspected,' said the king with a smile. 'You have come back empty-handed.'

'On the contrary,' said Perseus. 'I have done what you commanded.' He pulled Medusa's head out of the goatskin bag. Even in death, with her eyes wide open, the Gorgon had her powers. The evil king looked into her face and was turned to stone.

Perseus shows Medusa's head to the evil king, who instantly turns to stone.

Orpheus and Eurydice

Orpheus was born in Thrace, a part of ancient Greece where music was played and enjoyed by all the people. But no one could play like Orpheus. When he took up his lyre and began to sing, the birds in the trees were silent, so eager were they to listen to songs more beautiful than their own. No one could resist the beautiful music he made. Orpheus seemed to sing like one of the immortal gods, and the sounds he made were not of this world.

One day Orpheus fell in love with a beautiful young woman called **Eurydice**. Did she love him too? Of course, she could not help but love him when she heard the songs that he sang for her. They were married, and felt themselves happier and luckier than any other couple on earth. Then one day, a terrible tragedy befell them. Eurydice was moving through a field, dancing to the lovely sounds that came from her husband's lyre, when she was bitten on the ankle by a serpent who was sleeping in the grass. She fell down dead at her husband's feet.

Orpheus was overcome with grief and could not be consoled. His friends all feared that he would lose his mind, so terrible was his grief. He decided that one thing alone would satisfy him: he would go down to **Hades**, the land of the dead, and ask **Pluto**, lord of that dark and frightening place, if Eurydice could return to the sunlight. This was a brave thing to do, for no mortal had ever ventured into the underworld to mingle with the dead, but Orpheus was so full of grief that he could not feel fear.

Orpheus was shown the entrance to the underworld by **Mercury**, the messenger of the gods, and down he went, further and further into the darkness until he reached the gates of Hades. The servants of the great god Pluto were astonished to see a living mortal in their realm. The thin and smoky shades of the dead made little gibbering noises of surprise. What would their terrible master have to say!

Then Orpheus picked up his lyre and began to sing of his love for Eurydice, and how much he longed to hold her again. He sang of the kingdom of the dead, to which all must come in time, rich and poor, powerful and weak. This is the debt we all must pay to time. But please, he sang, please, Lord Pluto, give me back my lovely Eurydice, for she was taken before her time. She was cut down before the bloom was off her youthful beauty.

Pluto had a heart of stone. He had to be stern to rule his terrible kingdom, where love and pity had no place. But he could not resist the charm of Orpheus. Big, bitter tears ran down his cold, hard cheeks. The very ghosts themselves were weeping.

'Orpheus,' said Pluto, 'you have touched my heart in a way that no mortal man has ever been able to do. I grant your request. You may take your wife back to the sunlight. Soon enough you will both be joining me in my dark kingdom, but for now, enjoy your youth and be happy together.'

He called to Eurydice, who came timidly to him, limping where she had been bitten by the serpent.

'Follow your husband,' said Pluto, 'back to the world of light. You will be the first mortal who ever saw the realm of Hades and then returned to tell the tale. But hear me, Orpheus, there is one great command that I give you. As you lead your wife along the steep path, you must not, for any reason at all, turn to look behind you. You must not see her again until you both emerge into the realm of light again. Do you understand?'

'I do,' said Orpheus. 'I carry your command in my heart.'

And so he turned to begin the steep climb, up the long, dark path that led from Pluto's kingdom up to the world of light. He was tempted to turn to see his lovely wife again, but he knew he must not. At last, the gloom began to lift as the sunlight made its way through the darkness. Orpheus turned to face his wife. 'Eurydice, my love,' he said. But he was too early. Eurydice was still in the shadows. She began to fade away. He tried to grasp her beautiful form, but she disappeared as his arms went around her.

'Farewell!' was all she could say. Then she was gone.

Poor Orpheus! To lose his wife a second time. He ran as fast as his legs could carry him back down the path, but this time he could not come near the kingdom of the dead. His moment had passed.

He returned to earth, filled with a terrible grief. He could do nothing but sing of his lost love, and his songs were so beautiful that those who heard him said: 'His music was lovely before, but nothing could be more moving than these melodies of longing and regret.' He died of a broken heart, and was buried by the Muses on the slopes of Mount Olympus. The birds gathered around his grave, where it is said that they sing sweeter than they sing anywhere else.

The Sword of Damocles

Damocles looks up to see the sword.

This story comes to us from ancient Rome. Many people still talk of something dangerous or unpleasant that could happen to them at any moment as the 'sword of Damocles'.

Damocles [dam-o-KLEES] looked with envy on his friend **Dionysius** [die-oh-NISS-ee-us], the king of Syracuse. He believed that the king had a very good life – all the riches and all the power that anyone could want.

'You think I'm lucky?' Dionysius said to him one day. 'If you think so, let's trade places. You sit here, on the throne, for just one day and see if you still think I'm lucky.'

Damocles eagerly accepted his friend's invitation. He ordered servants to bring him fine robes and a great banquet of food. He ordered expensive wine and fine music as he dined. He sat back, sure that he was the happiest man in the world.

Then he looked up. He caught his breath in fear. Above his head, a sword dangled from the ceiling attached by a single strand of horse's hair. Damocles could not speak, could not eat, could not enjoy the music. He could not even move.

'What is the matter, my friend?' asked Dionysius.

'How can I enjoy myself with that sword hanging above me?' Damocles said.

'How indeed?' answered Dionysius. 'And now you know how it feels to be king. That sword hangs over my head every minute of every day. There is always the chance the thread will break. An adviser may turn on me or an enemy spy may attack me. I might even make an unwise decision that brings my downfall. The privilege of power brings dangers.'

Damon and Pythias

Here is another story about Dionysius, the king of Syracuse. It was used by the ancient Roman writer Cicero as an example of true friendship.

Dionysius condemns Pythias to death.

Dionysius, the king of Syracuse, heard rumours that a young man named **Pythias** [PITH-ee-us] was making speeches and telling people to question whether he, or any king, should have so much power. He called Pythias before him. The young man arrived with his best friend, **Damon**, by his side.

'You dare to stand before the king without bowing?' shouted Dionysius when he saw the two men before him.

'I believe that all people are equal,' Pythias boldly stated. 'No man should have absolute power over another.'

'Who do you think you are, to speak such a philosophy and spread it among my people?' Dionysius raged.

'I speak the truth,' Pythias answered bravely. 'There can be nothing wrong with that.'

Dionysius was outraged. 'You risk punishment, even death, by speaking like that.'

'My philosophy teaches me patience. I have no fear of punishment, or even death.'

'We shall see how much use that philosophy is to you in prison,' roared Dionysius. He commanded his soldiers to seize Pythias and lock him in the caverns of Syracuse until he promised never to contradict the king again.

Pythias stood strong and tall. 'I cannot make that promise, and so I will accept the punishment,' he said. 'But may I first go home to tell my family and put my household in order?'

'Do you think I'm stupid?' shouted the king. 'If I let you go, you will never return!'

Then up stepped Damon. 'Lock me up until he returns.'

'Very well,' said the king, 'but if Pythias does not return in three days, Damon will be executed.'

'I trust my friend,' said Damon. So Pythias travelled to his home, and Damon sat in the deep, dark cell, alone. Two days came and went. On the morning of the third, Dionysius ordered Damon to be brought before him. 'Your friend has not returned,' he bellowed. 'You know what that means? It means your death!'

'I trust my friend,' Damon repeated. 'Something has delayed him. He will come back. I am sure of it.'

At sundown, the soldiers led Damon to the place where he would be put to death. Dionysius watched with a sneer on his face. 'What have you to say of your friend now?' he asked.

'I trust my friend,' Damon replied.

Just then Pythias rushed in, his clothing torn and his face bruised and dirty. 'Thank the gods you are safe,' he said to Damon. 'My ship was wrecked in a storm. Thieves attacked me on the road. But I did not give up, and I finally made it here. Now I am ready to take my punishment.'

Seeing such friendship, Dionysius learnt an important lesson. He revoked Damon's death sentence, freed Pythias and asked the two men to teach him how to be such a good friend, too.

Androcles and the Lion

The ancient Romans thought it great sport to watch men fight wild animals to the death. This fight has a surprise ending.

Androcles [AN-droh-clees] was a Roman slave who escaped his master and ran away. He was delighted with his freedom but uncertain how he could make it on his own. As night fell, he found a cave carved out of the hillside. He crept into the cool darkness, lay down and fell asleep.

Suddenly, he awoke, hearing the loud roar of a lion nearby. It was no dream – it was a real lion, looking straight into the cave. Androcles shrank back, fearful for his life, watching the lion's every move.

Then he noticed that the lion was suffering. It was roaring in pain. The great beast limped into the cave and flopped down. It lifted its right front paw and licked it.

Androcles took a step towards the lion. The big cat gave him a sad look, as if asking for help. Androcles crouched next to the lion. He saw a thorn stuck in the middle of its paw. Gently, he pulled the thorn out. The lion looked him in the eye again and purred.

That was the beginning of a warm friendship between Androcles and the lion. They lived together in the cave and slept side by side, keeping each other warm.

But one day Roman soldiers discovered Androcles. The law of Rome said that runaway slaves must be punished, so Androcles was captured and shut into a prison cell in the city of Rome.

For ten days, Androcles sat alone in prison, fed nothing but water and crusts of stale bread. Then a soldier announced that he was to meet his death in the Colosseum.

Androcles knew what that meant. Runaway slaves were often made to fight vicious lions before crowds of Roman citizens. He knew, as he walked the path from the prison to the Colosseum, that he would soon die.

The crowd cheered as Androcles stepped into the arena. They cheered even more loudly as the lion appeared on the other side. Androcles walked into the ring and bravely faced his death.

Then he and the lion recognised each other. To the amazement of the crowd, instead of attacking, the lion began licking the slave's face – and the slave began stroking the lion!

The crowd cheered even more. They yelled: 'Free the slave! Free the lion!' The emperor agreed. Androcles and the lion lived a long life together in the city of Rome.

Androcles with his friend the lion

Horatius at the Bridge

This famous story about a Roman hero has stayed with us in part because the English poet Thomas Macaulay wrote a book called Lays of Ancient Rome, *which included a poem about the acts of heroism performed by Horatius. We use some of Macaulay's powerful verses to tell the story here.*

Lucius Tarquinius, the last of the Roman kings, was so cruel that the people called him Tarquin the Tyrant. Finally, they banded together and sent him out of Rome.

Brave Horatius defends the bridge.

Forced out of power, Tarquin visited Lars Porsena, king of the Etruscans, who lived to the north of Rome. Tarquin convinced Lars Porsena to assemble a huge army, much larger and more powerful than the Roman army, and attack Rome.

There was only one way for them to enter the city of Rome, over a small wooden bridge across the River Tiber. A soldier named Horatius guarded that bridge. When he saw the Etruscans preparing to attack his city, he came up with a plan.

He and two others would cross the bridge and fight off the Etruscans as they came down the narrow path toward the bridge. As they fought, Horatius suggested, the Romans could tear apart the bridge, making it impossible for the Etruscans to cross and storm the city.

'Horatius,' quoth the Consul,
'As thou sayest, so let it be.'
And straight against that great array
Forth went the dauntless Three.
For Romans in Rome's quarrel
Spared neither land nor gold,
Nor son nor wife, nor limb nor life,
In the brave days of old.

While the three soldiers held the Etruscans back, others chopped away at the wooden bridge. Just before the bridge fell into the river, Horatius commanded his two helpers to cross to the Roman side. He remained, fighting off the Etruscans until he could do so no longer. Then, praying to the River Tiber to take good care of him, Horatius threw himself into the water.

Every Roman soldier held his breath, afraid he had seen the last of brave Horatius. Then the crest of his helmet surfaced above the river, and all cheered. The current was high, the river was fast and Horatius, wearing heavy armour, had to struggle to survive.

And now he feels the bottom;
Now on dry earth he stands;
Now round him throng the Fathers
To press his gory hands;
And now, with shouts and clapping,
And noise of weeping loud,
He enters through the River-Gate,
Borne by the joyous crowd.

Thanks to Horatius at the bridge, Tarquin and the Etruscans could not enter Rome. For many generations after, men and women told the story of how Horatius saved the city of Rome in the brave days of old.

Learning About Literature

Biography and Autobiography

A *biography* is the true story of a person's life. We have read biographies of important scientists and explorers in other books in this series, and you can read more starting on pages 169 and 352.

Suppose you wanted to write the life story of someone you know. You could talk to her and ask her questions about what happened in her life. You could find out about her from her parents, relatives and friends who know her well. If she had old letters and scrapbooks, you could learn from them, too.

But suppose you wanted to write the life story of someone who lived two hundred years ago. You could use writing that he and other people left behind, like old letters, diaries and newspaper articles. You would have to read carefully and remember all that you learnt, then turn that information into a story about the person's life.

A person who was asked to write her own life story would probably do it in a different way from someone else who was writing it. When a person chooses to write her own life story, it is called an *autobiography*. The prefix 'auto-' means 'self'. An 'autograph' is your name written by yourself. Something 'automatic' works by itself. So an 'autobiography' is a biography you write yourself. We read autobiographies to learn about what people did, why they did those things, and what they thought about the people they knew and the times they lived in.

Anne Frank writing her autobiography

For example, in the eighteenth century, a former African slave called Olaudah Equiano wrote his autobiography to convince people that slavery was wrong. In the twentieth century, Nelson Mandela wrote *A Long Walk to Freedom*, about his struggle against the system of apartheid in South Africa, which discriminated against black people. Sometimes people record their thoughts and their lives in diaries that are later published as autobiographies, like Samuel Pepys, who tells us so much about life in London in the 1660s; and Anne Frank, who wrote about how she had to hide from the Nazis in a tiny attic during the Second World War because she was Jewish.

Fiction and Non-fiction

Fiction means stories that did not actually happen, such as fairy tales and myths or made-up stories like *Alice's Adventures in Wonderland* or *The Wind in the Willows*. Fiction can be so close to the truth that it seems real, or it can be so fantastic that it could never happen. When you make up a story, you are creating fiction.

Non-fiction, on the other hand, is all about true things – people who really lived and the things they really did. A biography is non-fiction. An autobiography is non-fiction. History is non-fiction. Articles in the newspaper and a science report are non-fiction, too. When you write about what you did during your summer holidays, you are creating non-fiction.

There is an old saying that 'truth is stranger than fiction'. Do you think that's true?

Learning About Language

Let's Write a Report

Let's imagine that you have to write a report about African elephants. You know some things about elephants, but you need to learn more in order to write a good report. So where do you go? For a start, you can go to books.

These children are reading different books to help them learn more for writing their reports. Let's say you look up elephants in a book called *Mammals of the World*. Open the book at the front, and you will find the table of contents. The table of contents tells all the subjects in the book, listed in the order that they appear.

Chapter 1. What Is a Mammal?   page 3

Chapter 2. Lions   page 5

Chapter 3. Gorillas   page 13

Chapter 4. Giraffes   page 21

Chapter 5. Elephants   page 26

Chapter 6. The World's Mammals   page 35

What page will you turn to in order to learn about elephants? For this chapter, go to page 26. Since elephants are mammals, you might also want to read the chapters on mammals. On which pages can you find those chapters?

You can also use the index of a book to look up subjects that interest you. The index is always at the back of the book, and it gives an alphabetical list of everything in the book. An index helps you find specific subjects that might not be named in the table of contents.

INDEX

African elephants, 30

baboons, 38

gibbons, 4

giraffes, 21-25

Indian elephants, 27

jaguars, 6

mammals, 3-4, 35-45

monkeys, 37

okapi, 41

panthers, 9

tigers, 11

To do some reading for your report on African elephants, which page will you turn to?

There are other books that can give you information about African elephants. One very helpful kind of book is an *encyclopedia*. Encyclopedias give information about famous people, places, things, ideas, events in history and more. Some examples are *The Kingfisher Children's Encyclopedia, Children's Illustrated Encyclopedia* and *The Kingfisher Encyclopedia of Life.*

To find out about African elephants in an encyclopedia, open the volume marked 'A' and look for 'African elephants'. But maybe you can't find that topic listed. Try looking in the volume marked 'E' for 'Elephants'. That article might include something about African elephants.

You can also search in online encyclopedias. With these, you just type in a word or phrase – like 'elephants' or 'African elephants' – to search for information on your topic. Wikipedia is a popular online encyclopedia that many people contribute to and edit to keep it up to date, but it relies on trusting others to make sure the information is correct. Once you have researched and written your report on African elephants, maybe you can add something to the Wikipedia page on African elephants, or help make sure the article's information is correct.

Dictionaries explain words. They show how to spell a word correctly, how to divide it into syllables, how to pronounce it (using symbols that stand for sounds) and what it means. Dictionaries also tell us what part of speech a word is.

If you were reading about elephants and saw the word 'species', where would you look to find out what it means? In a dictionary, under the letter 'S'. Why not look it up?

After you have read about African elephants, you'll need to plan your report. Let's say you have three big ideas you want to write about:

1. What African elephants look like

2. Where African elephants live

3. What African elephants eat

You could write one *paragraph* about each of these big ideas.

A paragraph is a group of sentences all written about the same idea. It's a good idea to start a paragraph with a sentence that states the topic, or the main idea, of the paragraph. Then you can write a few more sentences to explain the idea and give examples.

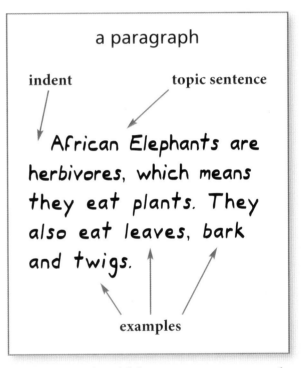

Every time you start writing about a new idea, you should *begin a new paragraph*. How do you show that it is a new paragraph? You *indent*. See the space at the beginning of this paragraph, before the word 'Every'? When you make a space like that, you're indenting. Another way to show that you are starting a new paragraph is to leave a blank line between one paragraph and the next.

Let's Write a Letter

Today a lot of people use computers, iPads and smartphones to send e-mail, but there are times when you will want to write a letter. For example, you could use a letter to thank someone for a present, send someone an invitation or make a formal request or statement, such as a letter to your local Member of Parliament, to tell him or her what you think about your local park.

Writing a letter is different from writing a report. It's a lot more like talking. Still, there are a few rules to follow.

- Begin by writing a heading, which gives your address and the date.

- Write a greeting to the person you're addressing. The greeting is like saying hello, and many people start formal letters with 'Dear'.

- Write the body of your letter in paragraphs. Indent each new paragraph or leave a line between the paragraphs.

- End your letter with a closing (such as 'Yours sincerely' or 'Your friend'). Then write your signature – your name in handwriting.

heading

10a Park Avenue
Watford, WD3 2HU
10 June 2013

Dear Tooth Fairy, ⟵ **greeting**

I have had a loose tooth for almost a month. Yesterday when I was playing hockey, I bumped into my friend really hard and fell on the ground. When I stood up, I noticed my tooth was missing!

body

We looked all over the ground. All my teammates looked with me. We still didn't find my tooth.

I'm putting a drawing of my missing tooth under my pillow anyway.

Yours sincerely,
closing Amelia

Parts of a Sentence: Main and Subordinate Clauses

You speak and write sentences all the time. A sentence is a group of words that expresses a complete thought. Is this a sentence?

Six silly spiders

No, something – a verb – is missing to tell you what is going on. Is this a sentence?

Sang songs in the shower

No, something – a subject – is missing here, to tell you who is singing. But if you put them together, you can make a complete sentence.

Six silly spiders sang songs in the shower.

What if you want to describe more about what is going on?

Six silly spiders sing songs in the shower after spinning their webs.

| main clause | subordinate clause |

A *main clause* can be a sentence on its own, and a *subordinate clause* adds more detail to the sentence. The subordinate clause also has a verb, but it can't be a sentence on its own. Since it *depends* on having a main clause with it in the sentence, some people call a subordinate clause a *dependent* clause. It usually starts with words like these:

| after | because | before | if | once | since |
| that | when | where | while | which | who |

These words are clues to help you know which part of a sentence is a subordinate clause. Let's look at some other examples.

When I am older I will ride in a hot air balloon.

| subordinate clause | main clause |

I have a fun granny because she teaches me how to paint and lets me make a mess.

| main clause | subordinate clause |

In these sentences, 'when' and 'because' are clues to tell you which part is the subordinate clause. It's not always at the end of the sentence either!

Can you write a subordinate clause to tell more about this sentence?

Eight enormous gorillas run through the forest before _____ .

Did you write 'they find their bananas' or 'the sun comes up'?

Now can you write a main clause to go with this subordinate clause?

_____ *if they go on holiday in France.*

Did you write 'My friends will go to the beach' or 'All mice feast on cheese'?

Every sentence begins with a capital letter. Do you remember other times when you use a capital letter? Capital letters start proper nouns, like names of people and places: for example, Oliver Cromwell and United Kingdom. You capitalise the main words in titles of books: for example, **We're Going on a Bear Hunt**. You capitalise holidays, days of the week and months of the year: for example, Hanukkah, **W**ednesday and **J**anuary. And you always use a capital letter for the word that stands for yourself: **I**.

What Kind of Sentence Is It?

Now let's find out about three different kinds of sentences. You make up sentences every day. The three basic kinds of sentences are:

- declarative
- interrogative
- imperative

Let's start with this sentence:

Julia took her pet crocodile for a walk.

That's called a *declarative sentence* because it *declares* or makes a statement about Julia and her pet. If Julia's friend visited and found her not at home, she might use an *interrogative* sentence, which is a sentence that asks a question.

Did Julia take her pet crocodile for a walk?

Interrogative sentences end with a question mark.

If Julia were sleeping late and had been ignoring her pet, then Julia's mother might use imperative sentences, which are sentences that make requests or give commands.

Wake up! Take your pet crocodile for a walk.

Both of these are imperative sentences. Look at the first one again: *Wake up!* Where is the subject in that sentence? You don't see a subject, but we say that the subject, 'you', is understood. In most imperative sentences, the 'you' is understood, such as in *Stop!* or *Please sit down.*

If Julia took her pet crocodile for a walk to the park, then the people who saw her might use exclamatory statements, which are incomplete sentences that show strong feeling:

Help! A crocodile! What a crazy girl!

Exclamatory statements often end with exclamation marks!

Parts of Speech

Let's review the parts of speech you already know and learn about some new ones.

Nouns

Can you find the *nouns* in this sentence?

My brother put on his swimming trunks, snorkel and flippers, but he forgot to bring a towel.

Remember, a noun names a person, place or thing. Here is that sentence again with the nouns printed in colour.

My **brother** put on his **swimming trunks**, **snorkel** and **flippers,** but he forgot to bring a **towel**.

Adjectives

Do you remember what *adjectives* do? Here's a hint. Look at this sentence, with the adjectives printed in colour:

*On **cold** mornings, Michiko likes to cuddle up in her **soft, fuzzy, purple** blanket.*

Adjectives are words that describe. Adjectives include words like *cold, soft, fuzzy* and *purple*, as well as *long, big, scary* and *beautiful*. Can you think of three adjectives to describe a puppy? How about an elephant?

There are three special adjectives you use all the time, called *articles* (or 'determiners'). The articles are:

a   an   the

You might say: 'Please hand me a glass', if you just wanted any glass. But if you wanted a certain glass, you would say, 'Please hand me the glass'. If you felt hungry for an apple, just any old apple, you might say: 'I would like an apple.' But if you wanted to eat a big, juicy, red apple sitting in the middle of a bowl of fruit, you might say: 'I would like the apple.' Notice that you use 'a' before words that begin with a consonant, but 'an' before words that begin with a vowel. You say 'a glass', but 'an apple'.

Verbs

Can you think of a good word to fill in the blanks in each of these sentences?

Jose _____ fast.

Alison _____ the football.

For the first sentence, did you come up with something like runs, swims or eats? For the second sentence, did you say something like kicked, dribbled or passed?

These words, and many more, show actions. Words that express action are verbs. Can you find three verbs in this sentence?

Henry carries his backpack and shouts to his friends while he rides his bicycle to school.

Adverbs

We use adverbs to add something to a verb. Adverbs describe the verb. Let's start by looking at this sentence:

Liz showed us her trophy.

What is the verb in that sentence? It's 'showed'. So how did Liz show us her trophy? You could say:

Liz proudly showed us her trophy.

Or you could say:

Liz secretly showed us her trophy.

Proudly and *secretly* are adverbs. They each tell us something about the verb, showed. Most adverbs end with the letters *-ly*, such as:

quickly	slowly	suddenly
quietly	politely	carefully

Here are two sentences. First find the verb. Then think of a good adverb to tell something more about the verb.

The cat crept towards the mouse.

I asked for permission to leave the room.

Now, can you find the adjectives and the adverbs in this next sentence? Adjectives first, then adverbs.

Melanie proudly showed her mother the fuzzy pink petunias
that she had carefully planted in the garden.

Pronouns

Do you like to talk about yourself? Most people do! What do you call yourself when you do? Sometimes you use your name, but most of the time you use pronouns. You call yourself 'I' and 'me', depending on what you are saying. *I* and *me* are both pronouns.

Pronouns are words that stand for nouns. *He, she, it* and *they* are pronouns. Here's a sentence without any pronouns:

James asked Sarah to tell James when Sarah was going to come over to James's house.

Would you ever say or write a sentence like that? No! You would use pronouns, like this:

James asked Sarah to tell him when she was going to come over to his house.

When you read that sentence, you understand that the pronouns 'him' and 'his' stand for 'James' and the pronoun 'she' stands for 'Sarah'.

More About Verbs

Some words help express action. They are called helping words, like:

does ride	*will* shout	*have* brought	*is* diving
has carried	*had* broken	*was* throwing	*am* thinking

Let's Punctuate!

Writing isn't just words and letters. All those little squiggles and symbols – like , ? ! .' – mean something, too. Some punctuation marks come at the end of a sentence. That last sentence ended with – what? – a *full stop.*

What other punctuation marks can end a sentence? That last sentence, which was a question, ended with – what? – a *question mark*.

There is only one more punctuation mark that can end a sentence! What punctuation mark ended that sentence? It ended with an *exclamation mark*. When a sentence ends with one of those, you know it's about something exciting.

The *comma* is a punctuation mark that comes inside a sentence. Consider the comma in these sentences:

I live in Tiverton, Devon.

A comma always comes between the names of a town and a county.

My favourite animals are earthworms, moles and eagles.

Commas always separate words in a series except when the word 'and' occurs between the last two words in the series.

Yes, I know that my favourite animals are strange!

Commas always come after the words 'Yes' or 'No' at the start of a sentence.

The *apostrophe* is a punctuation mark that comes inside a word. It has two different jobs. An apostrophe can show possession:

Emily's scarecrow costume

my puppy's name

Even when the word ends in -*s*, you add an apostrophe and an *s* to make it possessive:

St Thomas's Hospital

The bus's roof

(Some people just add an apostrophe to show possession with a word ending in -*s*. They would write 'St Thomas' Hospital', and they would be right, too.)

An apostrophe is also used to make *contractions*, when two words come together to make one.

did not → didn't

it is → it's

is not → isn't

In contractions, the apostrophe stands for a letter that has been dropped. In the contractions above, what letters do the apostrophes stand for?

Just Say No Once

Here are two good sentences that are easy to understand.

I didn't eat lunch today.

I ate no lunch today.

But what would it mean if somebody said:

I didn't eat no lunch today.

Would it mean that the person ate *no lunch,* or that the person *did* eat lunch? It's confusing, isn't it?

The third sentence has a *double negative*: both 'didn't' (which stands for 'did not') and 'no lunch' are negatives. If you say you did not *not* do something, that can only mean you really did it. Double negatives are confusing, and it's best not to use them.

Prefixes and Suffixes

Prefixes attach to the beginning of words to change their meanings.

re- **means 'again':**
refill means 'fill again'
reread means 'read again'

un- **means 'not':**
unfriendly means 'not friendly'
unpleasant means 'not pleasant'

un- **can also mean the opposite or reverse of an action:**
untie means the reverse of 'tie'
unlock means the reverse of 'lock'

dis- **means 'not':**
dishonest means 'not honest'
disobey means 'not obey'

dis- **can also mean the opposite or reverse of an action:**
disappear means the opposite of 'appear'
dismount means the reverse of 'mount'

See if you can find an example of your own for each of these prefixes.

Suffixes attach to the end of words to change their meanings.

-*er* and -*or* change verbs to nouns naming people:

sing + -er → *singer*
paint + -er → *painter*
act + -or → *actor*

-*less* makes an adjective meaning without that noun:

hope + less → *hopeless*
fear + less → *fearless*

-*ly* turns an adjective into an adverb:

quick + ly → *quickly*
calm + ly → *calmly*

Can you find another example for each of these three suffixes?

They Sound Alike, but They're Different

Can you solve this riddle?

Why was six afraid of seven?

Answer: Because seven eight nine

This riddle works because the words 'eight' and 'ate' sound alike, even though they mean different things.

Words that have the same sound but different spellings and meanings are called *homophones*. 'Eight' and 'ate' are homophones. Can you think of some others? What is the word for a female deer, and what word is its homophone? 'Doe' and 'dough'. Here's a silly sentence with *two* pairs of homophones:

I was asked by my father to buy a pair of pear trees.

Which words are the homophones in that sentence? Can you make up a sentence with a pair of homophones? Sometimes you just have to memorise the different words and their spellings. Here are a few to memorise.

Where are the bears? *They're there*, in *their* cave.

they're → they are
there → in that place
their → belonging to them

That *bear* would like to sit on a chair but *it's* standing up because *its* cave is *bare*.

its → belonging to it
it's → it is
bear → a big, furry animal
bare → empty, unfurnished

You're sure *your* hair is three feet long?

you're → you are
your → belonging to you

Here are two more sentences. Can you find the homophones?

Come over here so you can hear the bird better.

Those two tortoises are creeping too slowly to win the race.

Shorten Up with Abbreviations

Sometimes it's useful to find a short way to write a word that is used often. For instance, we use the word 'Mister' so often that we abbreviate it as 'Mr'. When you see the abbreviation 'Mr', you still say the whole word, 'Mister'. Here are some common abbreviations.

125 High **St** (street)   99 Mulberry **Rd** (road)

Born in the **UK** (United Kingdom)   Team **GB** (Great Britain)

99 **m** (metres)   66 **cm** (centimetres)   500 **kg** (kilograms)

Mr Magoo   **Mrs** Tiggy-Wiggle   **Ms** Manners   **Dr** Gizmo (doctor)

(abbreviations for people's titles)

Sayings and Phrases

PARENTS: Every culture has phrases and proverbs that make no sense when carried over literally into another culture. Their meanings come from metaphor and custom, not from literal definitions. The sayings and phrases in this section may be familiar to many children who have heard them at home. Their inclusion has been singled out by parents and teachers who work with children from home cultures in which they may be unfamiliar with these phrases and sayings.

Actions speak louder than words

This saying reminds us that what people say does not always show what they think, while what people do reveals their true thoughts or beliefs more clearly.

'Dad says he hates cats – even Tigger!' Stewart shook his head.

'But last night,' Tracy said, 'I saw Dad kiss the top of Tigger's head when he thought no one was looking.'

'Maybe he really loves Tigger but he keeps it a secret. Actions speak louder than words!'

His bark is worse than his bite

People use this saying to describe a person who speaks angrily or threatens but may not be truly mean or dangerous.

'Mr Baxter is bad-tempered,' said Jason.

'Yes,' said Mickey. 'They should call him 'Mr Whackster'!'

'You two are so silly,' Miyaka said. 'Mr Baxter would never whack anybody. He might get cross easily, but he's a kind man. His bark is worse than his bite!'

Beggars can't be choosers

People use this saying to mean that when you are in a weak or disadvantaged position, you shouldn't be fussy about the help that may be offered – even if it isn't exactly the sort of help you want.

'I didn't have time to eat breakfast,' Supriyo said, 'and I'm starving. But the only thing left in the canteen for lunch is spinach salad – eeugh!'

'Beggars can't be choosers, Supriyo,' Nikki said. 'Looks as if you'll have to eat something healthy for a change.'

Let bygones be bygones

People use this saying to mean letting go of whatever is bothering you so it becomes a thing of the past.

Jack and Imran were always arguing at school. The arguments had started on the first day of school when Jack had knocked a pot of water over Imran's painting. Since then they just couldn't get along. One day their teacher picked them to work together to build a model boat. The first pair to make a floating boat would win a prize! 'I really want to win the prize!' said Imran. 'We'd better let bygones be bygones.'

Last straw

This phrase describes the moment when things have gone too far one way and just have to change. It comes from a legend about a man who piled straw on his camel's back, one piece at a time. Even though each piece of straw was light, one piece was the 'last straw' that broke the camel's back.

'What's wrong, Paul?' Lenny asked. 'Do you need any help?'

Paul was kneeling down next to his bicycle, trying to remove his front tyre, which had gone flat. 'Just leave me alone,' he snapped. 'First I fell off my bike on the way to school and skinned my elbow. Then, once I got to maths class, I remembered that I left my homework at home. Then Rob Banks tripped me when we were playing football, and I bruised my knee. And now I have a flat tyre. This is the last straw!'

Beat around the bush

People use this phrase to mean that someone is avoiding direct discussion of a difficult subject by talking instead about related subjects that are less important.

'So how did you do in your maths test, Alex?' Mr Novak asked.

Alex cleared his throat. 'Three children were late, so the teacher didn't start the test until ten minutes after it should have started.'

Alex's father looked at his son, waiting for an answer to his question.

'I was supposed to bring in three pencils,' Alex said. 'I forgot.'

'Didn't you say you were going to have a test today, Alex?' said Mr Novak. He was getting impatient.

'I don't know how that teacher expects us to finish 20 problems when we only have 40 minutes.'

Mr Novak got up and put his arm around Alex's shoulder. 'Come on, Alex. Stop beating around the bush. Just tell me what mark you got.'

A feather in your cap

This expression indicates a person has done something to make him or her proud.

Angela loved to play the violin. She practised every day. One day during orchestra rehearsal, the string section was playing a piece that Angela had practised carefully.

'Angela, play that phrase again,' said the conductor. Angela played the phrase flawlessly.

The conductor told Angela that she played so well she would be the orchestra's leader in the concert next week. She ran home to tell her parents.

'Well done! That's a feather in your cap,' said her father.

One rotten apple spoils the whole barrel

This saying means that one bad thing can spoil everything connected with it.

Mr Small's class was known as the best-behaved class in the school. One day a new boy joined the class. He was noisy and rude, but he was also funny. Soon the other children in Mr Small's class started chatting, laughing and getting rowdy. Mr Small just shook his head and said: 'One rotten apple spoils the whole barrel!'

Clean bill of health

People use this phrase to express that something is in perfect shape, as if a doctor has just declared them fit.

Before the cycle ride, Latasha and Simon took their bikes to the group leader. Simon's chain was drooping and his brakes needing adjusting. He had to go to the garage for repairs, whereas Latasha could start straight away. 'Your bike has a clean bill of health,' said the leader.

Rule the roost

People use this phrase to describe a person who bosses other people around. It comes from the way a cockerel acts in a chicken shed or 'roost'.

Katie and Emily were watching television in their living room. When Olivia came in from playing, she grabbed the remote control and changed channels.

'Hey!' Katie said. 'We were here first.'

'Tough,' Olivia said. 'I'm the oldest.'

'You may be the oldest,' Emily said, 'but that doesn't mean you rule the roost!'

A stitch in time saves nine

If you do a small job before it is too late, it saves having to do a bigger one later.

Lucas's father had promised to take him to see the Spurs play at White Hart Lane if Lucas would help to redecorate the living room. This was too good an offer to turn down, but Lucas had promised to go over to his friend's house that afternoon, so he was really in a hurry. Just as he was about to start painting, his mother rushed into the room with some old sheets and spread them over the furniture.

'What are you doing, mum?' said Lucas, 'I don't have time for this.'

'Lucas, you're flicking paint all over the furniture and it will take ages to clean off,' she said.

'You're right,' said Lucas. 'It's quicker in the end to use the dustsheets.'

'Yes, Lucas,' said his mother, 'a stitch in time saves nine.'

The show must go on

This saying means that no matter what happens, things will continue as planned.

'We can't play in the finals next Saturday,' Karen said to her coach. 'Lisa sprained her ankle, Cecilia has the mumps and Jenny has to go away for the weekend. They're the best footballers on the team. We'll lose without them.'

'We've been practising all season,' answered her coach. 'We're not giving up. The show must go on!'

The writing is on the wall

When things are going wrong, and it looks as if something you don't want is going to happen, people say that the writing is on the wall.

Miss Reynolds told us that the school choir would have to close unless more children joined it, so when Jason and Rosemary said they were leaving, I knew the writing was on the wall for the choir.

We saw on page 178 how Belshazzar knew he was in trouble when he saw the handwriting on the wall!

Touch and go

This phrase describes a situation that is so difficult, no one knows how it will turn out.

Harold had been training to walk a tightrope, but today was his first day to perform for an audience. He took his first steps steadily and slowly, using a long pole to keep his balance. When he got to the middle, he looked down for a moment. He felt himself teeter. The crowd gasped. Then, just in time, he regained his balance. The rest of his steps were strong and sure.

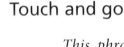

Later Harold said: 'Everything was fine until I looked down. For a few seconds there, it was touch and go.'

On its last legs

People use this phrase to say that something is about to die or is too worn out to be repaired.

'This has been a good old van,' Mr Johnson said to his grandson Josh. They drove down the bumpy road, and the van sputtered and groaned. 'I've had it for nearly twenty years.'

Josh was amazed to hear that the van was older than he was. 'But you hear those noises it's making, Josh? I'm afraid this van is on its last legs,' said Mr Johnson.

When in Rome, do as the Romans do

This saying suggests that when you are in an unfamiliar situation, it's good to behave like others around you.

Jason was really excited when his father asked if he would like to drive to Paris, taking their car onto the Shuttle. But when they came off the Shuttle at Calais, as soon as they got onto the road, other drivers were sounding their horns. 'Watch out Dad!' said Jason, 'You're driving on the wrong side of the road!'

'Sorry son,' said Jason's dad, 'it's just force of habit. Of course they drive on the right here. When in Rome, do as the Romans do!'

Rome wasn't built in a day

This means that it is no good expecting a big and difficult job to be completed quickly. The beautiful city of Rome contains many magnificent buildings, but they were created over many centuries.

Darren and Collette had volunteered to decorate the school hall for the Christmas party.

'These paper chains are taking ages,' complained Darren. 'I wouldn't have volunteered if I'd known it would mean being late for the big match on TV.'

'Don't be so impatient,' said Collette, 'it will all look fantastic when we've finished. Rome wasn't built in a day, you know.'

Cold shoulder

People use this phrase to mean that someone is being made to feel unwelcome. To people feasting on a lamb, a piece of cold shoulder meat was less appetising than a hot piece of leg.

'Ever since I told Daryl he should lose some weight, he pretends he doesn't know me,' Christina said. 'I called to him at break and he just walked away.'

'Maybe it's the way you said it,' Sara said. 'If you told me I looked like a hippopotamus, I'd give you the cold shoulder, too!'

Suggested Resources

Poetry

Heard It in The Playground by Allan Ahlberg (Puffin) 1991

Please Mrs Butler by Allan Ahlberg (Puffin) 1984

The Poetry Store by Paul Cookson (Hodder Children's) 2005

A First Poetry Book by Pie Corbett and Gaby Morgan (Macmillan Children's) 2012

Stories

Alice in Wonderland by Lewis Carroll (Wordsworth Classics) 1992

The Wind in the Willows by Kenneth Grahame (Egmont Heritage) 2012

One Thousand and One Arabian Nights (Oxford Story Collections) by Geraldine McCaughrean (Oxford University Press) 1999

The Butterfly Lion by Michael Morpurgo (HarperCollins Children's) 1996

Myths and Legends

D'Aulaires' Book of Norse Myths by Ingri D'Aulaire (New York Review Children's) 2006

Norse Myths and Legends by Cheryl Evans and Anne Millard (Usborne) 2006

Orchard Book of Greek Myths by Geraldine McCaughrean (Orchard) 2005

Classic Myths to Read Aloud by William Russell (Broadway) 1992

Romans: Gods, Emperors and Dormice by Marcia Williams (Walker) 2013

Jason and the Golden Fleece (Young Reading Series 2) by Claudia Zeff (Usborne) 2007

Learning About Language

Oxford Primary Grammar, Punctuation and Spelling Dictionary (Oxford University Press) 2013

Oxford Junior Illustrated Dictionary by Sheila Dignen (Oxford University Press) 2007

Junior Dictionary and Thesaurus by Cindy Leaney and Susan Purcell (Miles Kelly) 2011

Perfect Pop-Up Punctuation Book by Kate Petty and Jenny Maizels (Bodley Head) 2006

You Can Do It! Grammar by Andy Seed and Roger Hurn (Hodder Children's) 2011

The Butterfly Grammar by Irina Tyk (Civitas) 2008

Mobile Apps

Grammaropolis (Grammaropolis LLC) app for iPhone and iPad [Practising parts of speech; free]

Mad Libs (Penguin) app for iPhone [Practising parts of speech]

DVDs

Androcles and the Lion (Odeon Entertainment) 1952; 2010

Jason and the Argonauts (UCA) 1963; 2012

Magazines

Carousel by the Federation of Children's Book Groups: www.carouselguide.co.uk

History and Geography

Introduction

As anyone who has witnessed children's fascination with dinosaurs, knights in armour or kings and queens will know, young children are interested in other people, places and times. The idea at this stage is for children to become familiar with people, words and ideas so that, even years later, they can say: 'I know something about that'.

Learning history is not simply a matter of recalling facts – although getting a firm mental grip on a few significant dates, such as 1066 and 1688, is important. Dates reinforce a sense of chronology and establish a foundation for a more sophisticated historical understanding in years to come.

By Year 4, children are ready to make more subtle connections among historical facts. They are beginning to understand how ideas cause change. Still, the best history teaching emphasises the story. In some cases, it's hard – and perhaps not entirely necessary – to separate history from legend, as in the story of Romulus and Remus. We encourage parents and teachers to find art, drama, music and literature that help children to learn about history, too.

A special emphasis should be placed on learning geography. The primary school years are the best years in which to establish a lasting familiarity with the main features of world geography, such as the continents, the larger countries, the major rivers and mountains, and the major cities of the world. Especially when learnt in connection with interesting stories, these features and places will stay with a person throughout life. Knowledge can be reinforced through work with maps – drawing, colouring and filling in place-names. Maps offer children a foundation for understanding how geography influences world politics and economics.

World Geography

Quiz Time – How Much Do You Remember?

Let's see how many geographical facts you already know.

- Which continent do you live on?
- Which country do you live in?
- Which county do you live in?

Was that easy? Well, we're just getting started. Now look at this map.

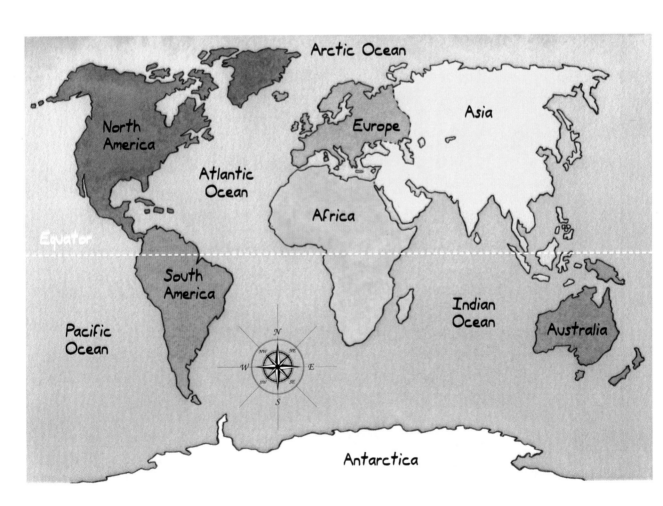

- Where is the compass rose on this map? What do N, E, S and W stand for?

- Which way is north? South? East? West?

- Can you point to and name the world's seven continents?

- Can you point to and name the world's four big oceans?

Did you remember all seven continents? And how about the four big oceans? Now, can you point to these on the map?

- Great Britain

- Ireland

- Scandinavia

- India

- The Equator

- The Northern Hemisphere

- The Southern Hemisphere

Do you have a globe? If you do, see if you can find the North Pole and the South Pole. That's the whole quiz. How did you do?

Look at the Key

Look at the map of Ireland on the next page. See the box in the corner? That's the map's *key*. The key explains the symbols used on the map. For example, it shows that a dotted line marks the boundary (or dividing line) between counties, while a solid line marks the boundary between countries: here, it shows the national boundary between the Republic of Ireland and Northern Ireland, which are the two countries in Ireland. Dublin is the capital of the Republic of Ireland and Belfast is the capital of Northern Ireland. Northern Ireland is part of the United Kingdom, together with Scotland, Wales and England.

Maps often have bar scales to help you read distances. For example, the scale on this map shows that 1 cm equals about 15 miles. If you travelled between Dublin and Belfast, about how far would you travel? You can estimate your answer by using this map and a ruler. Did you find it's around 6 cm? That represents about $6 \times 15 = 90$ miles.

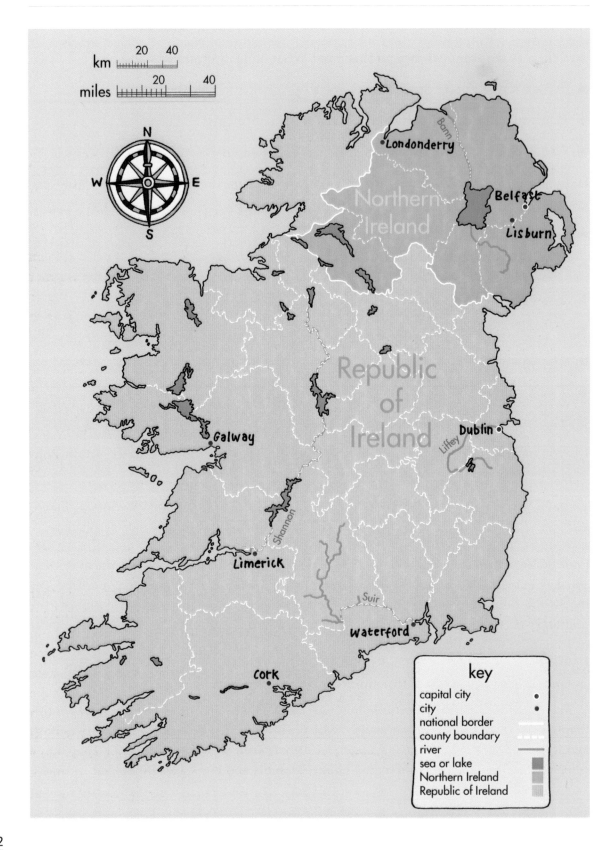

Mediterranean Europe

A Nice, Warm Climate

We have already learnt about Northern and Western Europe in Years 2 and 3, but now we can find out about the Southern part of Europe. Southern Europe is sometimes called Mediterranean Europe because it's near the Mediterranean Sea. 'Mediterranean' comes from the Latin words that mean in the middle of the land. The Mediterranean Sea is almost completely surrounded by the land of three continents – Asia, Africa and Europe.

Most countries in Southern Europe have a Mediterranean coastline. Portugal is an exception because it is on the Atlantic coast. Mediterranean Europe is generally warmer than the other *regions*, or areas, of Europe. The weather is usually hot and dry in places like southern Italy, Spain and Greece. This is because they are further south and closer to the Equator.

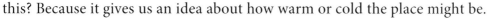

The *Equator* is an imaginary line that runs around the middle of the earth, right in the middle between the North and South Poles. Can you spot the Equator line on this globe? The Equator is also as far as possible from each pole. This means that the heat from the sun hits the earth more directly than at the poles, where the heat is more spread out. Because of this, places nearer to the Equator are warmer.

We measure the distance to and from the Equator using *latitude*. Knowing a place's latitude will tell you how far north or south of the Equator it is. Why might we want to know this? Because it gives us an idea about how warm or cold the place might be.

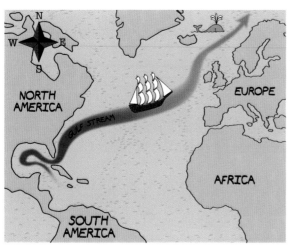

Mediterranean Europe has two other advantages besides latitude that make it warm: the Gulf Stream and the sea itself. The Gulf Stream is a current of warm water that flows from the Gulf of Mexico in Central America, all the way across the Atlantic Ocean to Europe. Northern Europe is less cold because of the Gulf Stream, so there is less cold air to blow chilly winds across the Mediterranean. Then the sea itself can hold a lot of heat

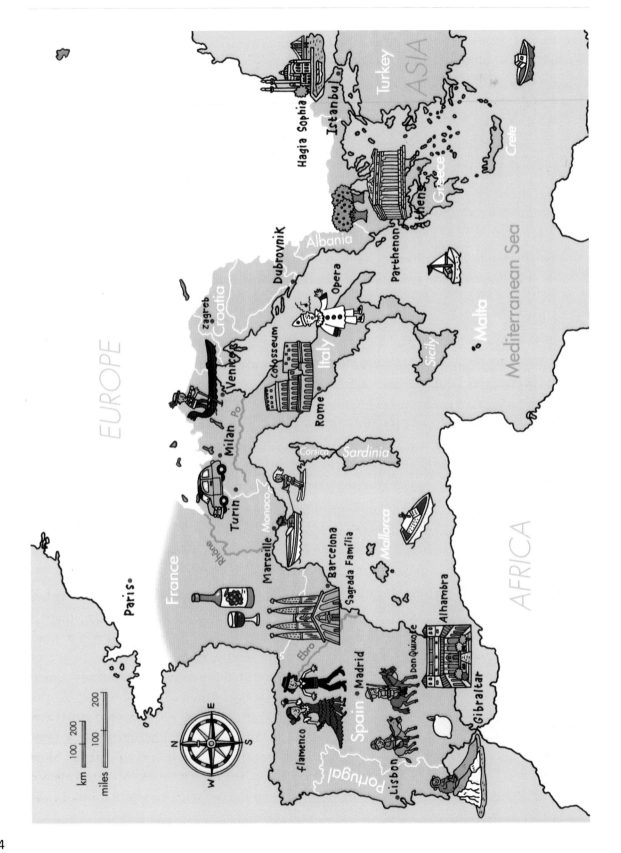

and acts like a room thermostat. It keeps the temperature fairly comfortable, neither too hot in summer nor too cold in winter.

Learn more about ecosystems on page 299.

Together, these different factors all come together to create the warm and dry Mediterranean climate. The climate affects what kind of plants and animals live in an area. This is called an *ecosystem*, and different types of plants and animals find it easier to live in certain conditions.

In Mediterranean Europe, the hot, dry summers and cooler, wetter winters mean that plants like shrubs and grasslands like to grow here. Some plants have to be tough to survive. The olive tree is very hardy and it can survive with not much water in the summer. Some of these trees live to be very old. In fact, there are some olive trees in Mediterranean Europe which are thousands of years old!

Olive trees can live in very hot and dry climates.

Some plants love to grow in this hot, dry climate. The weather is good for growing citrus fruits like oranges, lemons and limes, as well as grapes and olives. Have you eaten any of these? Well, these fruits are often used in the food eaten in Mediterranean countries. The grapes grown in Italy and southern France are used to make wine, and both Spain and Italy are well known for making olive oil. These countries send the wine and olive oil to be sold all around the world.

This farmer is inspecting the grapes he has grown.

Italy

There are many important mountain ranges in this part of Europe. Can you think of any you know already? We have learnt about the Alps. They are so big that they are in several different countries, including northern Italy. As you can imagine, it can be difficult to live in hilly places like this, but just to the south of the Italian Alps is the Po Valley. This is a fertile valley, meaning that crops grow very well there. The river Po, which starts in the

Alps and runs east, flows through the Po Valley and eventually into a part of the Mediterranean called the Adriatic Sea, not far from the famous Italian city of Venice. Venice is a very unusual city. It is an island in a calm area of the sea called a *lagoon*. In Venice there are no cars and, instead, people travel around the city by boat through the canals that snake through the city, or they have to walk across the many bridges that criss-cross the city. In fact, the whole city looks as though it is floating on the sea!

This gondola, *a traditional boat used along Venice's canals, is passing in front of the famous Rialto Bridge*.

There are lots of cities that have grown up in the large, fertile Po Valley, such as Milan and Turin. Some famous Italian cars are made in Turin. Milan is the biggest city in Italy, and it has many businesses and

See the Arch of Constantine on page 194.

factories. But Milan is not the capital of Italy. The capital is Rome, which used to be the centre of the Roman Empire, which we'll learn more about later in this chapter. There are still many buildings that survive from that time. People come to Rome to see the Colosseum, where ancient Romans watched gladiators fight (learn more on page 139) and the Arch of Constantine.

If you find Italy on the map on page 94, you will see why some people say it looks a bit like a boot, and the island of Sicily looks like a ball near the toe of the boot. There is a rhyme about this:

Big-booted Italy
Kicks little Sicily
Into the middle
Of the Mediterranean Sea.

St Peter's Basilica in Vatican City is the most important Roman Catholic church.

Running down the centre of Italy like a backbone, from north to south, is a mountain range called the Apennines. Italy is the only country in mainland Europe that still has active volcanoes. One volcano, called Mount Vesuvius, erupted in 1908 and 1944, but it is most famous for a huge eruption in ancient Roman times that covered the town of Pompeii in ash, killing everything but preserving it forever. Today you can visit Pompeii and see how the town was, just before the eruption.

You can read about the famous eruption of Mount Vesuvius on page 141.

Spain and Portugal

To the west of Italy is the country of Spain. In the north of Spain are the mountains of the Pyrenees. This mountain range forms a natural border between France and Spain, with the tiny country of Andorra nestled inbetween. Unlike much of the rest of Spain, which enjoys a Mediterranean climate, the height of these mountains means that it can be much colder here. It is called an *alpine* climate.

There is snow all year round on the very highest peaks of the Pyrenees.

In the south of Spain there is also another mountain range with snow on the top. It is called the Sierra Nevada, which means 'snowy mountains' in Spanish. It is in the region of Andalucía in the south of Spain and has the tallest mountain in mainland Spain, called Mulhacén [mul-ah-THEN]. But the south of Spain is better known for warm sunny beaches than snow-capped mountains. This region of Spain welcomes many tourists in the summer who come to enjoy the hot, dry weather and sunny Mediterranean beaches. Here the weather is so hot in the middle of the day that people sometimes sleep until it is cooler later on. This is called a *siesta*, which means 'nap' in Spanish.

Spain and Portugal together form a large *peninsula* to the south of France, called the Iberian Peninsula. A peninsula is an area of land almost completely surrounded by water except for a little bit, called an *isthmus*, connecting it with the mainland.

The capital of Spain is Madrid, which is also its largest city. Madrid is located in the middle of Spain, surrounded by the region of Castile. Another large, important city in Spain is called Barcelona.

Portugal has two major cities, Porto and the capital, Lisbon. Portugal has had a long seafaring history, starting the European age of exploration by sea. Portuguese explorers include the famous Vasco da Gama, who was the first European to sail to India.

The seaside along Costa Brava, Spain

We first learnt about peninsulas in Year 3.

Greece

Further east from Spain and Italy is the country of Greece. The mainland of Greece is another peninsula, extending into the Mediterranean Sea, but Greece also has hundreds of inhabited islands in a part of the Mediterranean called the Aegean Sea. *Inhabited* means that people live there, and people have lived on these islands for thousands of years. In fact, this is where the famous civilisation of

The modern city of Athens has been built all around the ancient Parthenon.

Ancient Greece began. There were many city-states on the different islands and in separate places on the Greek mainland, and altogether we call this civilisation ancient Greece. Do you remember in Year 3 learning about the Parthenon? It was built on a hill called the Acropolis and was an important temple in the time of ancient Athens.

We learnt about Ancient Greece and the Parthenon in Year 3.

Today the modern city of Athens is the capital of Greece and the Parthenon is still there. It remains one of the best examples of ancient Greek architecture. Athens attracts people from all over the world who come to see the Parthenon and visit the city.

The highest mountain in Greece is Mount Olympus. The ancient Greeks believed that this special mountain was the home of their gods. Unlike Italy, Spain and Portugal, which are traditionally Roman Catholic countries, many people in Greece belong to another strand of Christianity called the Greek Orthodox Church.

Read myths from ancient Greece in the Year 3 book and on page 52.

The Bosphorus divides two parts of the city of Istanbul, and the continents of Europe and Asia.

Turkey

Still further east from Greece across the Aegean Sea is Turkey. Turkey is a very big country that stands on the very edge of the European continent. Part of Turkey is in Europe and part is in Asia. Istanbul, the biggest city in Turkey, is at the crossroads of the continents of Europe and Asia. In fact, the city itself is split in two, separated by a narrow stretch of water called the Bosphorus. On one side lies Europe, with Asia on the other.

Because of its location, Istanbul is one of the most important cities in history. It has been the capital of four different empires. The culture of the city shows how it has been a gateway for people travelling between Europe and Asia, with both the East and West represented there.

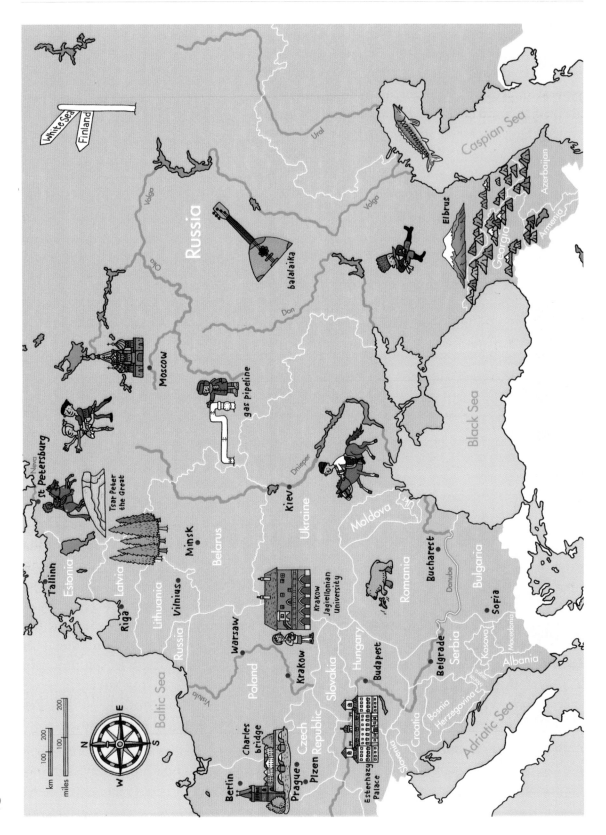

White Sea
Finland

Ural
Caspian Sea

Volga
Russia
Volga
balalaika
Elbrus
Azerbaijan
Georgia
Armenia

Don

Moscow
Black Sea

gas pipeline

Nova
St Petersburg
Tsar Peter the Great

Dnieper
Kiev
Ukraine
Moldova

Minsk
Belarus
Bucharest
Bulgaria
Danube
Romania
Sofia

Tallinn
Estonia
Latvia
Riga
Lithuania
Vilnius
Krakow Jagiellonian University
Macedonia

Russia
Warsaw
Belgrade
Serbia
Kosovo
Albania

Baltic Sea
Vistula
Poland
Krakow
Slovakia
Hungary
Budapest
Bosnia Herzegovina
Adriatic Sea

Charles bridge
Czech Republic
Pizen
Croatia
Slovenia

N E S W
km 100 200
miles 100 200

Berlin
Prague
Esterhazy Palace

Eastern Europe

Eastern Europe covers a wide area, with many countries, peoples, cities and rivers. It has a long, long border with the continent of Asia. Let's visit a few areas within Eastern Europe.

Russia

The biggest country in Eastern Europe, by far, is Russia. Not all of Russia is in Europe. Some is in Asia. Only a huge country could have borders with both China in the East and Finland in the West! At the very edge of Europe is a range of high mountains in central Russia, called the Urals [YUR-ahls] and a river, also called Ural, that runs off them and flows south.

West of the mountains is a *plain*, a large flat area of land. This plain is enormous, with no high mountains and not even many hills, where people riding horses can ride long distances and farmers can grow plenty of crops such as grain and vegetables. When we get an east wind, the cold air from Siberia blows across this plain and then to Britain. So sometimes the cold wind we can feel here has come a long way!

The Kremlin in Moscow

As the plain is quite flat, rainwater is gathered from miles around and flows into long rivers that eventually carry it to the sea. Cities have grown up on the river banks because ships can transport goods easily. The River Moscow has the same name as the capital of Russia. In Moscow the people in the government work in a place called the *Kremlin*, which means castle.

Further north, the icy River Neva [nyi-VAH] flows into the Baltic Sea at St Petersburg. This city was built by Tsar Peter the Great in a Western European style and it became the capital of Russia in 1713. A *tsar* is the name for a Russian king. Tsar Peter wanted his country to have closer links with the West and to have a navy, too. Because it is on the Baltic Sea, St Petersburg was in a good place to trade with other countries, but because the land was so low-lying, there were often floods. Can you see the statue of Tsar Peter the Great on the map on the opposite page?

Later in the eighteenth century, Catherine II became the Empress of Russia. She ruled Russia for over 30 years and was such a powerful woman that she became known as Catherine

You can find out about centuries on page 119.

the Great. Like Peter the Great, she wanted to make her country more modern and more like Western European countries. She built a magnificent palace called the Hermitage to display her great art collection. The Hermitage is now a museum and is visited by art-lovers from all over the world.

St Petersburg is so far north that in midsummer it is not completely dark even at night. Can you look at a globe and think why this might be? In 1918, Moscow became the capital of Russia but St Petersburg is still the second largest city in Russia. Both Moscow and St Petersburg have famous ballet companies.

The Hermitage Museum, along the River Neva, has one of the greatest art collections in the world.

Baltic Countries

West of Russia on the Baltic Sea are the three small countries of Latvia, Lithuania and Estonia and the large country of Poland. Because they are so far north, it isn't quite as warm to swim at their seaside compared to the Mediterranean's! These four Baltic countries have now joined the European Union but, in the past, they had to fight for control of their land

Warsaw's colourful Old Town

against powerful countries like Austria, Russia and Germany. Britain is an island, so its borders are clearer, but when countries are surrounded by other countries, there are often disagreements over where the boundaries between them should be. These disagreements have led to many wars.

In Poland, visitors can spend time at the Baltic seaside, explore the Old Town of the capital city Warsaw or go hiking in the mountains. A long time ago Krakow was the capital city. A famous university was founded there in 1364 called the Jagiellonian University. It was one of the first universities in this part of Europe and became the home of many great scholars. The River Vistula runs right through Poland and goes through both Krakow and Warsaw. Can you follow the path of the river on the map?

Balkans

South of the Danube are the Balkan countries, along the Balkan Peninsula. They are mountainous countries north of Greece. Many tourists enjoy visiting Croatia, on the opposite shore of the Adriatic Sea from Italy. It has attractive islands and a beautiful walled city called Dubrovnik that used to be a big trading city.

Other countries in the Balkans include Albania, Bosnia-Herzegovina, Bulgaria and Kosovo, amongst others.

The city of Dubrovnik juts out into the sea, and its sheltered harbour protects many boats.

Rivers and Seas

The countries of Eastern Europe are surrounded by four seas: the Caspian Sea, Black Sea, Adriatic Sea and Baltic Sea. The Caspian Sea is completely surrounded by land, so you could call it a lake. If so, it is the largest lake in the world! What is the difference between a sea and a lake? For one thing, seawater is salty whereas the water in lakes is called *fresh water*, meaning that it is not salty.

The Caspian Sea is a bit salty, but not as salty as other seas. That is because the Caspian Sea is fed by water flowing from 130 rivers, including the Volga River and the Ural River, but the water has nowhere to flow out again. Can you see the fish in the Caspian Sea on the map on page 100? It is called a *sturgeon*, and there are a lot of them here. The eggs of the sturgeon are used to make *caviar*, a sort of paste to spread on little bits of bread or biscuits. It is one of the most expensive things to eat!

This area has a lot of oil, and the Caspian Sea was the first place where people practised *off-shore drilling* – which means setting up an oil rig in the water and drilling down into the seabed. There are also islands in the Caspian Sea that have very large *reserves* (stores) of oil.

The Black Sea looks as if it could be a lake too, but if you look at the map very carefully, you will see that the water can flow out towards the Aegean Sea and then the Mediterranean Sea. The water flows through the Bosphorus, and we read on page 99 about how it divides Europe and Asia.

The Adriatic Sea has the Italian peninsula on one side and the Balkan countries on the other. Croatia, Albania and Slovenia all have coastlines on the Adriatic. It is quite shallow at the northern end but gets deeper as it joins with the Ionian Sea, which in turn joins with the Mediterranean Sea.

The Baltic Sea, like the Black Sea, is almost entirely surrounded by land, but it reaches the North Sea by going through narrow stretches of water called *straits* between Denmark and Sweden. Like the Black Sea and the Caspian Sea, is it slightly salty, but not as salty as most seas are. The weather in this northern part of Europe is so cold in winter that a lot of the Baltic Sea becomes covered with ice. There are some very large sheltered areas called *gulfs* on the edge of the Baltic, and these freeze first, but sometimes the whole of the Baltic is covered with ice. There are some very important shipyards on the shores of the Baltic, including a famous one at Gdansk in Poland.

As you can see from the map on page 100, there are some very long rivers in Eastern Europe. The Volga – which starts to the north of Moscow, the capital of Russia, and eventually reaches the Caspian Sea – is the longest river in

> We started learning about the Volga and the Danube in Year 3.

Europe. The Russian people call it Mother Volga. The Ural, the Don, the Dnieper and the Vistula are all long and important rivers, but the most famous river in this part of Europe is probably the Danube.

In Year 3, we learnt how the Danube River flows from the German mountains to the Black Sea. The river is so long that it flows through several countries in Western Europe and then flows into Eastern Europe. Four capital cities lie on its route. The Danube flows through Vienna, the capital of Austria; Bratislava, the capital of Slovakia; Budapest, the capital of Hungary; and Belgrade, the capital of Serbia.

This hydrofoil is travelling from Bratislava to Budapest on the Danube. Why do you think boats like hydrofoils go faster downstream than upstream?

Mountains

Where do you think we would find the highest mountains in Europe? Did you say the Alps? In fact, Europe's highest mountains are in the far south-east corner of Europe. They are called the Caucasus Mountains and they stretch out in two great ridges between Turkey and the Caspian Sea. The very highest mountain in this range is Mount Elbrus in Russia.

People enjoy skiing in some parts of the Caucasus Mountains.

On the edge of the great plain, between the Danube, Vistula and Dnieper rivers, the Carpathian range is a chain of mountains that crosses the Czech Republic, Slovakia, Poland, Hungary, Ukraine and Romania. Bears live up in the Carpathian Mountains in the north of Romania. Can you see the bear on our map? What is he trying to catch?

Religion and Alphabet

There are many different countries and many different cultures in Eastern Europe. People speak different languages, practise different religions and even use different alphabets.

The Russian Orthodox St Basil's Cathedral in Moscow is well-known for its 'onion domes'. Why do you think they are called that?

In Russia, most Christians belong to the Orthodox Church. Orthodox

The Cyrillic script on these stamps shows Russia's pride in its ships and space programme.

Christians sing together without musical instruments, and they use *icons* in church, which are pictures of Jesus and holy men and women painted in a special way that takes a very long time. They use the *Cyrillic* [si-RILL-ic] alphabet named after St Cyril, who translated the Bible into the Russian language. It has more letters than our alphabet and includes ten vowels.

There are other Eastern European countries that use the Cyrillic alphabet, but not all of them do. In some countries, where the Christians belong to Catholic or Protestant churches, they write with the Latin alphabet we know, using the same letters as the ancient Romans. The country where the language is most like the language spoken by the Romans is Romania. You might guess that from the name! When Emperor Trajan crossed the Danube and invaded, he made them part of the Roman Empire. There are many Muslims who speak Arabic in parts of Eastern Europe, like Kosovo and Bosnia, because the Ottoman Empire in Turkey used to have a strong influence on this area of Europe. Do you know how to speak or write in any other languages?

British Geography

Let's Explore London and the South East

You know that London is the capital of the United Kingdom. It is also the biggest city in the country, and one of the biggest in the whole world. People from all over the country

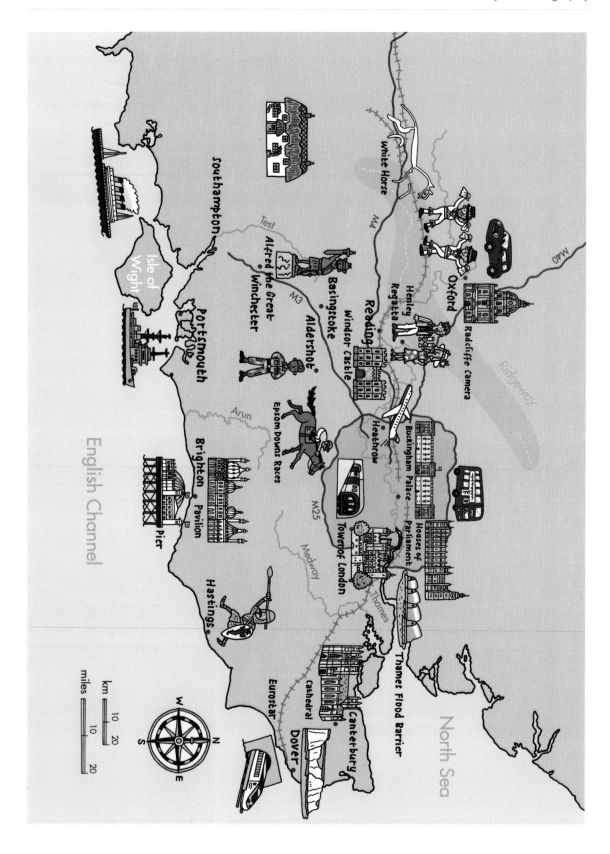

and from all over the world have moved to London to live and work, so there are lots of different languages and cultures in the city. In fact, there are so many people there that, to help everyone get around more easily, London has a network of trains in

The London Underground carries about three and a half million passengers per day.

tunnels underneath the city. This is called the London Underground, or the Tube.

People can also travel around this enormous city using London's famous red double-decker buses. London is a *conurbation*; do you remember learning about conurbations in Year 3? It means that the city has grown and spread out so that it also includes lots of other urban areas too. Because lots of people want to travel to London, it has one of the busiest airports in the world, called Heathrow. People come to London on holiday or to do business and there are other airports such as Gatwick and City Airport because having just one airport wasn't enough for all the people who wanted to travel to London.

We already know that the River Thames runs right through London on its way out to the North Sea. There are around 30 bridges across the Thames in London. The oldest is London Bridge, but it has been rebuilt many times over the centuries. The River Thames has been very important to London, helping people in the city to trade with countries all over the world, but it

The Thames Barrier can stop a high tide coming up the Thames to flood London.

can be dangerous too. To stop the city flooding during high tides and storms, the Thames Flood Barrier was built in the 1980s. It stretches across the river and can be raised when the sea might come too far up the river to London at high tide.

London was founded by the Romans, who called it *Londinium*, and since then it has grown to become one of the most important cities in the world. Today, London is home to the Houses of Parliament, which is where politicians meet to make decisions about how to run the country, but London is famous for lots of other things. Some of the most important art galleries and museums in the country are in

We first started learning about the Romans in Britain in Year 2.

London, as well as famous landmarks like Tower Bridge, St Paul's Cathedral and Buckingham Palace where the Queen lives. There are many theatres in London, and people come from all over the world to see their performances.

London's Financial District

Canterbury Cathedral

People in London do all sorts of different jobs and there are many different businesses in the city. The financial district, where many banks and other businesses offering *financial services* (relating to money) have their headquarters, is referred to as the City (with a capital 'C'). This is because many years ago there used to be two separate cities: the City of London (where the businesses were) and the City of Westminster (where the king and the government were).

London is in the South East of England, and there are lots of other interesting places in this region. Further south east in the county of Kent is Canterbury, where St Augustine brought Christianity to England, and to this day the Archbishop of Canterbury is the head of the Church of England. Canterbury's cathedral is beautiful, seen either close up or from the hills above the city.

The White Cliffs of Dover

On the south coast of Britain, the port of Dover is one of the places where you can sail across the English Channel to France. From the boat, you can look back towards England and see the famous White Cliffs of Dover. If you get seasick, however, maybe you would want to travel to France through the Channel Tunnel, which is also called 'the Chunnel'. This is a 30-mile long tunnel under the English Channel. It means that you can get a train from London to Paris.

Also on the south coast of Britain is the town of Hastings. Can you think of what Hastings is famous for? It is where the Battle of Hastings took place, when William the Conqueror defeated Harold to become the King of England in 1066.

> We learnt about the Battle of Hastings and William the Conqueror in Year 2.

Further along the south coast is the seaside town of Brighton, in the county of Sussex. For a long time, people have travelled to Brighton to be beside the seaside and enjoy its beaches. The weather is often warmer on the south coast too. Brighton has a famous *pier* called Palace Pier. (It used to have more but the others were damaged.) Piers are long walkways out into the sea lined with cafes and sweetshops, theatres and amusements. People

Palace Pier in Brighton

also come to Brighton to see its famous Royal Pavilion. It was built by the architect John Nash to be a royal *residence*, where the royal family could stay when they came to visit the seaside.

Further along the coast to the west, the ports of Southampton and Portsmouth both have strong connections with the sea. Southampton is where the doomed ocean liner *Titanic* set sail on her maiden (first) voyage in 1912. She sailed safely out of Southampton, only to sink after hitting an iceberg a few hundred kilometres from New York. The city of Portsmouth is famous for its naval dockyards. It has been an important base for the Navy since the time of Henry VIII. Further north, in Hampshire, the Army has a big base in Aldershot.

There are several old and new ways of travelling west through the region from London. On the River Thames, a boat could take you past Henley, where top rowers compete in the regatta, to the university city of Oxford, where the Mini cars are made. In the Thames Valley is a fast railway line to Bristol, designed by the famous engineer Isambard Kingdom Brunel. You can see farms from the railway, because the soil is ideal for growing fruit. Up on the line of chalk downs is the Ridgeway. 'Downs' seems like a funny word for hills, since they go up, but that is what they are called. Chalk lets rainwater drain quickly, so the hilltop route was dry and good for traders taking their farm animals to market.

Besides history, the South East of England is home to lots of companies and businesses. In fact, it has more than any other region outside of London. If you were to travel west from London along the M4 motorway you would pass by many towns and cities: Slough, Maidenhead, Bracknell and Reading. There are lots of companies here where people work with *technology*, which means doing useful things with science and often involves computers. This is sometimes called 'hi-tech' industry.

Let's Explore The South West

The South West of England is made up of the counties of Cornwall, Devon, Dorset, Somerset, Wiltshire and Gloucestershire. It is one of the warmest parts of Britain because it is the furthest south and the first area to be warmed by the Gulf Stream. This is one of the reasons why many places in the South West are popular with tourists from other parts of the UK and abroad.

Cornwall, for example, is famous for its beaches and beautiful coastline. You can see from looking at a map of the UK that the county of Cornwall juts out into the Atlantic Ocean. The strong ocean waves not only make it a popular place for surfing but also erode the coastline. *Coastal erosion* happens when strong waves batter the land, causing bits of rock and soil to break off into the sea. It happens wherever land meets the sea, but in places like the south-west coast it happens more quickly because of the Atlantic Ocean's

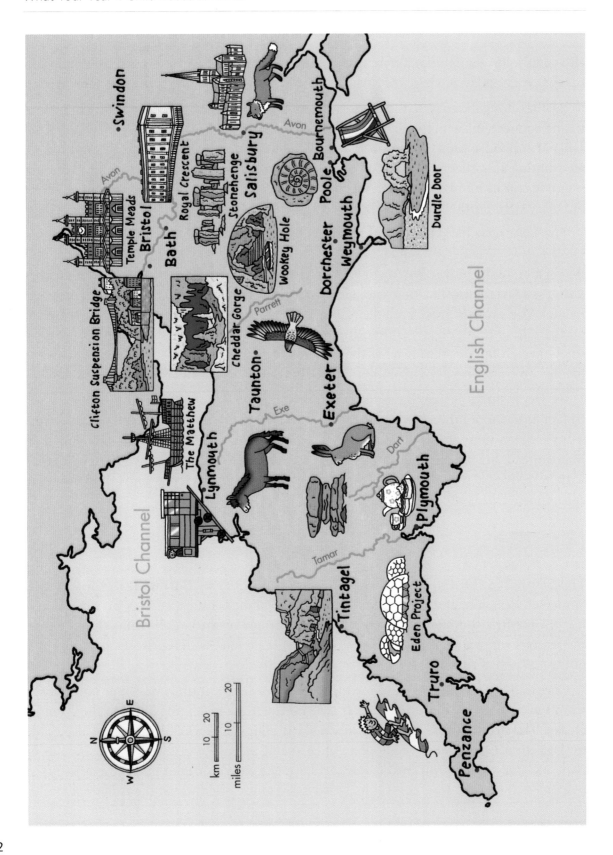

Waves batter the coastline at Land's End in Cornwall.

big waves hitting the land. The effects of erosion can be seen in places such as the jagged cliffs at Land's End, at the very south-west of Britain.

The warmer climate in the South West means that much of the land is well suited to farming. There are many different types of *agriculture* (this means farming) that take place in the South West. Where the land is flat and the soil is fertile, the warm weather makes it a good place to grow fruit and vegetables. The county of Somerset is well known for growing apples. It is also the home of the town of Cheddar, after which the cheese is named, and lots of cheese is made in this part of the country because of all the cows here. Just west of Somerset, in Devon, dairy products like cheese and cream are produced too.

The South West is a popular place to visit for more than its good weather and food: there are also many interesting natural and man-made landmarks to see. In the county of Wiltshire is the world-famous ancient monument Stonehenge. Stonehenge is a giant circle of standing stones that was built over four thousand years ago! Nobody really knows why (or how!) the huge rectangular stones were put up here.

Stonehenge is one of the oldest man-made things in Britain.

We learnt about Stonehenge in Year 1 and King Alfred burning the cakes in Year 2.

The region is rich in tall tales and legends. Tintagel Castle in Cornwall and Glastonbury in Somerset are linked with events in the life and death of King Arthur. Althelney, also in Somerset, is where King Alfred burnt the cakes.

On the Dorset coastline, coastal erosion has created many interesting and beautiful natural landmarks. One of these is Durdle Door, a giant rock arch made of limestone stretching out into the sea. The South West has many other popular natural landmarks, such as Cheddar Gorge in Somerset. A *gorge*

We read legends about King Arthur and Camelot in Years 1 and 3.

is a steep valley where the land has been worn away by a river and Cheddar Gorge is a very dramatic natural feature. The hilly land of Exmoor, Dartmoor and Bodmin Moor provide bleak but beautiful landscapes for people to enjoy.

Durdle Door was formed after softer rock eroded away, leaving a hard limestone arch.

Generally, the South West is quite a rural area of Britain, but there are some bigger towns and cities there too. Bristol is the largest. It has a rich seafaring history. Explorer John Cabot and engineer Isambard Kingdom Brunel both sailed ships from Bristol. It was a major port, trading in industrial products but also in African slaves. Large cargo ships still sail from Avonmouth.

Nearby, the city of Bath was an ancient Roman settlement and some ancient buildings still survive here, most famously the Roman Baths where the water is already hot as it comes out of the ground. Exeter was a Roman settlement too. It is now known for its cathedral and university.

On the south coast of Dorset, the town of Bournemouth has been a popular tourist resort for people to come and spend time by the seaside since the nineteenth century. The Dorset coastline was once home to Jurassic dinosaurs.

Read more about fossils on page 297.

Fossils are still being found there and the Natural History Museum has a Scelidosaurus from Dorset in its collection.

Let's Explore Northern Ireland

The northern part of the island of Ireland is called Northern Ireland. It is part of the United Kingdom and separate from the Republic of Ireland. Northern Ireland is sometimes referred to as Ulster. Ulster is one of the four provinces, or areas, of Ireland and is made up of nine different counties. Six of these counties make up Northern Ireland. They are Fermanagh, Tyrone, Londonderry, Armagh, Antrim and Down. The three other counties of Ulster – Donegal, Cavan and Monaghan – are part of the Republic of Ireland.

The climate in Northern Ireland is very similar to that of the north of England and Scotland. It is temperate and humid, and because of the Atlantic Ocean there are high levels of rainfall, especially over high ground. The Sperrin Mountains in the west and the Mourne Mountains in the south east are the main upland areas of Northern Ireland. Slieve Donard, the highest mountain in Northern Ireland, can be found in the Mourne Mountains, which are mainly formed out of granite rock. Whilst some crops are grown, the climate and geography of Northern Ireland mean that the upland areas are often used for animal farming.

Farmers grow crops at the foot of the Mourne Mountains.

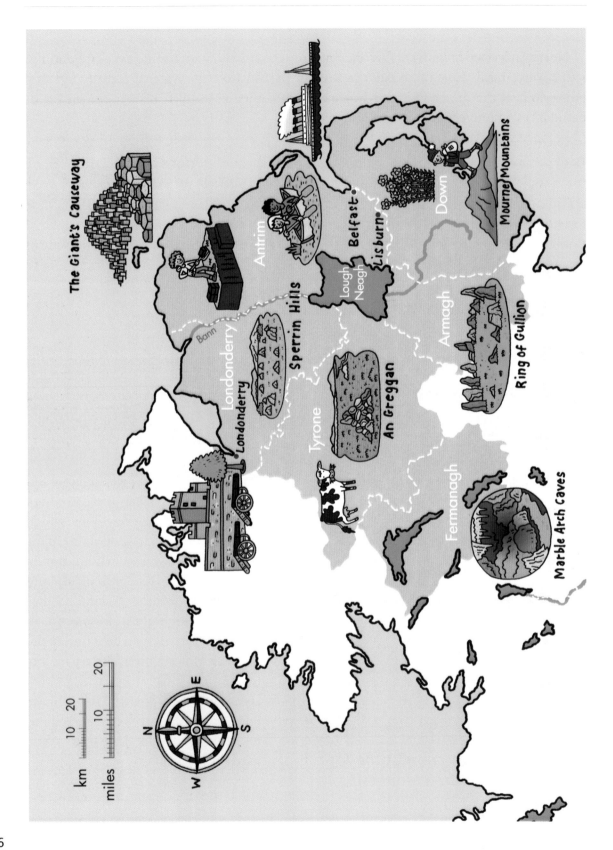

Northern Ireland has many other interesting natural features. It is home to the largest lake in the British Isles, Lough Neagh. The lake is about 20 miles long and nine miles wide and is

You can read about Finn MacCool on page 41.

used for recreation, as well as providing drinking water to many people in Northern Ireland. According to an old Irish legend, the lake was formed when a giant called Finn MacCool scooped up the land and threw it into the sea, creating the Isle of Man as well as Lough Neagh.

The Marble Arch Caves are a natural limestone cave system formed by an underground river. These amazing caves are over seven miles long, but are not the most famous natural feature in Northern Ireland. That prize almost certainly goes to the Giant's Causeway, which is one of the most popular tourist destinations in Ireland and one of the most unusual. It is a landscape of rock columns made of basalt. Each column is quite small, but together they create thousands of steps down from the surrounding cliffs into the sea. It was created by an ancient volcanic

Walk on paths through the Marble Arch Caves to explore them yourself.

eruption. However, legend has it that the same giant Finn MacCool built it as part of a causeway that connected Ireland and Scotland.

You can walk out on the Giant's Causeway and think of Finn MacCool.

117

Belfast is the capital and the largest city in Northern Ireland. It is also the most heavily *industrialised* part of Northern Ireland. This means that there are many factories in this area. Belfast was particularly famous for producing textiles and shipbuilding. The *Titanic* was built in Belfast, but now there are other important industries, such as engineering and electronics. Belfast is by far the biggest city, but the second biggest settlement is Londonderry, also called Derry. It is one of the oldest inhabited places in Ireland and is famous for its city walls, built to protect the city's inhabitants in the seventeenth century.

$e^{i\pi}+1=0$

See a picture
of Belfast and r(
its size on page

The city of Lisburn is best known for making linen. Tablecloths and sheets of the highest quality are made by spinning, bleaching and weaving fibres from the flax plant.

Learn about weaving
on page 188.

People have come from many other places to live in Northern Ireland. Many people in Northern Ireland can trace their families back to Scotland. These people are sometimes known as Ulster-Scots, and are mainly Protestant. The people who lived in Ireland before the Scots arrived were the Gaelic Irish community, and they were mainly Catholic. Northern Ireland remained part of the United Kingdom when the rest of Ireland became independent in 1922. Communities in Northern Ireland still disagree about whether Northern Ireland should be part of the Republic of Ireland or remain in the United Kingdom. Those who wish to remain in union with Britain are called Unionists and those who wish to be part of an Irish nation are called Nationalists.

Fibres from the flax plant are spun and then woven together to make linen.

What is a century?

How do we know when things happened in the past? We read on page 122 about the way in which we use B.C. and A.D. to describe things that happened either before or after the birth of Jesus Christ. But suppose we want to be more exact about when things happened? Then we talk about the *century* they happened in.

A century is a hundred years long. On page 257 we learn that the letter that the Romans used to show 100 was C, because the Latin word for a hundred is *centum*. But how do we know which century is which? This sounds strange, but the *ordinal number* of the century always sounds like it's one ahead of the first one or two numbers in the exact date! So, the dates 1603, 1642 and 1688 were all in the *seventeenth* century. Do you remember the date of the Norman Conquest? It was 1066 – in the *eleventh* century. King John agreed to Magna Carta in 1215 – in the *thirteenth* century. In which century was 1776? Or 1851? Which century are we in now?

$$e^{i\pi} + 1 = 0$$

We learn about ordinal numbers on page 232.

The little princes were murdered in the Tower of London in 1483 – in the *fifteenth* century

Sir Francis Drake defeated the Spanish Armada in 1588 – in the *sixteenth* century

Charles I was beheaded in 1649 – in the *seventeenth* century

| 1400 | 1500 | 1600 | 1700 |

Ancient Rome

Do you remember the saying 'When in Rome, do as the Romans do'? When people use that saying today, they aren't really talking about the great city in Italy, are they? Here's another saying: 'Rome wasn't built in a day'. Again, when people use that saying today, they aren't really referring to Rome. Instead they mean: 'Be patient. It takes a long time to complete a great task.'

Read about the saying 'When in Rome, do as the Romans do' on page 85.

These and other sayings about Rome are still around because Rome is still important to us. Like the civilization of ancient Greece, ancient Rome still affects us today. In our laws and government, in the design of many buildings, in our calendar, even in many words of the English language, ancient Rome lives on in these modern times.

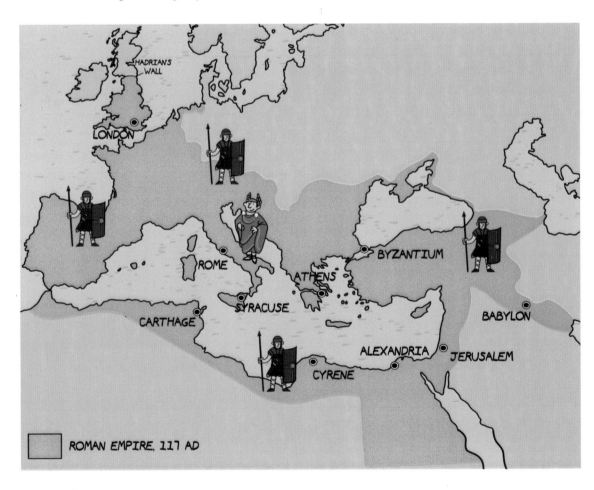

The Legend of How Rome Began

Almost three thousand years ago, people chose seven hills above the River Tiber in Italy as a good place to build their little huts and to farm the land. Those villages grew together into the city called Rome. As Rome grew, its army conquered other countries. The boundaries of Rome's empire spread. Look at the map to see how, at its biggest and strongest, the Roman Empire included most of today's Europe and some of Africa and the Middle East as well. Sixty million people lived under Roman rule, many of them far from the city of Rome, in places that we now call Great Britain, Germany, France, Spain, Greece, Egypt and Turkey.

The ancient Romans believed that they were born to rule the world. They told a story about how their city was founded by two brothers, Romulus and Remus.

In the legend, there was a jealous king who feared that if his niece had children, they might take his kingdom from him when they grew up. To make sure that she never had any children, the jealous king made his niece become a priestess. That way she would devote herself to the gods and never marry any man.

Imagine the king's anger when his niece gave birth to twin boys, Romulus and Remus. She explained that the father of these two boys was not a man but Mars, the Roman god of war. The angry king put the babies into a basket and threw them into the River Tiber to drown.

But Romulus and Remus were rescued from the river by a mother wolf. She took them back to her lair and fed them as if they were her own babies. When a passing shepherd happened to see the two boys, he took them to his village and cared for them until they grew to be men.

Romulus and Remus agreed that they should start a city. As brothers will do, though, they argued over many things. Where would they put the city? Who would be its ruler? During one terrible argument, Romulus killed Remus.

Legend has it that Rome was founded by two brothers, Romulus and Remus, who were raised by a wolf.

121

Romulus went on to build his city on the seven hills overlooking the River Tiber. The city took its name from his: Rome. He ruled as king for many years. Then one night, in the midst of a huge thunderstorm, Romulus disappeared. The Romans believed that he became a god.

As with most legends, there is some truth in the story about Romulus and Remus. As early as 950 B.C., almost three thousand years ago, shepherds and farmers lived on those hills overlooking the River Tiber. About two hundred years later, around 750 B.C., those communities joined to form the one city of Rome.

Talking about time in history

When we talk about ancient history, we're going back a long time, sometimes more than 2,000 years. That means we're going back to the year with the number 1, or even further. How do we number those years more than 2,000 years ago?

We give years their dates based on the birthday of Jesus, whom Christians call Christ, starting to count from the year Jesus was born. The years before Christ was born are called B.C., which stands for 'before Christ'. If we say Rome was founded in the year 753 B.C., we mean 753 years before Jesus was born.

Every date after the birth of Jesus is called A.D., which stands for *anno Domini*, or 'in the year of the Lord' in Latin, the language of the Romans. 'In the year of the Lord' is another way of saying 'after Christ'. If you were born in 2005, then another way to name your birth year is A.D. 2005, meaning that you were born 2,005 years after the birth of Jesus.

Religion, Roman Style

Like the ancient Greeks, the ancient Romans worshipped many gods and goddesses. The Romans believed that their gods and goddesses looked and acted like people but held powers greater than those of any human being. Like the Greeks, the Romans built temples in which they worshipped their gods.

We first learnt about the ancient Greek gods in Year 3.

They carved beautiful statues to show what they thought their gods looked like. Today in some museums we can see those statues, and in the city of Rome we can see the ruins of those temples.

Also like the Greeks, the ancient Romans believed that different gods ruled different parts of their world. The king of all the gods, who ruled the sky, was named Jupiter by the Romans. He behaved a lot like the Greek god Zeus. The Romans believed that Neptune ruled the sea, just as the Greeks believed in Poseidon.

The Roman Forum includes ruins of very old Roman buildings and temples.

Learn more about another ancient Roman temple, the Pantheon, on page 194.

Romans performed ceremonies to please the gods. They would pray, offer food and wine and sacrifice animals such as sheep or goats. These ceremonies took place at home, led by the head of the household, or at temples, led by the priests.

The ancient Romans also believed that godlike spirits lived in nature. When birds flew overhead, Romans saw them as messengers from the gods. Priests would watch the way birds flew and decide what the gods were saying.

Rome's Powerful Location

What made Rome so powerful? One answer is location. Let's look at the map on page 120. First find the country we now call Italy. It is a peninsula, shaped like a boot, sticking out into the Mediterranean Sea. Its long eastern coastline faces the Adriatic Sea. Now find Rome. What are the advantages of its location?

Rome sits at a crossroads on both land and sea. It is on a river, so boats can leave Rome and reach the Mediterranean Sea. It is far enough south for Romans to enjoy a mild climate. Further north, the mountain range called the Alps runs from one edge of the boot shape to the other. The Alps protected the ancient Romans. Their rocky, snow-covered peaks kept out most invaders – but not *all*, as you will see.

Can you spot the mountains in the distance beyond the city of Rome?

Rome's Early Republic

For 250 years, Rome was ruled by kings. Some were strong and some were kind, but the last king was so proud and cruel that the people drove him away. To be sure that no bad king came to power again, the Romans invented a new form of government. They called it a *republic*, from the Latin words for 'a thing of the people'.

Read about this last king in 'Horatius at the Bridge' on page 63.

Every year the wealthy men of the Roman republic would select two leaders, called *consuls*. Having two people to make important decisions meant that no one man was likely to grab all the power. In times of war, the consuls led the army. In times of peace, they ran the business of the city. To make decisions, both consuls had to agree. If one disagreed, he would say 'Veto', which means 'I forbid' in Latin.

The Romans had a *Senate*, which advised the consuls. The Senate was a group of as many as three hundred wealthy landowners. Once a man became a Roman senator, he held that position for life.

Who's Got Class?

Some people who lived in Rome were considered citizens, but some were not. Slaves and foreigners and, in the early times, people living in conquered lands were not considered citizens. Women were not considered citizens either, no matter how clever or wealthy they were.

Some Roman gods

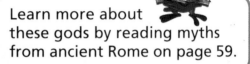

Jupiter: the King of the gods and god of the sky

Learn more about these gods by reading myths from ancient Rome on page 59.

Juno: Jupiter's wife, the goddess of women and marriage

Minerva: the goddess of wisdom and crafts

Mercury: the god of trade

Mars: the god of war

Venus: the goddess of love and beauty

Diana: the goddess of hunting

Apollo: the god of art and medicine

Pluto: the god of the underworld

Saturn: the god of farming and time

Neptune: the god of the sea ▶

Vulcan: the god of volcanoes and fire

Members of all classes came to the Colosseum for entertainment, but they sat in separate sections.

Among the Roman citizens, there were two classes: the *patricians* [pat-TRISH-uns] and the *plebeians* [pleb-EE-ans]. Patricians were wealthy men who owned a lot of land. They became consuls and senators. Plebeians were ordinary people who owned a little property but were still poor. The poorest people in Rome were the slaves, who did hard work for both patricians and plebeians.

The plebeians wanted more say in how they were governed. As Rome conquered more lands, the patricians needed the plebeians more, since they fought in the army. Over time, the plebeians gained rights nearly equal to those of the patricians. A plebeian council was established to allow ordinary people the chance to discuss policy. It elected tribunes who could veto decisions of the Senate. Initially there were two 'tribunes of the people', but later there were more.

Rome and Its Provinces

Rome grew by taking control of land in every direction. Any area conquered by the Roman army became a province of Rome. Roman rulers assigned a governor to each province to rule the people and report back to Rome. They collected taxes, either food or money, from the people in the provinces and sent them to Rome.

Some of the conquered people became slaves. In other provinces, the Romans allowed people to follow their own customs and religions. They even let wealthy men from the provinces become Roman citizens. Those who did business in the provinces had to speak Latin, the language of Rome.

Latin Lives!

Some people call Latin a dead language because no one speaks or reads it in everyday life. Plenty of people study Latin, though, because it has played an important part in the history of many

Isaac Newton wrote science books in Latin.

of the languages spoken around the world. In that way, Latin is far from a dead language.

Latin was the language spoken and written in ancient Rome. As Rome conquered its provinces, Latin became the language spoken throughout the Roman Empire.

Look at these Roman letters chiselled into stone and see how many letters in the Roman alphabet are the same as ours today. Can you find the name 'Claudius' on the stone?

Foreign merchants and local town rulers used Latin to communicate with the Roman soldiers, businessmen and governors. Over centuries, the Latin language spread far, and words in Latin influenced the words spoken in the languages of all those regions.

Some of our English words come from Latin, such as 'family' (*familia* in Latin) and 'mother' (*mater* in Latin). Many other English words have a connection with Latin. 'Library' comes from *liber*, the Latin word for 'book'. It's fun to find the Latin roots of English words in the dictionary. (Even 'dictionary' comes from *dictio*, Latin for 'speech'.)

Conquering Carthage

By 265 B.C., Rome had conquered most of the peninsula of Italy. Next, the Romans decided to conquer lands that were further away. To the north, that meant invading by land. But to the south, that meant invading by sea, and it meant facing the biggest threat to Roman power, the strong and wealthy city of Carthage. (Find Carthage on the map, page 120.)

Carthage was a city on the north coast of Africa, in the country we now call Tunisia. The city of Carthage began at just about the same time as Rome. By 265 B.C., Carthage controlled much of North Africa. The Carthaginians [car-thuh-JIN-ee-uns] were great shipbuilders and sailors. One of the lands they had conquered was the island of Sicily.

Take a look at the map on page 120 to find Sicily. (Here's a clue – its capital city was Syracuse.) Which is closer to Sicily: Italy or Carthage? Sicily is less than ten miles from Italy. The Romans thought that Carthage was a threat because it was so close.

A war broke out between Carthage and Rome over who would control Sicily. Battles were fought at sea. Who do you think had the advantage? Not the Romans! They could fight a ferocious battle on land, but on the water they were in big trouble.

Once the Romans learnt to build ships, they began waging battles at sea.

But those Romans believed they were born to rule the world, so they weren't about to give up and go home. They found a wrecked Carthaginian warship and, with the help of Greek shipbuilders, made one hundred copies of it in 60 days.

When a Roman ship pulled alongside the enemy, the sailors lowered a drawbridge with a hook that attached to the deck of the enemy ship. Roman soldiers crossed the drawbridge and attacked the Carthaginians on board their own ships, wielding swords and spears and winning many battles.

> Rome's wars against Carthage were called the Punic Wars because the Romans used the Latin word *Punicus* to mean a person from Carthage.

After more than 20 years of struggle, Rome won its first war against Carthage, called the First Punic [PYOO-nick] War. The proud Carthaginians did not want to be conquered by the Romans. One man was so angry that he made his son promise to battle Rome for the rest of his life. That promise begins the next chapter in ancient Roman history.

Hannibal Keeps His Promise

Hannibal was only nine years old when his father, angry over the Roman conquest of Carthage, took him to a temple. 'Swear by the gods that you will be the enemy of Rome until the day you die!' he demanded. The young boy agreed, and from that day forward, his life was shaped by the promise. By the age of twenty-five, Hannibal had already led an army of Carthaginians across the Mediterranean and into Spain, capturing a city that was friendly with Rome. That's how the Second Punic War started.

When word arrived in Rome that Hannibal was attacking the city in Spain, the Senate sent soldiers out to find him. It took those soldiers a long time to reach Spain and, when they got there, Hannibal was nowhere to be found.

'He's headed east,' everyone told them.

'East?' questioned the Romans. 'Across the mighty Alps? Even if he were foolish enough to scale those icy slopes, his men would die trying.'

The Romans had no idea how courageous Hannibal was. He did lead his army across the Alps, which were icy, steep and dangerous. And what an army it was! Hannibal started out with sixty thousand soldiers, marching all the way from Spain, through France (then called Gaul), across the Alps and into Italy. Along with those men came 40 massive beasts — animals that frightened the Romans, who had never seen them before. They were huge and heavy, much taller than a human, with big ears, thundering feet and long trunks. Elephants!

Hannibal and his soldiers crossed the Alps on rocky pathways. They marched across icy streams, up and down snow-covered slopes. Many soldiers and most of the elephants died, but that didn't stop Hannibal. He had made a promise to his father and he was going to keep it.

Imagine leading thousands of soldiers and dozens of elephants along the narrow, icy paths of the Alps, as Hannibal did.

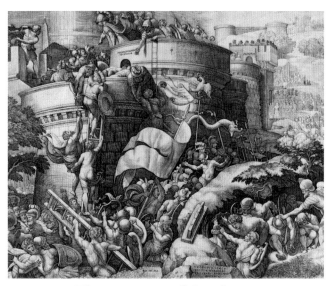

The capture of Carthage

At last, he and his soldiers made it into Italy. They camped in the villages and countryside outside Rome. They befriended the villagers who hated Rome, and banded together to attack Roman villages. Hannibal stayed in Italy for more than 16 years, tormenting the Romans but never actually capturing Rome. No matter what they tried, the Romans could not defeat Hannibal.

The Romans finally decided that if they could not defeat Hannibal on their own soil, maybe they could defeat him on his. They sent a mighty army across the Mediterranean to Carthage. They thought that if Hannibal's own city were under siege, he would rush home to defend it.

The plan worked. Hannibal returned to Carthage, but he was too late. In 202 B.C., Rome defeated the Carthaginians again, ending the Second Punic War. The Romans demanded large sums of money, and they made the Carthaginians promise to keep a smaller fleet of ships.

But they still hadn't captured Hannibal. He lived in hiding for years, refusing Roman rule because of his boyhood promise. When it looked as if Roman soldiers were going to capture him, Hannibal killed himself, choosing to die rather than to live under Rome.

The Final Defeat of Carthage

Rome and Carthage just wouldn't stop fighting. Fifty years later Rome burned Carthage to the ground. The Carthaginians who survived were sold into slavery. With this victory, Rome now ruled over North Africa and Spain, and the islands of Corsica, Sardinia and Sicily.

All Roads Lead to Rome

Many roads were built to connect the city of Rome to the places it ruled. As soon as Rome conquered a new territory, soldiers and slaves would build roads from there to Rome.

Imagine building a road where there are only trees and rocks and earth. And without trucks or bulldozers! The Romans wanted their roads as level and straight as possible. They dug tunnels through hills. They built bridges over rivers. Even today, more than two thousand years later, people still use the roads and bridges that the Romans built.

> Do you remember from Year 2 how the Roman roads in Britain were important in changing society?

You can still walk along this ancient Roman road today.

Good roads and strong bridges helped Rome to become powerful. The Romans had no cars, trucks, trains or planes, yet they controlled an enormous area. You could travel on a Roman road to North Wales or to the edge of the desert in North Africa. Good roads helped the Romans travel rapidly to the faraway provinces. If there was a rebellion against the Romans anywhere, good roads and bridges meant that messages got to Rome more easily and Roman soldiers could reach the province more quickly to crush the rebellion.

Good roads and bridges also helped business. Romans could carry what they grew or made to the provinces to sell, and they could bring goods from the provinces back to Rome. We know that the Romans traded many things with their provinces, such as pottery and wool, gold and silver, olive oil and wheat, copper, tin and iron. The further the

Roman roads reached, the more materials could be brought back to Rome, making the city richer all the time.

By 100 B.C., Rome was ruling many people in many lands. These people paid taxes to Rome. Romans did business with the conquered peoples. Thousands of foreign slaves worked on roads, bridges and buildings. It sounds like a time of prosperity but, in fact, it was a time of war and unhappiness. Then a man named Julius Caesar came on the scene, changing the course of Roman history forever.

Julius Caesar Shows the Pirates Who's Boss

Julius Caesar

Julius Caesar was born in 100 B.C., the son of a wealthy man. In those days, if a rich young man wanted to make a name for himself, he would go off and fight in foreign lands. Julius Caesar did just that.

Roman ships carried gold from other territories back to Rome. Young Julius Caesar was given the job of protecting the gold from pirates. He was captured and held prisoner. Rome paid a high ransom to make the pirates set him free. Later Caesar tracked down those pirates and killed them.

Julius Caesar became a great hero to the Romans. He was sent to fight in Gaul (the country we now call France) which he conquered. He tried to invade Britain twice but didn't stay very long.

Pompey, Caesar's Rival

While Julius Caesar was off fighting in foreign lands, a man named Pompey became powerful in Rome. Like Caesar, Pompey was a great soldier.

At first, Pompey and Julius Caesar believed they could rule in Rome together, but Pompey grew jealous of Julius Caesar's power and popularity. While Caesar was fighting in Gaul, Pompey convinced some senators that Julius Caesar was a dangerous man who might try to take over Rome. The Senate declared Pompey 'a protector of the state' and called Julius Caesar 'a public enemy'. They ordered Caesar to give up his leadership, disband his army and come home to Rome.

Crossing the Rubicon

Can you imagine how Julius Caesar felt? If he obeyed the Senate's command, he lost all power. But if he chose not to obey their orders, what was he to do?

Caesar thought over his decision as he and his troops camped along the River Rubicon, on the border between Gaul and Italy. He and his soldiers had left Rome to conquer new territories. If they turned back and crossed the Rubicon, it would be like invading their own country.

'The die is cast,' Caesar said. 'I have made my decision.' He marched his army across the river and on to Rome. Ever since then, people have used the phrase 'crossing the Rubicon' to mean making a decision from which you can never turn back.

Julius Caesar makes his important decision and crosses the Rubicon.

Soldiers fought against the approaching army, but Julius Caesar took control of the city and became ruler of the Roman republic. Later he got himself named not emperor but 'dictator for life', governing the army and all the provinces. Elections continued, but only people chosen by Julius Caesar stayed in office. The consuls became less important. Rome's republic was coming to an end.

Caesar Meets Cleopatra

As you can imagine, once Julius Caesar seized power, Pompey decided to get out of Rome. He had turned the Senate against Caesar, after all. First he fled to Greece. Caesar's troops followed and defeated his

We first learnt about ancient Egypt in Year 2.

army. From there he fled to Egypt, where he hoped the king, Ptolemy XII, would protect him. But Ptolemy's army met Pompey and killed him. Ptolemy wanted the powerful Julius Caesar on his side.

Caesar invaded Egypt anyway. There he met Ptolemy and his sister, Cleopatra.

*Julius Caesar made Cleopatra
the ruler of Egypt.*

There was something about Cleopatra – her beauty, her power, the way she spoke her mind. Whatever it was, Julius Caesar fell in love with her. He ordered his army to overthrow her brother, making her the one and only ruler of Egypt. She was glad to have a way to unite her country with the powerful city of Rome.

Back home, the Romans had become worried. What if their leader, Julius Caesar, married Cleopatra? What if he brought her home and made her queen of Rome? Had Caesar lost his mind? He had even ordered a gold statue of Cleopatra to be placed in a Roman temple! What would the gods think?

Julius Caesar stayed with Cleopatra in Egypt for a year. Then, when an uprising occurred in an eastern province, Caesar rushed his troops there and defeated the enemies. Back in Rome, Caesar celebrated his victory with a grand parade and a big sign that said, 'Veni, vidi, vici' [WAY-nee, WEE-dee, WEE-chee]. Those are the words in Latin for 'I came, I saw, I conquered'. It was Caesar's way of saying, 'I'm such a hero, winning that battle was not a problem'.

Pride Comes Before a Fall

Julius Caesar's behaviour as an army general and a dictator scared many Romans. They didn't believe in letting one man rule the city and its territories. They didn't want Julius Caesar to be dictator for life, nor did they want Cleopatra as queen. They liked the old system of government, and they wanted their republic back. Some of the senators were so worried they plotted to kill Julius Caesar.

They planned the *assassination*, killing him, for the Ides of March, which was the Romans' name for 15th March. That day, in the year 44 B.C., as Julius Caesar walked out of the Senate, a group of men jumped out from the shadows and stabbed him 22 times.

Julius Caesar was killed at the foot of this statue of Pompey.

Caesar tumbled down, right at the foot of a statue of Pompey. As they attacked him, he looked up and saw his old friend Brutus, who had helped to plot his death. It is said that Caesar's last words as he died were: *'Et tu, Brute?'* [et too BROO-tay]. It means 'You too, Brutus' and shows how shocked he was to be betrayed by his friend. People now use those words to accuse someone else of betraying them.

All for Love – and Power

Those who killed Julius Caesar thought they had rescued their republic, but they were in for a big surprise. Many people, including soldiers in the army, did not support the senators' actions. They supported two men who had been close to Julius Caesar: Mark Antony (*Marcus Antonius*) – one of Caesar's best friends – and Octavian, Caesar's great nephew and adopted son. Mark Antony and Octavian took control of Rome and divided the responsibilities for governing all its territories.

Octavian ruled the west. Mark Antony ruled the east and moved to Alexandria, the capital city of Egypt. There he met the famous Cleopatra. Like Caesar before him, Mark Antony fell in love with her. Soon they were married. Back in Rome, there was a problem. Mark Antony was already married to Octavian's sister! 'How dare he?' the Romans cried. That was the end of Octavian's friendship with Mark Antony.

Octavian went to the Roman Senate and warned that Mark Antony planned to make Cleopatra queen of Rome. The senators had heard that story before, and they didn't like it any better the second time.

There was a great sea battle in which Octavian defeated Mark Antony, who went back to Egypt with Cleopatra. Soon, believing that he had lost all hope of achieving power, Mark Antony killed himself by falling on his sword. Cleopatra also killed herself by letting an asp – a poisonous snake – bite her.

Octavian became the sole ruler of Rome. The senators welcomed him and soon they gave him a new name of honour. They named Octavian *Augustus*, which was like calling him 'Your Majesty'. From 27 B.C. on, this great Roman leader was known as Augustus Caesar.

Our Calendar: A Gift from Rome

We have the Romans to thank for making up the calendar and the names for months we use today.

JANUARY – from Janus, the Roman god of entrances and exits

FEBRUARY – Latin for 'the month for cleaning'

MARCH – from Mars, the Roman god of war

APRIL – possibly from the Latin word *aperire*, which means 'to open'

MAY – from Maia, the Roman goddess of spring

JUNE – from Juno, queen of the gods and the Roman goddess of marriage

JULY – from Julius Caesar, the Roman dictator

AUGUST – from Augustus Caesar, the Roman emperor

SEPTEMBER – from the number 7 in Latin

OCTOBER – from the number 8 in Latin

NOVEMBER – from the number 9 in Latin

DECEMBER – from the number 10 in Latin

$$e^{i\pi} + 1 = 0$$

Do you remember learning about the calendar in Years 1, 2 and 3?

Because of the power granted him by the Senate and the people, Augustus Caesar is considered Rome's first emperor. His name has stayed with us in another way as well, because the Senate decided to honour him by naming a month after him. Can you guess which month they named after Augustus Caesar?

Augustus Caesar, Rome's first emperor, 63 B.C. — A.D. 14

Roman waterworks

As Rome and its provinces grew, people in the cities needed more water than nearby streams and rivers could provide. Romans built aqueducts, which were stone troughs that carried water many miles, from a spring or river to the city where water was needed. The Romans built their aqueducts so well that you can still see some today. In France, cars now drive over the lowest of the three levels of the Pont du Gard [pohn dyoo GAR] aqueduct, which was built by the Romans in 19 B.C.

With plenty of water brought into the cities, Romans could enjoy public fountains and baths. For them, having a bath was something you did in the middle of town with a lot of your friends. How would you like that?

Romans built the Pont du Gard (or bridge of Gard) aqueduct in 19 B.C.

Pax Romana

We often think of an emperor as someone who is cruel and selfish. Not so with Augustus Caesar. He made many decisions that were good for the people. He ruled for more than 40 years and created peace that lasted two hundred years. Historians call those two hundred years the *Pax Romana*, which means 'Roman peace' in Latin.

Augustus made soldiers' lives better by paying them more and taking care of them when they retired. He created a strong police force in the city of Rome, which meant less crime and fewer riots. Life in the provinces changed, too. Augustus appointed governors in the provinces and found ways to tax more fairly. He made sure that the tax collectors didn't steal any money, and he insisted that tax money be spent to help the people, by building new roads, bridges and public buildings.

The Baths of Caracalla in Rome were built during the Pax Romana

No big wars upset the government. Cities and roadways were safer than ever. Trade increased and both Rome and its provinces prospered. Everyone felt the benefits of the *Pax Romana*, but the Romans still worried about letting one man make so many decisions.

Augustus Caesar was also concerned with how people behaved towards each other. Family and marriage were important to him. He encouraged people to participate in religious festivals. He constructed temples and other great buildings. He boasted that he found Rome a city of brick and left it a city of marble. In this time of plenty, Rome was named the Eternal City, because it felt as if the good times might last forever. People still use that name for Rome today.

The Roman City Centre

Does your home town have a market square, an open place where people gather to meet their friends and to buy and sell things, with shops and important buildings like the town hall around it?

Rome did, too. Rome's market square was called the *Forum*. You can still visit the ruins of the Forum in the city of Rome today.

Let's walk through the Forum and see what it's like to live in ancient Rome. Look, there's a merchant selling pottery, and another selling woven cloth. Mmm – I smell cinnamon. This shop must sell spices from Africa and the East. Here's a shop selling food. I see grapes and apples and olives.

The Roman Forum was the busy centre of the city. See another photo of the Roman Forum on page 123.

137

There are dried fish hanging from the ceiling. Here's a big pot filled with wheat. You grind it yourself to make flour. Now I can smell the aroma of bread baking in an oven. Look, next door – there's the baker. He is pulling round, brown loaves out of the stone oven.

Let's pass these shops and visit the temple, around the corner. Do you hear that man shouting in Latin? He is debating an issue on the steps of the courthouse. People are listening and answering him. They all have opinions on how the government should be run. There, in front of us, is the beautiful white marble temple to Saturn, a god of farming. I'll bet those two men in togas, carrying pitchers towards the temple, are bringing gifts of wine for the god.

This man is wearing a toga.

Where's the Spaghetti?

As we stroll through the Forum, we might see a vendor cooking pieces of meat over an open fire and selling them to the men, women and children passing by. Most Roman houses were built of wood, very close together, so ovens were considered fire hazards. Many Romans bought cooked food from vendors. Along with meat or fish, they might eat bread or cheese, onions or garlic, and a piece of fruit.

These are the ruins of Hadrian's Villa (Villa Adriana in Italian) in Tivoli, Italy.

A Roman family with plenty of money could build a big, spacious house – called a *villa* – with enough room for an oven. These Romans often hosted big banquets. Slaves prepared enormous amounts of fancy food. Guests began arriving in the late afternoon. They wore nice clothes, often pinned with jewellery. They usually took their shoes off as they entered a home. When they ate, they leant back on couches near tables low to the ground. They ate with their fingers. Slaves stood nearby, ready to wipe the rich Romans' hands clean. Guests brought cloths to wrap leftovers and took them home for later.

Are you wondering what the Romans ate? Don't picture mounds of spaghetti covered with tomato sauce. Pasta and spaghetti were not made in Italy at that time, and the ancient

Romans had never seen a tomato. They ate some things we still eat today, and many things we would never dream of eating. Take a look at this menu, which lists things that wealthy ancient Romans really did eat.

Menu from a Roman Banquet

Pig Udders	Stuffed Dormice
Stuffed Jellyfish	Snails
Flamingo	Fig Wine
Roasted Parrot	Dates Stuffed with
Boiled Ostrich	Chopped Apples and Spices

Roman Sports – Play at Your Own Risk

The ancient Romans loved sports. They seem to have preferred violent and bloody spectacles, like gladiators fighting to the death. From Greek architects, they learnt to build *amphitheatres*, which were huge sports arenas with a field in the middle and seats raised all around it. One of the most famous Roman amphitheatres, the Colosseum that we saw from the outside on page 125, was so big that fifty thousand people could sit on its marble seats and watch athletic events. You can visit the remains of the Colosseum in modern-day Rome.

Crowds entered the Colosseum through any one of 76 doorways. Canvas awnings stretched above the seats, to shield spectators from the sun. The arena was covered with sand, which would become so soaked with the blood of men and animals that slaves had to bring in new sand. Complicated stairways, and even mechanical lifts, brought people up to their seats and brought wild animals, caged in dens below, up to the arena when an event was due to begin.

You can still see the seats where the spectators sat at the Roman Colosseum. Competitors waited in the bottom and then appeared on the arena in the middle that no longer survives.

A typical show day at the Colosseum might start out with a wild-animal fight. Roman officials paid lots of money for animals from far away. They bought polar bears, tigers, rhinoceroses, elephants and leopards. Sometimes the sport was to make a ferocious animal fight a gladiator until one or the other died.

Gladiators were slaves or criminals who had been trained to fight. A gladiator who was an excellent fighter might win his freedom. Some fought animals, but more often two gladiators would fight each other to the death. Sometimes the spectators took a special liking to a gladiator. If they wanted to see him fight again another day, they might cheer and give him the 'thumbs-up', meaning 'Let him live!', or they might give him the 'thumbs-down', meaning 'Death to the loser!' We still use 'thumbs-up' or 'thumbs-down' to signal that we agree or disagree with someone or something.

A gladiator

The crowd gave the thumbs-up to Androcles and his friend the lion! You can read the story on page 61.

Roman games

Children in ancient Rome played with dolls made of cloth rags and with marbles made of glass. They also used knucklebones to play with. They tossed the knucklebones on the ground and played a guessing game to see which side the bones would land on.

Do you also enjoy playing with marbles?

Let's Go to the Races!

Romans also loved watching chariot races. Each racer stood in a chariot, holding the reins and driving a team of horses at top speed around a huge racetrack. In Rome, the main racetrack was called the Circus Maximus, which means 'very big circle' in Latin. I expect you can tell what English word comes from the Latin word *circus*!

Romans raced chariots drawn by horses that looked like this.

The racecourse at the Circus Maximus was more than 600 metres long, longer than five football pitches. Can you imagine the noise and excitement of all those chariots, pulled by snorting, stomping horses?

You can visit the ruins of Pompeii and see the columns from a building destroyed by the eruption of Mount Vesuvius. See the volcano in the distance?

Pompeii: A City Frozen in Time

As you can see, we know a lot about the history of Rome and how the early Romans lived. How do we know so much? For one thing, the Romans made a good job of writing things down. For another thing, they built things well – statues and buildings, bridges and aqueducts – so we can study the remains of things from the days of ancient Rome.

We also have a volcano to thank for much that we know about ancient Rome. Thanks to Mount Vesuvius, a volcano that erupted one summer afternoon in A.D. 79, we know how people lived in Pompeii, about one hundred miles south of Rome.

Pompeii was a little town on the coast of Italy. Romans would go there to enjoy the sea breezes and the beautiful view of nearby Mount Vesuvius. Imagine their surprise the day

141

when they felt the rumble, heard the blast and looked out to see Mount Vesuvius erupting! The volcano spewed gas, stones and hot lava all over Pompeii.

Some lucky people escaped to tell the tale, but many in Pompeii were smothered by poisonous gases or buried under layers of hot ash. People considered the eruption of Vesuvius to be a punishment from the gods. They believed that the smoke, flames and ashes were caused by Vulcan, the god of fire. They were afraid to return to Pompeii. It took many years before anyone returned to build a new city on the ruins.

What can you tell about how this person might have been feeling during the eruption of Mount Vesuvius?

A first-hand account of the eruption
(written by a Roman named Pliny)

'By now it was dawn, but the light was still dim and faint. The buildings around us were already tottering. We also saw the sea sucked away and apparently forced back by the earthquake. On the landward side, a fearful black cloud was rent by forked and quivering bursts of flame, and parted to reveal great tongues of fire, like flashes of lightning magnified in size. Many besought the aid of the gods, but still more imagined there were no gods left, and that the universe was plunged into eternal darkness evermore.'

Over time, people forgot about Pompeii. Then, in 1748, archaeologists began digging and discovered something astounding. The molten (hot liquid) lava that had destroyed Pompeii had also preserved it. Hot ashes had hardened around people's bodies, preserving the very positions they were in when the volcano erupted. The bodies had long since rotted, but by pouring plaster into the holes in the hardened ash, archaeologists could

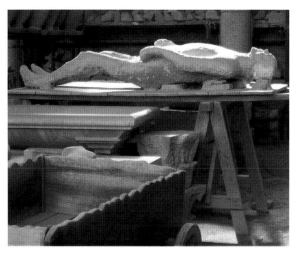

Lava from Mount Vesuvius's eruption helped to preserve the city of Pompeii, helping us learn about ancient Roman society.

make out the shapes of men, women, children and even a dog. In some cases, they could even see the expression on a person's face. Inside the houses, they found impressions of a cake on the table, a half-eaten loaf of bread, an egg and a kettle on the fire.

That hot lava preserved much more: shops, temples, a theatre, paintings on the walls. Today you can visit the ancient city of Pompeii. In the paved streets, you can see the tracks made by the wheels of chariots. In the hallway of one house, you can see a sign, written almost two thousand years ago. The sign says CAVE CANEM — 'Beware of the dog'.

Claudius: The Emperor who Brought Britain into the Empire

Emperor Claudius

We read about the Romans in Britain in Year 2.

Now that you have learnt a little about what it was like to live in ancient Rome, let's go back to Augustus Caesar.

Augustus ruled for a long time. When he died, millions of people across the empire felt sad, because he had done many good things for them. He was followed by other emperors, some of whom were cruel and lived only for their own pleasure. But some were good rulers who tried to do the best for their people. One of these was called Claudius.

Both the people and the soldiers in the army liked Claudius. Under his rule, the Romans built more roads, aqueducts and buildings. They also conquered more people, including the people of Britain. Claudius came to Britain himself in A.D. 43 to lead the Roman army against the British leaders.

Nero: Not a Hero

Claudius did not reign long. His second wife poisoned him and then she placed Nero, her son from another marriage, on the throne. That was a dark day for Rome. Nero wasted money on big parties. He built an enormous golden palace and decorated it with a giant statue of himself, 120 feet tall! But Nero did worse than that. He tortured and killed people he didn't like, and he even ordered his teacher, his mother and his wife to be killed.

Nero thought he was something special. He considered himself a brilliant actor and poet. Whenever he performed, the audiences were so scared of him they cheered. In A.D. 64, a terrible fire burned down half of Rome. Some claimed Nero started it, just for a dramatic backdrop as he recited his poetry. 'Nero fiddled while Rome burned,' they cried, meaning that Nero didn't care about how the people suffered.

We don't know the truth. We don't know how the fire started, and we don't know whether Nero played music or recited his poems while Rome burned. Nero blamed the fire on Christians living in Rome, and he began to kill and torture them.

Leaders in the Roman army hated Nero. When they named a new emperor, Nero knew he had lost control. He ordered a slave to stab him to death.

Christians During the Days of Ancient Rome

Augustus Caesar became emperor of Rome in 27 B.C., or twenty-seven years before the birth of Jesus Christ. Rome burned during Nero's reign in A.D. 64, or sixty-four years after the birth of Jesus Christ. Between those dates, something big had happened. The man named Jesus had lived, died and inspired a new religion. He lived in the area of the Middle East that we now call Israel. Jesus had ideas that changed the way many people thought about religion, but leaders of his time considered his ideas dangerous.

Can you spot the symbol of the cross in this mosaic of Jesus at the Hagia Sophia?

Jesus taught that there was one God. He said all people should love God more than anyone or anything else. He also said that people should love others as much as they love themselves. Jesus said that he was the son of God and that those who believed in him would live forever.

Jesus talked about a kingdom in heaven. Some people got excited, mistakenly thinking that Jesus planned to overthrow the Romans and set up a kingdom on earth. The popularity of Jesus scared the leaders where he lived. They worked out a plan to kill Jesus by crucifying him, which means to kill by hanging on a cross.

Jesus's death did not stop his followers. They said that Jesus came back to life three days after his crucifixion. They also said that, before Jesus went back up to heaven, he told them to invite the people they met to become his followers, too. They travelled through all the Roman Empire, preaching about Jesus. That was why Christians were in Rome during the reign of Nero.

Usually, Romans let the people in the provinces practise their own religions. But Christian beliefs presented a problem. Romans wanted all people to believe their emperors were gods, but the followers of Christ disagreed. They believed in only one God. They would worship only that God. They refused to worship any emperor.

Some Romans were willing to allow the Christians to have those beliefs, but other Romans, like Nero, were not. He ordered Christians to be jailed, tortured and killed. Nero persecuted the Christians, which means that he was cruel and made them suffer, all because of what they believed.

Constantine Sees a Cross in the Sky

In A.D. 310, a man named Constantine became emperor of Rome. He grew up worshipping the Roman gods and goddesses. On a night before leading his army to battle, though, Constantine said that he had a vision – something like a waking dream. A cross of light appeared in the sky with the words: 'In this sign you will conquer'.

Constantine seeing the sign of the Cross before leading his army to victory.

Constantine knew that the cross was a symbol for Jesus. He ordered his soldiers to paint crosses on their shields. When they won the battle, Constantine took it as a sign from the Christian God.

Constantine declared that all religions could be practised in Rome, and he ordered that Christians should not be persecuted. He may have become a Christian himself, and he is known as the first Christian emperor. Christianity became the official religion of Rome.

This mosaic shows Constantine presenting a model of the city of Constantinople.

Constantinople:
A City Full of Art

During his reign, Constantine moved the capital of the empire from Rome to Byzantium, an ancient Greek town. The city became known as Constantinople, which means 'Constantine's city' in Greek. Today it is named Istanbul, a city in the country of Turkey.

Can you find Istanbul on the map on page 94? Notice how the city sits right on the Bosphorus Strait, which is a long, narrow water passage between the Black Sea and the Mediterranean Sea. The city was a connecting point between Europe and the western part of Asia, called Asia Minor. It had pleasant weather, good soil and a safe harbour. Constantinople was a perfect centre for trade.

Constantine divided his empire into two halves: the western half, called the Roman Empire, and the eastern half, called the Byzantine Empire, named after the old city of Byzantium. The people of the Byzantine Empire blended Roman traditions with Greek and Asian culture.

The Byzantine Empire continued for another thousand years. Constantinople became one of Europe's most beautiful cities, its churches and palaces filled with art. It became especially famous for its mosaics, which are artworks made by arranging small coloured tiles on walls or ceilings. The images of Jesus and Constantine that you saw on pages 144 and on this page are both mosaics.

Hagia Sophia

The Hagia Sophia is massive in size and is beautifully decorated with mosaics.

This is Hagia Sophia [HAGGY-ar so-FEE-a], the most famous building from the Byzantine Empire. It is in the city of Istanbul, Turkey, which is the modern name for Constantinople. Hagia Sophia was built as a Christian church. Fires and earthquakes damaged it, but the people of Constantinople rebuilt it. Its largest dome is 102 feet across and arches 180 feet above the floor. Later Hagia Sofia became a mosque, a holy building for Muslims. Today it is a museum.

The Fall of the Roman Empire

The Roman Empire was destroyed when it was invaded by fierce tribes called Huns and Visigoths. In A.D. 410, the Visigoths marched into Rome. They stole, killed and burned everything in sight. Romans hadn't seen anything like it since Hannibal, six hundred years before.

The days of Rome's glory were over. Historians name A.D. 476 as the date when the Roman Empire gasped its last breath. In that year, a German general forced the emperor to give up his power. That emperor was a sixteen-year-old boy named Romulus Augustulus.

Do you recognize that name? Oddly enough, the last emperor of Rome had the same name as the city's founder.

Roman history: a timeline

753 B.C. Legendary founding of Rome by Romulus

509 B.C. Beginning of the Roman Republic

300s B.C. – 200s B.C. Rome expands throughout Italy and begins conquering other lands

100s B.C. Rome conquers territories in Greece, the Middle East, Spain and North Africa

55 and 54 B.C. Julius Caesar attempts to invade Britain

44 B.C. Death of Julius Caesar and end of Roman Republic

27 B.C. Augustus becomes emperor; beginning of Roman Empire

About A.D. 1 Birth of Jesus

A.D. 43 Claudius's soldiers invade Britain

A.D. 54 Nero becomes emperor

A.D. 64 Much of Rome is destroyed by fire

A.D. 79 Mount Vesuvius erupts and destroys Pompeii

A.D. 122 Hadrian visits Britain

A.D. 310 Constantine becomes emperor

A.D. 394 Roman Empire makes Christianity the official religion

A.D. 395 Empire splits into Byzantine (Eastern) and Roman (Western) Empires

A.D. 410 Roman legions leave Britain

A.D. 410 Rome is sacked by Visigoths

A.D. 476 Germanic invaders sack Rome; end of Roman (Western) Empire

A.D. 527 Justinian becomes emperor of Byzantine Empire

Justinian's Code: A Gift from the Byzantine Empire

Although the Roman Empire collapsed, the Byzantine Empire prospered. People built magnificent buildings and made beautiful art, which we still appreciate today. They also wrote important books about philosophy and law.

You can see the Emperor Justinian in the middle of this mosaic, wearing a crown.

A man named Justinian, who ruled the Byzantine Empire for almost forty years, from A.D. 527 to 565, began with the law of the Romans and organised it into ten books of law, called the Justinian Code. Some of the laws in the Justinian Code were:

1. A person is innocent until proved guilty.

2. Above all, the court should consider the rights of the individual.

3. No one should be punished for what he or she thinks.

4. When you are deciding on a punishment, you should consider the guilty person's age and experience.

These ideas are still regarded as important rules of law, and they can be found in the laws that govern our country. They were first written down by Justinian in the Byzantine Empire.

See a mosaic of Justinian's wife, empress Theodora, on page 180.

British History

James I & VI: The Union of the Crowns

James VI of Scotland enjoyed hunting when he was a child and throughout his life.

'James the first' is written James I and 'James the sixth' is James VI. Learn about Roman numerals on page 255.

$$e^{i\pi} + 1 = 0$$

James became King of Scotland in 1567 when he was just a baby, only a year old! He was the sixth King of Scotland to be called James. At this time, Elizabeth I was still the Queen of England. There had been lots of wars between England and Scotland for the past few hundred years, but now things were more peaceful. James's mother, Mary Queen of Scots, was Elizabeth's cousin. You might think that because the kings and queens of England and Scotland were now related to each other, there would be less fighting between them. Although the two countries were certainly more stable, it didn't stop Elizabeth having her cousin Mary's head cut off!

Do you remember learning in Year 3 about what Queen Elizabeth's reign in England was like? It was quite peaceful compared with what came before (and after). Elizabeth never married and spent all her time and energy making sure her country was stable and well governed. It was still unusual at that time for a queen to be in charge without a king, so Elizabeth wanted to prove that she could do the job just as well as a man.

Elizabeth proved her point but, because she never married, she did not have a child who could become the next king or queen. This meant that when she died in 1603, King James VI of Scotland kept that title and also became King of England and Ireland. This is called the *Union of the Crowns*. England and Scotland

Monarchs of the House of Stuart

James I of England or VI of Scotland reigned for 58 years:
    36 years as King of Scotland only, from 1567 to 1603
    22 years as King of Great Britain and Ireland, from 1603 to 1625

Charles I reigned for 24 years, from 1625 to 1649

The Commonwealth lasted for 11 years, from 1649 to 1660

Charles II reigned for 25 years, from 1660 to 1685

James II of England and VII of Scotland reigned for 3 years, from 1685 to 1688

Mary II and William III reigned together for 5 years, from 1689 to 1694

William III reigned alone for 8 years, from 1694 to 1702

Anne reigned for 12 years, from 1702 to 1714
(We will be learning about Queen Anne in Year 5.)

Coat of Arms of the House of Stuart in England, 1603 onwards

were still separate countries, but now they shared the same king. James had been the sixth King of Scotland called James, but he was the first King of England to be called James.

James moved from Edinburgh, the capital of Scotland, to London. James wrote a book called *The True Law of Free Monarchies*. It claimed that kings and queens should have all the power to rule a country because God had said so. This idea became known as the *divine right of kings*. James felt very strongly about this and it caused problems in the years to come because it had never been a widespread view in England. Most people thought that the king should always wait for parliament to agree to decisions before making big changes. These disagreements about how the country should be run would eventually lead to a war across England, Scotland and Ireland.

The gunpowder plot

Adapted from *Our Island Story* by Henrietta Marshall

Although his mother, Queen Mary, was a Roman Catholic, James had been brought up as a Protestant. The English Roman Catholics thought however that, in memory of his mother, James would be kinder to them than Elizabeth had been. They soon found out that James had no intention of being kind to them, and they became very angry. So angry did some of them become that they formed a plot to kill the King and all the chief Protestants in the country. Having done this, they intended to make Britain a Roman Catholic country once more.

The first thing to be done was to kill the King and all the chief Protestant gentlemen. To do this the *conspirators*, as the people who form a plot are called, thought of a very dreadful plan. They decided to wait until Parliament was sitting, until the King and all his wise men were gathered together in one place, and then they would blow them up with gunpowder.

Underneath the Houses of Parliament there were cellars. These cellars were let to merchants and other people who wished to store goods. It was quite easy for the conspirators to rent one of these cellars, and into it they carried thirty-six barrels of gunpowder.

Besides the gunpowder, sticks and firewood were piled into the cellars by the conspirators. This was done partly to hide the barrels, and partly, no doubt, to help to burn the Houses of Parliament when they were set on fire. Nobody paid much attention to the barrels as they were being taken in, and nobody thought of asking with what they were filled.

At last everything was ready. Guy Fawkes, one of the most fearless of the band, was chosen for the most difficult and dangerous part. He was to set fire to the gunpowder. Having done so, he meant to try to escape, but if he could not, he was quite ready to die in what he thought was a good cause. The day was fixed for the 5th of November, when Parliament would be opened.

A gentleman called Francis Tresham had joined the plot. He had a friend, a Roman Catholic nobleman, who was sure to be among the lords who would attend this Parliament.

Tresham could not bear to think of his friend being killed, so he wrote a letter to him in a disguised hand, warning him not to go to this Parliament. 'My lord,'

Everyone was worried after reading Tresham's letter.

said the letter, 'out of the love I bear to some of your friends, I have a care for your life. Therefore, I advise you, if you love your life, to make some excuse so that you need not go to this Parliament. God and man are agreed to punish the wickedness of this time. Do not think lightly of this warning, but go away into the country where you may be safe. For, although there is no sign of any stir, yet, I say, they shall receive a terrible blow this Parliament, and yet they shall not see who hurts them.' Tresham's friend was very much disturbed by this letter. He took it to Lord Salisbury, who took it to the King.

The King, who was afterwards very proud of his cleverness, said that the terrible blow which was to be given, without the person being seen, must mean 'gunpowder'. About midnight, on the 4th of November, the day before Parliament was to meet, the cellars under the Houses of Parliament were searched. With hushed voices, drawn swords and dim lanterns, the searchers moved from cellar to cellar. All seemed empty, silent and dark, till in a far corner, a faint light was seen, and near it the dark figure and pale face of Guy Fawkes.

Guy Fawkes was taken prisoner.

In a moment they were upon him. He tried to defend himself, but it was useless. Stern men with drawn swords closed in upon him, and he was soon a prisoner.

He could not deny his guilt. Round him were the barrels; in his pockets were those things which he needed to set fire to the gunpowder. He knew he must die. 'Oh, would I had been quicker,' he said, 'would I had set fire to the powder. Death would have been sweet had some of my enemies gone with me.'

Guy Fawkes was taken to the Tower. In the cruel manner of those days he was tortured to make him tell the names of the others who were with him in the plot. But Guy Fawkes was very brave, although he was wrong, and he would not tell.

The Roman Catholics in the country did not rise to help the conspirators as they had expected, and soon all hope of success was lost. There was great rejoicing at the discovery of the plot. Bells rang and bonfires blazed, and even now, the day is not forgotten. On the 5th of November people still have fireworks, and bonfires on which they burn a figure made of straw and old clothes, which is meant to represent Guy Fawkes.

King James VI of Scotland and King James I of England

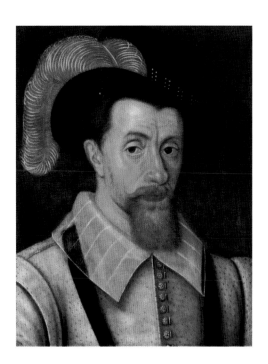

James wanted parliament to agree to collect more money in taxes from the people. Because James thought that kings could do anything they wanted, he wasn't happy when parliament refused to give him more money. There were lots of arguments between the King and parliament during James's rule, and James kept closing parliament down and sending everyone home. This made the members of parliament angry and less likely to help the King.

*King James VI of Scotland
and King James I of England*

What is a tax?

Imagine you get £2 every week for doing the washing up after dinner. Your Dad says he is going to take 50p away from you to pay for petrol for the car. You need him to drive you to football practice so you agree. You earned the £2 but some is taken away to pay for things your family needs. This is a bit like a tax. Adults pay tax when they earn money, and the tax is used to pay for things such as schools, hospitals and roads. Imagine if King James decided he was going to take £1.50 of your hard-earned money and you only had 50p left! How would you feel?

155

Who was Charles I?

When King James died in 1625, his son Charles became the King of England, Scotland and Ireland. Like his father, Charles believed in the divine right of kings. Do you remember the problems that James had with parliament? Well, Charles was soon in the same position, arguing with parliament over his right to make decisions on his own.

The King and parliament argued over money more than anything else. At this time, most of Europe was involved in a big war called the Thirty Years War. Since it cost a lot of money for Charles to send soldiers to fight in Europe, he wanted to increase taxation more and more. He collected taxes from people without parliament's agreement. Many members of parliament were very angry because they did not agree that a king could make people pay taxes without parliament's permission.

King Charles eventually became tired of arguing with parliament and sent all its members home. Kings usually called parliament quite a lot to discuss how to run the country, but Charles didn't ask parliament to meet for eleven years! He ruled on his own for all this time, doing exactly what he wanted. This became known as the 'Eleven Years Tyranny'.

To raise even more money, Charles made people pay new taxes without asking parliament's permission. But that

Charles I

What is a tyrant?

A *tyrant* is the name given to a ruler who is powerful, but uses his or her power to do cruel and nasty things. *Tyranny* means that the country is ruled by a tyrant. Tyrants don't have parliaments because they make all the decisions themselves.

was not the only reason people became angry with King Charles. Some people were worried that Charles was going to make the country Catholic again. Do you remember learning about how Queen Elizabeth tried to stop the religious fighting between Catholics and Protestants in England? People started to worry that Charles might start this fight all over again. Charles married the French Princess Henrietta Maria just after he became King. Henrietta Maria was Catholic, but this was just the beginning.

Although Charles was not a Catholic himself, he wanted to make the Church of England more like the Catholic Church. In particular, he didn't like very strict Protestants, such as the Puritans. The Archbishop of Canterbury – the most important person in the Church of England – agreed with Charles, and together they tried to change things about the Church of England to make it more like the Catholic Church. The Archbishop also tried to make it harder for Puritans to meet and worship together.

The Civil War

In Scotland, some people were so angry about these changes to their religion that they led a rebellion against the King. Charles sent an army but he couldn't stop the rebellion spreading across Scotland. The King was getting nervous and knew that he needed parliament's help if he was going to regain full control of his kingdom, so he commanded parliament to meet in 1640. However, it refused to allow him to raise taxes unless he agreed to rule with parliament's approval of his decisions. After three weeks, Charles realised that parliament would not give him the money he wanted, so he stopped the discussion and sent everyone home. As a result, it was called the 'Short Parliament'.

Things then went from bad to worse for Charles. The Scottish rebels marched south into England and took the city of Newcastle. They were in control of a large part of the north of England. Charles was running out of money and so he asked parliament to meet again. This parliament would last longer than Charles himself and was later called the 'Long Parliament'.

Charles wanted the members of parliament to raise money for him, and parliament wanted the King to deal with the concerns of the ordinary people. The members of parliament tried to cut down the King's power and made the King agree that parliament would meet at least every three years. Parliament then confronted the King with what members called their 'Grand Remonstrance'. This was a list of all the things they thought Charles had done wrong.

The King was so angry that he decided that he would arrest five members of the House of Commons who were the ringleaders. He went himself with guards to arrest the men.

When King Charles wanted to arrest five members of parliament, William Lenthall, Speaker of the House, would not tell King Charles where they were.

However, William Lenthall, the Speaker of the House (who leads it and chooses who can speak in debates in parliament) refused to tell the King where the men were. Charles stormed out of Westminster and left London with his Queen, Henrietta Maria, and their family. Parliament was now in control of the capital and the two sides were headed for war.

People across the country were divided over whether they should be loyal to the King or to parliament. People loyal to parliament became known as Roundheads (or parliamentarians) because some soldiers had their hair cut short. People who supported the King were known as Cavaliers (or royalists).

The first battle in the Civil War was the Battle of Edgehill in 1642, but neither side could claim a *victory* (that they had won). In 1644, however, the Battle of Marston Moor was an important victory for the Roundheads. Led by a dedicated officer called Oliver Cromwell, the Roundheads' *cavalry* (soldiers on horses) charged at the Cavaliers, and the Roundheads won. Despite this victory, the war was far from over.

Cavaliers vs. Roundheads

There were some key differences between the Cavaliers and the Roundheads:

The Cavaliers

- Fought for the King
- Some were Catholics
- Often had long hair
- Often wore fancy clothes and hats with feathers in them

The Roundheads

- Fought for parliament
- Most were Protestant
- Often had their hair cut short, which gave them their name!
- Often wore round helmets

Can you tell the difference between the Cavaliers and the Roundheads in this battle scene?

The Roundheads and other armies supporting parliament were brought together into one 'New Model Army' that was led by Sir Thomas Fairfax. The New Model Army won the Battle of Naseby in the summer of 1645 when Oliver Cromwell's cavalry charged at the Cavaliers. The Cavaliers *surrendered*, saying that they gave up and that the New Model Army had won, which meant that the parliamentarians were much closer to winning the Civil War.

Charles was then captured, but at the moment of victory there was a big disagreement within parliament. Some members wanted to keep Charles as king, but only if he would ask parliament before making decisions. Others wanted to put Charles on trial in a court. Unhappy with parliament, the New Model Army removed the members of parliament who did not want the King to have a trial. The remaining members were called the 'Rump Parliament' by the King's supporters. In the end, the King was tried in a court.

The Battle of Naseby

The Execution of Charles I and the Commonwealth

On 30 January 1649, Charles I (King of England, Scotland and Ireland) stood in front of the Banqueting House in Whitehall. It was a cold wintry day, and Charles wore several shirts to keep warm; he didn't want to shiver in case the crowd thought he was scared. A court had decided that King Charles should be beheaded to punish him for *treason*, which means not being loyal to his country and his people.

Some people were happy to have the chance to run the country in a new way, but others still wanted a king. After the old king's death, Charles's son, who was also called Charles, was invited to Scotland, where he was made King Charles II. He was now the hope for people who still wanted a king to rule. However, parliament saw him as a threat and wanted to capture him.

Charles II was able to get some people – mostly the Scots – to support him, and he fought the New Model Army (led by Oliver Cromwell) at the Battle of Worcester. This was to be the last battle of the Civil War and Cromwell won a clear victory. After fleeing the battlefield, Charles had to hide in an oak tree to avoid being captured! Eventually Charles II escaped to France where he had to live in *exile* (being forced to live away from his own country) while Oliver Cromwell ruled Britain.

The King in an oak tree

Adapted from *Our Island Story* by Henrietta Marshall

Charles fled from Worcester, and had many adventures before he reached safety. Great rewards were offered to anyone who would tell where he was hiding; punishment and death threatened those who helped him. Yet so many were faithful to him that he escaped.

He cut off his beautiful hair, stained his face and his white hands brown and, instead of silk and satin, he put on coarse clothes which were much patched and darned, so that he looked like a labouring man. Then with an axe over his shoulder, he went into the woods with four brothers, who really were working men, and pretended to cut wood.

All day long they stayed in the wood, and at night the four brothers guided the Prince to another place. There they found so many of Cromwell's men that it was not safe for Charles to stay in a house. That night he slept in a hay loft. Next day, finding that even there he was not safe, he climbed into an oak tree, and lay among the branches. As it was September, the leaves were very thick and hid him well.

Charles lay very still and quiet. His heart thumped against his ribs, and he held his breath when some of Cromwell's soldiers rode under the tree. They were so close that he could hear them talk.

'The Lord hath given the ungodly one into our hands,' said one.

'Yea, he cannot be afar off.'

'We will use well our eyes. Perchance the Lord may deliver the malignant even unto us.'

Charles II hid in the oak tree and narrowly escaped being found by Cromwell's soldiers.

161

But the kind green leaves kept close, and little did the Roundheads think that the very man for whom they were looking was close above their heads and could hear every word they said.

For a whole long day Charles lay in the oak, and at last Cromwell's men, having searched and searched in vain for him, went away. Then Charles climbed down from the tree and walked many weary miles till his feet were blistered and sore, and his bones ached.

After many dangers, often being recognised in spite of his disguises, the Prince arrived at Lyme Regis, and there a little boat was found to take him over to France. But when the captain's wife heard who was going to sail in her husband's boat, she was afraid. She was afraid that Cromwell might hear of it, and perhaps kill her husband. So she told him he must not go.

'I must go,' said the captain, 'I have promised.'

'You shall not go,' said his wife, and, seeing that talking did no good, she locked him into a room and took the key away.

Charles and his friends waited in vain for the captain, and at last they left Lyme Regis in despair. After more adventures they reached Brighton, and there they really did find a boat and a captain willing to take them over to France.

Very early the next morning, while it was still almost dark, the little party crept down to the shore. In the grey dawn Charles stepped on board the boat, the sails were set, and slowly he was carried away from his kingdom which he was not to see again for many long days.

In May 1649, parliament passed an Act declaring England to be a Commonwealth. A *commonwealth* is an old word for a government created for the good of the people. There were lots of different ideas about how people should live and how the leaders should rule, but the real power lay with the army. Parliament could not agree on the best way to move forward. Members were always arguing, especially about religion, until Oliver Cromwell dissolved parliament.

Some people wanted Oliver Cromwell to become the king as a way of solving these problems, but he had just got rid of a king and didn't want to become one himself.

In the end, Cromwell received the title 'Lord Protector'. Being the Lord Protector was quite similar to being a king and Oliver Cromwell had a lot of power.

Oliver Cromwell died in 1658 and his son took over as Lord Protector, but he was not as good a leader as his father. Where Oliver Cromwell had been respected and listened to, his son Richard was not. Soon, the Commonwealth started to fall apart. Richard Cromwell was Lord Protector for only nine months. Again many people were afraid, because no one knew what would come next.

Oliver Cromwell

The Restoration:
Politics and Society, Religion and Science

There had been nearly twenty years of war and uncertainty for the people of England, Scotland, Wales and Ireland and nobody really wanted to fight any more. There were elections for a new parliament, and that parliament decided that Charles II, who was still living in exile in France, could come back as king if he would give parliament more power than his father had allowed, and if he would forgive people for whatever they had done during the Civil War.

The return of Charles II in 1660 was greeted by cheering crowds as thousands of people came to see the new King and celebrate what they hoped was the end of so many years of problems and fighting. Charles was crowned in London in 1661, but he was a *chosen* king. This meant that if he did things the people didn't like, they could *choose* a new king. In less than thirty years' time, this is exactly what they would do.

Charles was not interested in the details of politics and so didn't get into too many arguments. He was more interested in relaxing and enjoying his hobbies. One of these hobbies was science, and Charles agreed to set up a new organisation to encourage it. He called it the Royal Society. Top scientists became members and held meetings in London to discuss their new discoveries.

Thousands of people welcomed Charles II when he returned from exile

Learn more about Isaac Newton and the force of gravity on page 354.

We first learnt in Year 3 about how Aristotle created the idea of the scientific method.

Isaac Newton was one of the earliest members. He was one of the most important scientists who ever lived. One of his great achievements was to discover the force of gravity, which is the force that makes things fall when you drop them. However, Newton was quite modest. He once said that his discoveries had been possible because he was 'standing on the shoulders of giants'. This was his way of saying that he couldn't have made his discoveries without learning from the work of scientists and thinkers who had gone before him. One of these great thinkers was Francis Bacon, who lived around a hundred years before Newton. Francis Bacon was important because he encouraged people to use the 'scientific method'. We learnt in Year 3 that this was a way of discovering how things in the world worked. It involved making experiments and recording their results. It also meant keeping an open mind about what might be found. Bacon made changes to Aristotle's original ideas about science. He also made the scientific method popular, and it allowed scientists to make all sorts of important discoveries.

The Great Plague and the Great Fire

In 1665, the Great Plague spread across London. It was a horrible disease called the *bubonic plague* that was spread by the fleas carried by rats. The King was able to get away from the city to keep safe, but most people couldn't. People who caught the disease had swollen lumps on their body and their fingers and toes turned black. There was no cure. Probably as many as 100,000 people died from the disease in London alone. Just think how scary it must have been to have lived through that!

Then, when the plague was coming to an end, another terrible disaster hit the people of London. During the night of 2 September 1666, at a small bakery on Pudding Lane in the City of London, a baker called Thomas Farinor found his shop filled with black smoke and flames. By the time he had alerted his neighbours, the fire was already spreading between the wooden buildings in the narrow streets nearby. Soon, helped by warm winds and the dry summer, the fire spread across the city.

The fire burnt down the homes of thousands of ordinary families. It even destroyed St Paul's Cathedral, as well as many other important buildings. Over 100,000 people were made homeless by the fire. There were some very grand ideas about how the city should be rebuilt, but in the end it was decided to keep most of the same streets. Christopher Wren and Robert Hooke were the two architects who took charge of rebuilding many of the important buildings in London. Christopher Wren rebuilt St Paul's Cathedral as it stands today.

St Paul's Cathedral was completely destroyed in the Great Fire of London.

Sing 'London's Burning' on page 217. It was written about the Great Fire of London.

We learnt in Year 3 how Wren's design for the new St Paul's Cathedral was inspired by ancient Greek architecture.

Did you know?

You can visit Pudding Lane in the City of London and see where the bakery stood. Everything has been rebuilt after the Great Fire so the buildings are all made of bricks and concrete now. You can also climb to the top of the Monument which was built to remember the Great Fire of London.

Can you spot the flames at the top of the Monument?

King James II

When Charles II died in 1685, his brother James became king. James II was a Catholic and many people were afraid that he wanted to make everyone become a Catholic. For this reason, as soon as James became King, some people tried to *overthrow* him, which means to force him to step down. The rebellion was led by the Duke of Monmouth, but it was easily defeated.

James then issued the 'Declaration of Indulgence' to abolish the laws that discriminated against people on the grounds of their religion, especially Catholics. This Declaration was against the laws that had been passed by parliament, but James claimed that he had the power as king to overrule parliament. There was a trial in a court to find out who was right, and the judges decided that the King was in the wrong. People lit bonfires in celebration all over London.

James was quite old and he had no son, so his eldest daughter, Mary, would be crowned as queen after his death. Mary had been brought up as a Protestant, so people thought that, even if James was not a very good king, he wouldn't be king for much longer and the next queen would be better. This all changed in 1688 when King James's Catholic wife gave birth to a baby boy. This boy would grow up to be the next king, since at that time boys would be given the crown before their sisters, even if the sisters were older. The baby was called James Francis Edward Stuart and he was going to be brought up as a Catholic, so his birth meant that the country would soon have a Catholic king again.

Queen Mary of Modena and baby James Francis Edward (both baby girls and boys wore dresses at this time!)

The Glorious Revolution and the Bill of Rights

William III and Mary II were joint monarchs.

Many people wanted to get rid of King James II and to have his daughter Mary on the throne. Mary had been brought up as a Protestant and was married to William of Orange, the Dutch Prince who had been a strong defender of the Protestant religion. Seven English lords secretly invited Prince William to invade England with an army and then take the throne from James, so that William would become the new king. The people and the parliament had removed one king before; now they were going to do it again. They still wanted a king, but they would choose which one.

William of Orange set sail to invade Britain along with many soldiers and ships.

William of Orange prepared 15,000 soldiers and over 500 ships to invade Britain. He had to wait until the wind was blowing in the right direction before he could set sail for Britain, and so it was not until the late autumn that he eventually arrived. He landed at Torbay in Devon in early November 1688.

Once William was on British soil, James started to get scared. His army was big enough to fight William's, but James thought he would never win. Even though some people advised James to stay and defend his crown, he fled to France. The news that the King had abandoned his position and his throne shocked the whole country. There was rioting in London as Prince William and his army marched towards the capital city.

Since James had escaped to France, there was now nobody really in charge. In this odd situation, cheering crowds greeted William when he arrived in London. William couldn't rule on his own because he had no right to, but his wife Mary was the daughter of James II, and so, in February 1689, William and Mary were crowned together as joint monarchs, a king and a queen ruling together. They were King William III and Queen Mary II.

The next step for the members of parliament was to make sure that the country would never have the same problems again. Charles I's rule led to civil war, and James II had been

forced to leave the country. To make sure that no other king in the future could have so much power, parliament decided to pass a Bill of Rights, which put in writing some important things that kings and queens could and could not do. Can you remember reading about the Magna Carta of 1215, when the barons tried to limit the power of King John?

> We learnt about the Magna Carta in Year 3.

The Bill of Rights was passed in December 1689 and said that kings and queens couldn't tax the people without the agreement of parliament (as Charles I had done), and that there would be no permanent army like Cromwell's New Model Army. Monarchs also had no power to overrule laws passed by parliament, elections had to be free and fair and parliament needed to meet every year. Later it was agreed that no future king or queen could be Catholic or even marry a Catholic.

These events were called the 'Glorious Revolution'. The result of the Glorious Revolution was to make it clear that the king or queen did not have control over parliament, which was meant to speak for the people. King William and Queen Mary were on the throne not because of their own power, but only because the people of the country thought they should be. This was not the sort of full democracy that we enjoy today, but it was an important step towards it. There would be no going back to being ruled by all-powerful kings and queens.

Sir Francis Drake

A great explorer:
Sir Francis Drake

In Year 3, we read about the Elizabethan Era, and one of its most important sailors, Sir Francis Drake. He was a *privateer*, which we learnt means that he was like a pirate but was loyal to one country – Britain. Do you remember the story of how he played bowls as the Spanish Armada came over the horizon? He famously said: 'Plenty of time to finish the game and beat the Spaniards too.' He was right!

Drake was born in Devon where his father was a farmer. He was an independent child and first went to sea when he was only 12 or 13 years old. He was an *apprentice* – someone who works to learn a skill – to a trader who owned a small ship. Drake learnt to sail well and to *navigate* ships, which is using a compass and other tools to steer them in the right direction. His master recognised Drake's skills. Later, when the master died, he left Drake his trading ship.

Drake went on voyages to distant places, and even sailed to the New World in the Americas when he was in his mid-twenties. Because the seas were dangerous, with privateers from different countries trying to kill each other, Drake had many fights, especially with the Spanish, who became his enemies. Drake also sailed to the West Indies to attack Spanish ports there, and he returned home with Spanish treasure for himself and his Queen. One part of Drake's story makes him a villain by today's standards. He was one of the first Englishmen to trade in slaves, taking people from West Africa and selling them to work for nothing in the Caribbean.

Drake had proved his success as a sailor and privateer when, in 1577, Queen Elizabeth I secretly sent him on an expedition to fight against the Spanish, who had settlements on the west coast of the Americas. Drake sailed away with five ships. Just after setting off from Plymouth, great storms set back Drake's journey, but he then sailed to the Cape Verde Islands off the coast of Africa. They made the long trip across the Atlantic Ocean, reaching San Julian in what is now Argentina as their first stop on this trip to the New World. Drake had now lost two of his five ships, and he and his sailors spent the winter in San Julian to prepare for the difficult next step of their journey.

In the spring, they set off for the Straits of Magellan, at the southernmost tip of South America, where Drake became the first Englishman to sail successfully through these Straits. They sailed through tremendous, gusty storms and, by the time they reached the Pacific Ocean on the other side of the Straits of Magellan in October 1578, two more of their ships had been lost. Now Drake and his small group of just 58 sailors travelled together on the one remaining ship, which had been called the *Pelican* although Drake renamed it the *Golden Hind* at this point.

The *Golden Hind* sailed north along the western coast of South America, stopping to plunder Spanish ports along the way. He stopped in Valparaíso in Chile and then sailed farther north to Lima in Peru, where Drake captured a ship full of Peruvian gold! After hearing of a ship that was full of treasure, Drake led the chase and eventually captured the ship, called the *Cacafuego*, and all its gold and silver.

Can you trace Sir Francis Drake's expedition around the world?

Drake travelled further north, eventually reaching what is now California. He had sailed further north along the west coast of the Americas than any other European. Drake was trying to find a passage that would lead east – back to the Atlantic Ocean – but he never found one. In 1579, he turned west and headed across the Pacific Ocean instead.

The *Golden Hind* reached the East Indies, which were also known as the 'Spice Islands', where Drake and his sailors filled the ship with six tons of cloves, which are a type of spice. Unfortunately, later during their voyage, the *Golden Hind* became stuck in shallow water and they had to throw half of the cloves off the ship to lighten it and free themselves! From there, they sailed past Java, which they discovered was an island and not a whole continent as other explorers had believed, and then eventually back to Britain.

Drake had successfully *circumnavigated* the globe – which means that he had travelled all the way around it. His journey took three years, from 1577 to 1580. Just think of all of the things he saw in that time! The *Golden Hind* had returned

home full of Spanish gold and silver as well as spices from the East Indies. Drake's sailors were in surprisingly good health, which showed how well he was able to look after them during the long journey. Drake had not only brought home treasure and valuable goods but also a wealth of knowledge about the new lands he had seen on his expedition.

Queen Elizabeth I came aboard the *Golden Hind* to dine with Drake when it dropped anchor in the River Thames, and she made him a knight so he became known as Sir Francis Drake. If you are walking along London's South Bank, you can climb aboard a replica (a copy) of Drake's *Golden Hind* to see for yourself what it was like.

You can explore a replica of Drake's famous ship on London's South Bank.

Suggested Resources

Geography

Starting Geography: Maps by Sally Hewitt (Franklin Watts) 2009

Mapping (Investigate Geography) by Louise Spilsbury (Heinemann) 2010

Ancient Rome

See Inside Ancient Rome by Katie Daynes (Usborne) 2006

Spend the Day in Ancient Rome: Projects and Activities That Bring the Past to Life by Linda Honan (Jossey Bass) 1998

Ancient Rome (Eyewitness) by Simon James (Dorling Kindersley) 2008

Julius Caesar: The Life of a Roman General by Gary Jeffrey and Kate Petty (Book House) 2005

Ancient Rome (Eye Wonder) by Lorrie Mack (Dorling Kindersley) 2009

Solving the Mystery of Pompeii (Digging into History) by Charlie Samuel (Franklin Watts) 2010

A Visitor's Guide to Ancient Rome by Lesley Sims (Usborne) 2009

Hail! Ancient Romans by Philip Steele (Wayland) 2012

British History

The Usborne History of Britain (Usborne Internet-linked Reference) by Ruth Brocklehurst (Usborne) 2008

Tracking Down the Tudors and Stuarts in Britain by Moira Butterfield (Franklin Watts) 2010

Don't Know Much about the Kings and Queens of England by Kenneth Davis (HarperCollins) 2002

Children of Winter by Berlie Doherty (Catnip) 2007

Life of Guy Fawkes by Emma Lynch (Raintree) 2006

Our Island Story by H.E. Marshall (Civitas/Galore Park) [1905] 2005

Britannia: 100 Great Stories From British History by Geraldine McCaughrean (Orion Children's) 2004

Cavaliers and Roundheads: The Story of the Civil War with Stand-up Scenes by Bob Moulder (Tarquin) 1997

Avoid Being in the Great Fire of London (The Danger Zone) by Jim Pipe (Book House) 2011

Extraordinary Lives: Oliver Cromwell by Philip Steele (Wayland) 2010

Tudors, Stuarts and Civil War (British History) by Philip Steele (Miles Kelly) 2002

History on Your Doorstep: Roman Britain by Alex Woolf (Franklin Watts) 2012

Visual Arts

Introduction

For Year 4 children, as in earlier years, the primary experience of art should come by doing: drawing and painting, cutting and sticking, working with clay and other materials. A few such activities are suggested here, but many more can be developed to complement your child's discovery of images with respect to light, shape and colour.

No book can offer the experience of actually viewing works of art in person by visiting museums and galleries. This chapter suggests how to introduce concepts and vocabulary to Year 4 children, helping them talk about what they see, what the artist decided and how it affects them. By looking closely at these works of art, both classic masterpieces and fine examples of contemporary craftwork, you help to enlarge your child's mental museum of our culture's finest works.

Caught in the Light

Basking in Sunlight

Think about waking up on a bright sunny day. As the sunlight pours through the windows of your room, it makes every detail stand out and every colour seem brighter. You feel bright and alive inside, ready to face the day.

Now think about waking up on a dark and cloudy morning. Your room looks grey and blurred. Do you wish you could pull the covers over your head and go back to bed?

Light can affect the way you feel. It can lift your spirits and make you feel happy. Without light, you can feel sad and dull. The way that artists use light in their paintings can affect your emotions as well.

Let's look at the painting called *The Milkmaid* by the Dutch artist Jan Vermeer [YON fair-MEER]. Vermeer has made this milkmaid's kitchen feel bright and pleasant to be in.

Sunlight pours through the window. It brightens the woman and all the objects in the room. It makes the metal lantern shine and highlights the rim of the jug.

Of course, there is no real sunlight in this painting. Vermeer has made you think that there is. By carefully studying how different surfaces reflect light, he painted what you would expect to see in a sunny room. The light seems to reflect off shiny objects. Even the white wall and the wood of the foot warmer on the floor seem to shine. He also made sure that some things in the painting were quite dark. The sharp contrast between dark and light makes the bright things look even brighter.

The Milkmaid

Look at the way Vermeer has varied the colours. He knew that the colours we see depend on how much light is falling on them. He makes us think that sunlight is coming in through the window by making the white of the milkmaid's cap, the yellow of her dress and the blue of her apron brightest on the side facing the window. The bottom of her apron and her skirt are darker, because the light does not reach them. Compare the bright wall behind the milkmaid to the dark wall under the window. Brightest of all is the white trickle of milk. That is the central part of the story as she adds just enough to soften the bread for a pudding.

> Look again Vermeer's *The Music Lesson* that we saw in Year 2 to observe how he also used elements of light in that painting.

Painting with Light and Shade

If you are drawing on ordinary paper with a pencil, you start white and add dark marks and lines. If you are using chalk on a slate, the picture is dark until you add white to it because slate makes a dark background. *Chiaroscuro*, an Italian word that means 'light and shade', describes a way of doing both.

Activity 1: Capturing the light in your still life

On a sunny day at home, find some objects you would like to draw. What can you find? Some apples, books or toys? Sit in a sunny spot by a window and arrange your items in a pleasing way. Will you make a small tower of books or arrange some apples like Paul Cézanne did? Draw the outlines of your items on a piece of paper, but don't shade them in just yet. Now, like Cézanne and Vermeer, observe how the sunlight hits the items (it can be helpful to turn off any inside lights to do this). The side closest to the sun will be bright and shiny, and the side furthest from the sun will be dark. How would you show this in your drawing? Would you have a shiny white spot on an apple fading into bright red on its sides, and then very dark red or even dark brown or black on the side away from the sunlight? Now look at the shadows on the objects. How would you draw those? Experiment with shading and drawing shadows to show light in your still life as you see it. Once you have tried this, try drawing and shading in a person and their shadow like Vermeer did.

We learnt about still lifes, including Paul Cézanne's *Still Life with Apples*, in Year 3.

The Supper at Emmaus

Have a look at *The Supper at Emmaus* by the Italian artist Michelangelo Caravaggio [MIK-al-AN-je-low ca-ra-VAJ-ee-o]. The artist began by covering the canvas in a light brown colour, called ground. There's not much left showing but there are places on the lower cloth on the table where you can see some. Then he could make a contrast by adding either dark or light paints quickly. Speed was important since the people he was painting, called *models*, had to stand still while he painted. Caravaggio needed to cover the ground with paint for light colours, but for darker colours he could let some ground show through the paint, allowing shadows to get darker bit by bit.

The characters show contrast between light and dark. Jesus had met two of his disciples earlier that day, but they did not recognise him. While having supper at Emmaus, Jesus reveals his identity to them. Can you spot Jesus, who is capturing everyone's attention? His disciple, wearing green, looks as though he is about to spring out of his chair, just as the patch of white shirt is straining through a tear at the elbow of his green shirt. The man on the right has a face, two arms, a shell and a napkin. His other features matter little and vanish into the shadows. But the clearest part of the picture is the still life of the meal on the table, suggesting that it was important in the story. The bowl of fruit is horribly near the edge of the table. Maybe a hand has knocked it. Are you ready to reach forward and catch it, or is something more important happening here?

Out of the Shadows

Belshazzar's Feast

Have you ever been surprised by a flash of lightning in a dark, stormy sky? The man standing in the centre of the next painting looks as though the same thing has just happened to him!

Belshazzar's Feast was painted by the Dutch artist Rembrandt van Rijn [REM-brant fahn RINE]. The painting tells a story from the Bible. While King Belshazzar was giving a great feast, a hand suddenly appeared and wrote a message on the wall, predicting that the King would be overthrown. Belshazzar could not read the message, but he was astonished by that hand. This painting makes you see how surprised he was.

 Do you remember listening to William Walton's *Belshazzar's Feast* in Year 3 to hear the percussion in the orchestra? That music and this painting tell the same story.

178

Rembrandt was very good at showing sharp differences between light and shadow. You can clearly see King Belshazzar, but it is harder to see the shapes in the dark shadows. You can see all the details of Belshazzar's robe, but little of the clothes of the woman or the bearded man behind him. Is it a person writing, or just a hand with no body attached? Rembrandt has used the contrast between dark and light to make the scene look more exciting.

Rembrandt applied dabs of white paint to indicate reflections from the light. There are glints of light on the metal surfaces, silky fabrics and sparkling jewels. Can you find the strands of pearls, the crown and the plate of grapes that Rembrandt has highlighted as well?

The Fighting Temeraire

In his painting *The Fighting Temeraire*, Joseph Turner is showing this warship which had taken part in the great Battle of Trafalgar, but Turner shows it years later being towed away by a tug boat. It has been sold for scrap and will be broken up into pieces. The artist uses light to show what he feels is a very sad moment for the ship.

The Fighting Temeraire

The sun is setting, the moon is just barely visible and we are looking straight at them, a technique called painting *against the light*. Small, bright reflections of light from the setting sun and the rising moon come from the *wash* – the disturbed waves around the tug. Shadows are faint because, apart from the sun's disc, there is nothing bright for contrast. We can only see shadows. In very dim light, your eyes cannot make out colours. We are nearing that level in this picture.

In the ghostly shadows, the ship has been painted in pale colours. The real ship was more like the *H.M.S. Victory* that can still be seen in Portsmouth today, but Turner wanted to tell a different story. Sunset, masts without sails and pale colours all combine to suggest that the *Temeraire* is fading away.

A Wall Filled with Light

Let's take an imaginary trip to the beautiful city of Ravenna in Italy to visit the church called San Vitale, where we can see world-famous mosaics. A *mosaic* is made from thousands of tiny pieces of coloured glass, jewels, stones or precious metals that are fitted together like a puzzle.

Mosaic of the Empress Theodora and her court

Mosaics cover the walls of San Vitale. The mosaic you see here shows the empress Theodora and her court. This mosaic is a good example of Byzantine [buy-ZAN-tine] art. Many great works of art were created when the Byzantine Empire was strongest (from about the year 400 to 1400). Christianity was very important at that time, so much of this art was made for churches. This mosaic honours the Empress Theodora because she and her husband built many new Christian churches.

This mosaic in San Vitale looks as if it is filled with light. Much of the background is made of gold, which catches and reflects the light coming through windows of the church or from candles. Byzantine artists used gold to remind people of heaven. Imagine how it would feel to be in a room full of mosaics shimmering with all the colours of the rainbow!

This close-up view of Theodora's face lets you see the tiles that make up the mosaic.

You can read about Theodora's husband, the Emperor Justinian, and the Byzantine Empire on page 148.

Can you tell which figure is Theodora in the mosaic? She is the tallest figure, carrying a golden cup to one side. What else makes her more noticeable than the others?

If you actually visited San Vitale, you would see that this mosaic is quite large. The figures are almost life-size. Just think how many tiny squares it took to make Theodora!

Activity 2: Make your own mosaic

You will need a pencil, a piece of cardboard, glue and construction paper of many colours. Cut the paper into tiny squares. Decide what picture you want your mosaic to show, and draw it on the cardboard. Keep the design simple to start with. One by one, glue the paper squares to the cardboard, fitting them next to one another to make the design inside the outline you have drawn.

Filling a Space

Filling Plane Figures

Circles, triangles and squares are plane figures. Spheres, pyramids and cubes are solid figures. A painter starts with a flat plane – a wall, a piece of paper or cloth – and paints shapes that are supposed to look solid. Just like we did in Activity 1, an artist begins in two dimensions – height and width – and creates something that looks like it has three dimensions: height, width and depth. How does a painter make something that looks round, or thick, or deep, or far away? We used light to help us do this before, and now we'll learn other techniques.

$$e^{i\pi} + 1 = 0$$

Plane figures and solid figures are also important parts of geometry. Learn more in Year 3 and on page 276.

Try this experiment. Look out of a window. Some of the things you see are farther away than others. Those things appear smaller, and they may be partially blocked from your view by other things that are closer to you. Next time you are in a park, have a look at the things closest to you. Can you see some trees close by, and more trees farther away?

Can you see anything beyond the trees, such as buildings? How clear are those things? The trees far away are not as clear, and their colours are not as bright. They seem smaller, even though you know that they are as big as the trees closer to you.

What you are seeing can be divided into three parts:

- the foreground (those things closest to you, like the trees nearby)

- the background (those things farthest from you, like the buildings)

- the middle ground (those things between the foreground and the background like the trees farther away)

Many paintings also have a foreground, background and middle ground. For example, let's look at a farm scene called *The Gleaners*, painted by the French artist Jean-François Millet [MIL-ay]. The central figures in the painting are three women who are *gleaning*, which means gathering what is left in a field after the harvest.

The Gleaners

Millet makes you focus on the women by placing them in the foreground, larger and more brightly coloured than anything else in the painting. While their faces are not visible, you can see the detail of their clothes and the stalks they hold in their hands.

These figures are in the foreground.

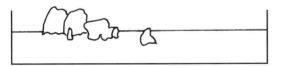

This wagon and stacks of grain are in the middle ground.

These buildings and trees, and a person on a horse, are in the background.

Behind them (in the middle ground) you see a cart, several large haystacks and many people. There is hardly any detail in these shapes, and the colours are paler. They seem little more than dabs of paint. The buildings and trees far in the background are even smaller. They seem out of focus, so pale they seem to fade away.

Activity 3: Big things far away

This man is holding up the Leaning Tower of Pisa!

Get a friend and a digital camera and go to where you can see a local landmark, like a clock tower or a historic building. Get your friend to stand so that when you look through the camera it seems as if your friend is leaning up against the landmark and is just as big as it, or you could make it seem as if your friend is holding the landmark between finger and thumb. If the moon is out – it doesn't have to be full – you could also try the second trick with that. Hold up a coin beside the moon so it looks the same size to the camera.

Now have a think. Small things near you can look the same size as big things far away. You are mixing up the foreground with the middle ground and background. Why? If an artist did this, it would be to make you laugh when you saw the picture. If you didn't want people to laugh, then you would want to balance the foreground, middle ground and background so that people could tell which was which.

Now let's look at a painting called *Peasant Wedding*, which gives us a view of a room filled with people. These are *peasants*, poor farm people like the women in *The Gleaners*.

Have you ever heard of a wedding in a barn? When the Flemish artist, Pieter Bruegel [BROY-gul] the Elder, was painting in an area that is now part of Belgium, peasant families would hold weddings in barns.

Peasant Wedding

Bruegel has kept the picture from looking too crowded by placing people in the foreground, middle ground and background. What happens to the size of the faces and bodies of the people as you look down the table? Can you see the people waiting to enter the room? Did Bruegel paint them with the same amount of detail as the people in the front?

Bruegel used the brightest colours in the foreground. The colours in the background almost blend with the walls. The bride, wearing what looks like a crown and seated in front of the dark cloth, has pale skin. The hat hanging above her head makes her stand out. What are the guests looking at?

Design

What is Design?

What have we been looking at in these paintings? Light and shadow, bright colours and dark colours, shapes and lines, a sense of space. All these different elements work together in every painting. We use the word 'design' to refer to the way the artist made the elements of a piece of art work together. Let's look at some more artworks and think about their design.

Drawing with Scissors

For years, the French artist Henri Matisse [on-REE ma-TEECE] painted bright, colourful pictures.

Icarus

184

Activity 4: Using a colour wheel

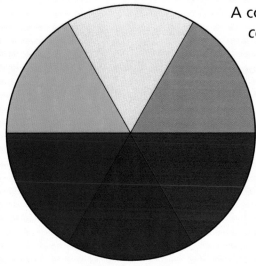

A colour wheel

A colour wheel shows the three *primary colours* (red, yellow and blue) and, in between them, the *secondary colours* (orange, green and purple) that are made by mixing the primary colours. *Complementary colours* are found opposite one another on the colour wheel. Can you name the three pairs of complementary colours on this colour wheel?

Taking a piece of paper, draw two lines to divide it into quarters – you know from your maths fractions that you are making four equal parts of the paper. In the first quarter, draw the outline of a basic picture, maybe a person or an animal or a flower, and repeat the same outline in each of the other three quarters. On the first, colour it in using only primary colours. On the second, only use secondary colours. Next, in the third and fourth quarters, shade in each of your drawings with a different pair of complementary colours. Once you have finished, examine the different effects of your colouring. Which ones do you prefer, and why do you think you like those best?

When he became too ill to stand at an easel, he started cutting out paper figures and gluing them onto a background. Matisse said he was 'drawing with scissors'. He made *collages*, works of art made of pictures and papers pasted together in a design. One of Matisse's collages is called *Icarus*, after the Greek myth.

A lot of art tells stories from myths. Do you remember how, in this story, Icarus's father – Daedalus – made wings out of wax and feathers to help them escape from King Minos's Labyrinth? They fastened the wings to their bodies and began to soar, but Icarus forgot his father's warnings and flew too close to the sun. What happened next?

Which part of this story do you think Matisse's collage tells? The arms and shoulders of the figure are curved like wings, but he does not seem to be flying. It looks as though gravity is pulling his body down. His right leg hangs a bit below the blue background. What do you think Matisse meant by this? Do you think the blue is the sky or the sea?

Did you notice the bright yellow shapes? They could be feathers or stars. Which do you think they are? Their sharp, straight lines contrast with the curves of the figure. They seem to be moving right off the page. And what about that tiny, red oval? In his design, Matisse chose to show Icarus's heart instead of his face. It's interesting to consider why.

Activity 5: Make your own collage

Collages are fun and easy to make. Let's make a piece of artwork that shows the cover of a book written by you. What is your book called, and what image will you show on the front cover?

To start, ask to see if your family or friends have any old magazines or newspapers that they have finished reading. Now take your scissors and cut out the letters or even the whole words of the title of your book that you find in any of the magazine articles, and don't forget to spell out 'by' and then your own name. For example, it could be: 'My Cat and I, by Sean McIntire'. It is fun to have letters and words of different colours and font styles. Write out the book title and author with these cut-outs, then glue them on to your paper.

Now return to the magazines and cut out things that catch your attention – parts of pictures, drawings or even more words or letters – that you can use for the picture to show what your book is about. In Sean's case, he might be making a purring cat. Start with some of the larger cut-outs and glue them down to make the outline of your figure, then use smaller cut-outs to add detail and colour to your collage.

When you were younger, did you read any of Eric Carle's children's books, such as *The Very Hungry Caterpillar*, *The Very Busy Spider* or *Brown Bear, Brown Bear, What Do You See?* Did you know that the artworks that Eric Carle made for these books are actually collages? Work with friends to make new collage artworks of your own for a children's book you know, and then read it to a younger brother, sister or friend in Reception or Year 1!

Pictures from Stitches

Stitching Icarus

Icarus

Artists work in different ways to share their work and their ideas about a story. This picture combines several techniques from embroidery to show us an important moment in the story of Icarus.

There are lots of things in this embroidery that make us look, along with Icarus, towards the hottest part of the sun. The sun's rays all point back towards the centre of the sun. Circles in ever-hotter colours lead inwards like a target. Two diagonal lines – one along Icarus's back and one from his feet to his head – point like everything else to the middle of the sun. Are you feeling hot yet? Can you tell what is going to happen next?

The artist, Kate Farrer, has studied and taught at the Royal School of Needlework at Hampton Court. She chose this story for her picture because her father read it to her as a child. Compare her embroidery with Matisse's *Icarus*. How do they tell this story differently?

Activity 6: Cross stitch your own picture

A cross stitch is two diagonal stitches that make an X. You can buy a children's cross stitch kit at a craft shop, some toy shops or online. If you are feeling adventurous, you could buy a plain piece of cross stitch fabric and some coloured threads. Thread a large needle and make two stitches to make an X across a group of four holes. With a kit, follow the colouring provided to fill in the picture with these crosses or, if using plain fabric, build up your own picture using crosses of one or more colours.

Tapestry – Art to Keep the Room Warm

Imagine if a picture could keep you warm! Better still, imagine you could fold or roll it up without damaging it and carry it from house to house or castle to castle. That is exactly what you can do with a *tapestry*, and this is why they became so popular. Pictures could be made of coloured wool, then hung on the wall to decorate a room and keep it warm. Tapestries are *woven*. Taut, plain threads, called *warp*, are

Raphael's cartoon of Christ's Charge to Peter

held on a *loom* from top to bottom. The weavers pass coloured threads, called *weft*, in and out, up and down, covering the warp and making a picture.

To make a tapestry, first of all an artist would make a drawing called a *cartoon*. (The word didn't mean a funny picture in those days!) The weaver would look through the warp threads to see the cartoon and copy it with the weft threads. Because the weaver works from the back, the tapestry will show the cartoon facing in the opposite direction.

King Charles I's Tapestry of Christ's Charge to Peter. *This can be seen in Chatsworth House in Derbyshire.*

King Charles I liked tapestries very much. He set up a place for making tapestries in Mortlake, beside the river Thames. He bought a set of cartoons that had been drawn by the great artist Raphael, which were used to create beautiful tapestries. You can still see these cartoons in the Victoria and Albert Museum in London.

Look at *Christ's Charge to Peter*. Strong design is important because weavers cannot use colour in the same way as painters. The apostles stand on the left in front of Jesus and are dressed in different colours. Their heads form a line pointing to Jesus, who is also framed by the line of trees and the shoreline. His right hand points down to Peter, who kneels to receive a set of keys. Jesus's other hand points to the sheep behind him. They are the 'flock' that Peter must look after. What do you see that's different as a result of the tapestry being the other way around compared with the cartoon?

Activity 7: Tracing pictures

Let's use tracing paper to make some images and see how images can be reflected. You will need a pencil, tracing paper, plain paper and a picture to trace.

1. Place the tracing paper over the picture and fasten the two together with a paperclip. You can now see the lines of the picture through the tracing paper.

2. Carefully trace over the lines of the picture with the pencil, making sure you press quite hard.

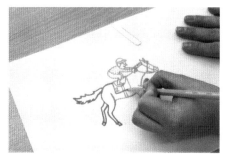

Trace the original picture.

3. Unfasten the tracing paper from the picture and place it face down on the plain paper. Fasten the two together with a paperclip to make sure the tracing paper does not slip.

4. Use the pencil to draw over the lines on the tracing paper. You are drawing over your original lines from the back. You can check carefully to see if your picture is transferring to the plain paper, but make sure the paper doesn't slip. If the lines on the plain paper are too light you may need to press harder on the tracing paper.

With the tracing paper face down on a new sheet, draw over the original lines from the back and shade them in.

5. When you have drawn over all of the lines, take away the tracing paper and your picture should now be on the plain paper.

Take a peek to check your image is transferring to the plain paper.

Discard the tracing paper and see how your new image is a reflection of the original.

What do you notice about your picture? Is it exactly the same? Your picture should be a reflection. Where else do we see reflections?

Tracing paper is also used by artists who want to make a picture or pattern on fabric by embroidering it. *Embroidery* is a type of sewing. Instead of transferring their picture onto plain paper like you did in this activity, some artists decide to transfer the picture to their fabric to make a large tapestry or a small piece such as a pillowcase or needlework that will be framed. They may use a needle to make small holes in the tracing paper, where the lines of the picture or pattern are. Then they drop coloured powder, usually black or white, through the holes in the paper. This leaves a copy of the picture on the fabric so the artist can then sew over it.

Dressing Up for an Important Occasion

Throughout history, important men and women have used the clothes they wear to let people know how important they are. Fabric can be made to look grand and more important by applying emblems and *motifs* – patterns or images that are often repeated. Your school jumper probably has an emblem or motif on it. Motifs can be sewn onto uniforms and clothing, just like Scouts and Guides sew embroidered badges onto their uniforms to show their achievements. Would that work with paint? (Please don't try!)

Queen Elizabeth was crowned in 1953. She is Queen of many different countries. She is the second Queen

Queen Elizabeth II in Coronation Robes

Which details can you spot in the Queen's coronation dress?

Elizabeth in England but only the first in Scotland, and she is Queen of many Commonwealth countries. Her gown was stitched with symbols of Britain and the Commonwealth. You know from Year 2 history and geography that a shamrock often represents Northern Ireland, a thistle for Scotland and a rose for England. Sometimes a daffodil stands for Wales but on this dress a leek was used instead. Each of these designs was embroidered into Queen Elizabeth II's coronation dress which she wore when she was crowned.

Nearer the hem of the dress are the symbols of countries in the Commonwealth such as a golden wattle for Australia and maple leaves for Canada. There are also olive branches embroidered into the dress, which stand for peace. Can you spot them?

Norman Hartnell designed the Queen's coronation dress and the Royal School of Needlework made her robes. Embroidery takes a very long time, and a lot of patience, too. The Queen's coronation dress was embroidered during just three months with people working on it for 3,500 hours!

Activity 8: Choose your badge

Here are some badges that Girl Guides can earn by taking part in activities to learn about different things. Once a Guide earns the badge, it can be sewn onto their uniform. Which badge would you be most likely to earn?

A Patriotic Wedding Dress

In April 2011, Prince William married Catherine Middleton. One day they will be the King and Queen of our country, so their wedding was a very special and public occasion. Many people all around the world watched the event on television and were excited about seeing the design of the white bridal gown. The decoration on the bride's dress could say things about the country in the same way as the Queen's coronation dress that you have just looked at.

The dress designer Sarah Burton chose emblems that resembled the flowers of countries of the United Kingdom: the daffodil, thistle, shamrock and rose. These emblems were shown on the dress as lace flower motifs.

Motifs were appliquéd on Catherine Middleton's wedding dress and on Prince William's military uniform.

These motifs were cut out from lace and sewn on, just like badges are sewn on uniforms. This kind of embroidery is called *appliqué* – from a French word meaning 'applied' or 'fastened'. When we say something is embroidered, we mean the material has been decorated with stitches.

Catherine Middleton's dress was made of a type of silk called gazar, and lace. They have different textures so a pattern can still show up even though all the material is white. Each motif was applied with tiny stitches by a team of clean- and nimble-fingered embroiderers from the Royal School of Needlework. Nobody wanted dirty finger marks on a white dress!

You have to look closely to see the different flowers but then a lot of people have looked very closely at that dress.

Roman Monuments: Art to Impress the People

Trajan's Column

In the second century, Emperor Trajan conquered the land of Dacia for the Roman Empire. Dacia was mostly where Romania is now. The name Romania tells us that the Romans took over and changed the name of the country.

To remind the Roman people of his success, Trajan put a column in a new *forum*, or marketplace, in Rome. A spiral of carved pictures tells the story, just as with the Bayeux Tapestry that we saw in Year 2. Trajan's Column shows soldiers marching, ships crossing the Danube and leaders taking hostages. Many of the later pictures are too high up to be seen easily. A copy of this huge column is in the Victoria and Albert Museum in London. It is too tall to fit inside so it has been made in two parts.

What do you see happening in this close-up view of Trajan's Column?

Learn more about Ancient Rome on page 120.

Arch of Constantine

Trajan's column was quite an unusual way of showing that his army was very powerful. A triumphal arch was much more common in ancient Rome. Generals who had won battles liked to remember their victories by building an *arch*.

Trajan's Column in Rome

An arch is a strong shape and can cross a space with enough room for several people to walk under it. They were often decorated with carvings. The Arch of Constantine, finished in year 315, is from the late Roman Empire and reuses some pictures from earlier buildings in the designs on the arch.

The Arch of Constantine in Rome

The Pantheon

Do you remember what a *dome* is? It's a round roof on a building, supported from its rim. It's a strong shape, so domes can be large, even without being held up by metal bars. The dome of the Roman pantheon was big enough to impress anyone who saw it. For hundreds of years it was the biggest dome in the world. Its shape is a *hemisphere*, which is like half of a hollow ball, resting on top of walls that are in the shape of a cylinder.

You can see the sky from inside the Pantheon's dome.

The ancient Romans knew about the strength of domes, and also about a strong material called concrete. The difficult part is getting the walls to keep the

$e^{i\pi} + 1 = 0$

We learnt about cylinders and spheres in Year 2

roof up from its sides, since they are not directly under it. Having a hole in the top makes it weigh less. It lets light and rain in and serves an artistic purpose, too. Some places of worship may have a hole in the top of their dome, like an opening to heaven.

Suggested Resources

Artistic Techniques and Activities

My Art Book: Amazing Art Projects Inspired by Masterpieces (Dorling Kindersley) 2011

Art Activity Pack: Matisse by Mila Boutan (Chronicle Books) 1996

Eyewitness: Perspective by Alison Cole (Dorling Kindersley) 2000

Draw 3-D: A Step-by-Step Guide to Perspective (Learn to Draw) by Doug DuBosque (Peel) 1998

The Little Bruegel: An Interactive Journey through Bruegel's World by Catherine de Duve (Happy Museum) 2011

Hello Matisse: Get to Know Matisse Through Stories, Games and Draw-It-Yourself Fun by Catherine de Duve (Birdcage Press) 2007

Discovering Great Artists: Hands-On Art for Children in the Styles of the Great Masters by MaryAnn Kohl and Kim Solga (Bright Ring) 2008

Complete Book of Art Ideas (Usborne Art Ideas) by Fiona Watt (Usborne) 2009

Mini Art Projects (Usborne Activity Books) by Fiona Watt (Usborne) 2009

13 Art Techniques Children Should Know by Angela Wenzel (Prestel) 2013

Looking At and Talking About Art

Introduction to Art (Usborne Internet-linked Reference) by Rosie Dickins and Mari Griffith (Usborne) 2009

How Artists Use Colour by Paul Flux (Raintree) 2007

How Artists Use Line and Tone by Paul Flux (Raintree) 2007

The Museum Book: A Guide to Strange and Wonderful Collections by Jan Mark (Walker) 2010

Rembrandt (Ticktock Essential Artists) by David Spence (TickTock Books) 2009

A Children's Book of Art by Sonia Whillock-Moore, Pamela Shiels and Deborah Lock (Dorling Kindersley) 2009

Look! Seeing the Light in Art by Gillian Wolfe (Frances Lincoln) 2010

Collages

Collage (Step-by-step Children's Crafts) by Judy Balchin (Search Press) 2002

Collage in the Classroom by Ann Manie (A & C Black) 2008

Start with Art: Collages by Isabel Thomas (Raintree) 2012

Mosaics

Mosaic Madness (Dover 3-D Coloring Books) by Jessica Mazurkiewicz (Dover) 2011

Mosaics (Step-by-step Children's Crafts) by Michelle Powell (Search Press) 2001

Embroidery

Simple Embroidery by Marilyn Green (Klutz) 2003

Where to Find the Works of Art in this Chapter

Jan Vermeer, *The Milkmaid*, 1657-1658 (Metropolitan Museum of Art) New York, USA

Michelangelo Merisi da Caravaggio, *The Supper at Emmaus*, 1601 (The National Gallery) London, UK

Rembrandt van Rijn, *Belshazzar's Feast*, 1636-1638 (The National Gallery) London, UK

Joseph Turner, *The Fighting Temeraire*, 1839 (The National Gallery) London, UK

Empress Theodora and Her Court, mid-6th century (San Vitale Basilica) Ravenna, Italy

Jean-François Millet, *The Gleaners*, 1857 (Musée d'Orsay) Paris, France

Pieter Bruegel the Elder, *Peasant Wedding*, 1567 (Kunsthistorisches Museum) Vienna, Austria

Henri Matisse, *Icarus*, plate VIII from 'Jazz', 1947 (Scottish National Gallery of Modern Art) Edinburgh, UK

Kate Farrer, *Icarus* (Artist's Collection, currently on display at the Royal School of Needlework) Hampton Court, UK

Raphael, *Christ's Charge to Peter*, cartoon, 1515-1516 (Victoria & Albert Museum) London, UK

Mortlake Workshop, *Christ's Charge to Peter*, an important set of three English Biblical tapestries from the Acts of the Apostles after cartoons by Raphael, c. 1635-1639 (Chatsworth House) Derbyshire, UK

Sir Herbert James Gunn, *Queen Elizabeth II in Coronation Robes*, 1954 (Royal Collection) London, UK

Royal School of Needlework, *Catherine Middleton's Wedding Dress*, 2011 (Royal Collection) London, UK

Apollodorus of Damascus, Trajan's Column, AD 114, Rome, Italy

Arch of Constantine, AD 315, Rome, Italy

Apollodorus of Damascus, The Pantheon, AD 126, Rome, Italy

Music

Introduction

In music as in art, Year 4 children will benefit from learning by *doing*. Singing, tapping out rhythm, playing musical instruments, counting to the beat or dancing to rhythm are all activities that sharpen a child's sense of how music works and what goes into its creation. In this chapter, we continue to teach musical notation so that, as children grow, they learn to read music for themselves and become more sensitive to the choices made by composers.

This chapter introduces some vocabulary and concepts that you can use to talk about music with your child. You can also help your Year 4 child learn about the lives of composers, the times in which they lived and the stories that inspired their music. No talking or reading, though, can substitute for a live performance. We encourage you to share good music with your child by playing music at home, attending concerts when possible and tuning in to performances online or on the radio or television.

Elements of Music

Have you ever whistled a tune, just making it up as you go? Or sat in the park and hummed just for fun? Maybe you found a phrase that was fun to say, then you said it over and over again until it sounded like music. If you have, then you have been a composer. You have created music.

What if you liked your musical creation so well that you wanted to share it with your friends? You could sing it for them and teach them to sing along. But what if you wanted to share it with a friend who had moved to another city? Of course, you could sing it for them over the telephone or you could create a podcast or video of your performance and share it online. But you could also write the music down. That way your friend could read the music and sing or play it.

Just as you are learning how to write and read the words you say, musicians learn to write and read music. You can, too. It's like learning a code. Different symbols tell you when to sing high or low, whether to play your instrument loudly or softly, and what kind of beat the music has. Let's learn some of those symbols.

Reading and Writing Musical Notes

Each sound in a piece of music is represented by a musical *note*. Notes are written on a *stave*, which looks like five lines running across the page. Here are the notes, on a stave, of a song you probably know.

A note sits high or low on the stave, depending on its *pitch*. When you sing, you make some sounds that are low and some that are high, don't you? When you talk about how low or how high you can sing, you are talking about the pitch of the notes you are singing.

In Year 3, we learnt that musical notes take their names from the first seven letters of the alphabet: A B C D E F G. When you get to G, you start again with A.

Try this. Instead of speaking those seven letters of the alphabet, sing them. Start low with A and go a little higher with each letter you sing. After you sing G, go a little higher and start with A again. That's the way letters name the notes in music.

Going backwards is not so easy. Can you say the alphabet backwards from G to A? Starting up high with G, go a little lower with each note. It's not much of a melody, but it's a start.

Now it's time to match the lines with the letters. On a musical stave, each note sits either on a line or on a space between lines, starting low and moving up.

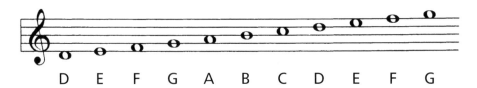

D E F G A B C D E F G

Here's one way to remember where the notes come on the stave. See the fancy swirling symbol on the left side of each stave? That is called a *treble clef*. It's a fun shape to draw. Try it.

When you draw a treble clef on the five lines of the stave, it curls around the second line up. The note that sits on the line inside the curl is always G. In fact, sometimes the treble clef is called a G clef. If you remember that G is on the line where the clef swirls, you can figure out all the other notes around it. A stave with a treble clef is called a *treble stave*.

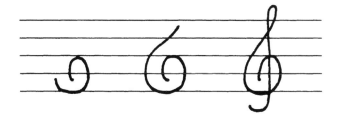

What happens if the song you are composing has a note lower than E? The next note down, D, sits just below the lowest line. The next note down, C, gets drawn with a short extra line through it. B sits below that. Lower still, you have the choice of more extra lines or using a different clef.

This note looks different from all the others. We call it middle C. To find this note on the piano, you play the C key that's nearest to the middle of the keyboard.

Middle C

Do you know the *Marseillaise* [mar-say-aise]? It is the French national anthem. It begins with D, to the words 'Come on you' and G, 'children'. Those are the same pitches as *London's Burning*. 'London's' is a D, 'Burning' is a G. The same pitches make a different song, depending upon the *rhythm* you give them. Rhythm is the way you keep time as you make music. To write down rhythm, musicians use different symbols in the notes.

Remember that piece of music you saw at the beginning of this chapter? Let's look at it again. See all those dots with tails, like tadpoles? Each of them represents a note. The dot is called a 'head' and the tail a 'stem'. Some heads are filled in and others are empty. That is one way musicians represent the rhythm of the notes.

In Year 3, we first learnt the names of these three different types of notes. Do you remember them? The notes with filled-in heads and stems are called *crotchets*. *Minims*, with their empty heads and stems, last for two crotchet beats. *Semibreves* are also not filled in, but they don't have a stem and they last for four crotchet beats.

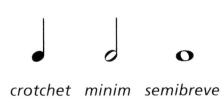

crotchet   minim   semibreve

Every piece of music has a beat. You have to listen carefully to find it. Pick a song that you know how to sing and see if you can clap to the beat. The beat stays steady, like a ticking clock.

When you march around the room, one-two, one-two, you are following a steady beat. If you start to skip or run, you're not following that beat anymore. Whether fast or slow, most music has a steady beat.

Let's try an example. Let's sing the first two lines of 'Yankee Doodle', clapping out a steady beat. Clap for every beat, even if you don't sing for each time you clap.

Yan - kee   Doo - dle   went   to   town,
clap   clap   clap   clap   clap   clap   clap

A - rid - ing   on   his   po   -   ny
clap   clap   clap   clap   clap   clap   clap   clap   clap

Did you notice any time that you clapped without singing a new sound? It happened when you sang the two syllables of the word 'pony', didn't it? If we want to use musical notes to write the rhythm of this part of 'Yankee Doodle', it would look like this:

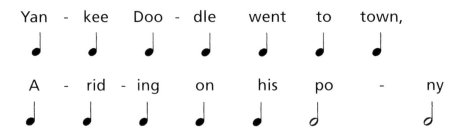

Let's put those notes on the treble stave where they belong.

Now you can sing the song and point to the notes as you sing them.

 Maybe you want your music to go faster. Then it's time to learn about another note, called the *quaver*. It looks something like a crotchet with a small flag on the stem. 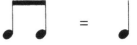 Sometimes quavers get joined together when they're written. Each quaver lasts half the time of a crotchet, so two quavers take the same time as one crotchet.

What if we were going to put all the notes for all the verses of 'Yankee Doodle' onto the treble stave? That would be a lot of notes, all in a row. To make it easier to read so many notes, musicians divide the music into *bars*. They show each bar by drawing a line down through the stave. The line is called a *bar line*. They draw two thick lines, or a double bar line, to end a piece of music. Let's use bar lines to divide the first part of 'Yankee Doodle' into bars.

Every bar in a piece of music has the same number of beats. In 'Yankee Doodle', every crotchet gets one beat. So how many beats per bar are in 'Yankee Doodle'? How do you find that out? Try clapping again as you sing. This time, notice how many times you clap between the bar lines. What's your answer? Four? That means there are four beats per bar in 'Yankee Doodle'.

There's another way to find the answer to that question. Musicians write down numbers called the *time signature* to tell about the *metre* of a piece of music.

The time signature is made of two numbers. The top number tells how many beats are in each bar. The bottom number tells what kind of note equals one beat as you count the rhythm. Since 'Yankee Doodle' has four beats per bar, and each of those beats equals a crotchet, the time signature for 'Yankee Doodle' is $\frac{4}{4}$. You read it 'four-four', but you know it means 'four crotchet beats per bar'. Look at the very first piece of music you saw in this chapter, on page 198. Can you see the time signature?

$\frac{4}{4}$ is just one time signature. There are many more. What would the time signature be if you saw $\frac{3}{4}$ written on the stave? Three crotchet beats in a bar. Can you count out that rhythm? One-two-three, one-two-three. Make the 'one' slightly louder. It feels like a swing. Sway to and fro as you count: up-two-three, back-two-three, up-two-three, back-two-three.

Many songs have a $\frac{3}{4}$ metre. Remember 'My Bonnie Lies Over the Ocean'? Clap along and see if you feel the rhythm divide into three. 'My BON-nie lies O-ver the O-cean, My BON-nie lies O-ver the SEA.'

Rests

Music is made of silences as well as sounds. Musicians use symbols called *rests* to show when and for how long the singer or instrumentalist should be silent – and rest!

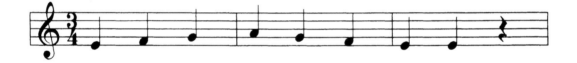

Look at this musical notation and see how many things it tells you. The treble clef and the lines and spaces tell the pitches of all the notes on the stave. The time signature says that each bar has three crotchet beats, so a crotchet equals one beat. The crotchets tell you how long to hold the sounds. The bar lines divide the music into regular bars.

What's that squiggly sign at the end? That's a *rest*. It's a crotchet rest, which lasts the same amount of time as a crotchet. It tells the musician to keep quiet during that beat. If you were singing, that might be a good time to breathe, but you mustn't take too long and be late for the next note. Getting rests right can sometimes be harder than singing or playing notes.

In Year 3 we first learnt that rests have different rhythms, just as notes do. Let's review a chart of the most common notes and rests, paired to show you which ones last the same number of beats.

| semibreve | semibreve rest | minim | minim rest | crotchet | crotchet rest |

You could sing 'Yankee Doodle' in a whisper or at the top of your voice. Musicians have special ways to write down how loud the music should sound. They use Italian words, as spoken in Italy. When the music should be quiet, musicians say it should be *piano* [PYA-no]. When the music should be loud, they say it should be *forte* [FOR-te].

In Italian, you can add '-issimo' [EES-si-mo] to a word to emphasise its meaning. In music, *pianissimo* [pya-NEES-si-mo] means 'very soft' and *fortissimo* [for-TEES-si-mo] means 'very loud'. Sometimes a composer might write the whole word in the music, but abbreviations do just as well.

$$p = \qquad\qquad f =$$

$$pp = \qquad\qquad ff =$$

Now you have learnt everything you need in order to read the piece of music with which this chapter began, on page 198. Have you guessed what it is? It's the first four bars of 'Yankee Doodle'! You have learnt about notes and their pitch and rhythm, about the treble clef, time signatures, rests and bars. Turn back to that page and point to the notes as you sing along. Congratulations! Now you're reading music.

Let's Join the Orchestra

Let's pretend you're going to join an orchestra. Look at all the instruments you could play: *strings*, *brass*, *woodwinds* or *percussion*.

Guitar

French Horn

Clarinet

Snare Drum

Maybe you want to bang on a drum and help keep the beat. Then join the *percussion* section of the orchestra! You might get to shake a tambourine or ring the bells or tap on the cymbals, because all those noisemaking instruments are in the percussion family.

Maybe you would rather make the beautiful singing sound of a *stringed instrument*, like the violin, the viola, the cello or the big double bass. Usually, musicians use bows to play stringed instruments, but sometimes they pluck the strings. What other stringed instrument is played that way? Did you think of a guitar? A harp?

We learnt about stringed and percussion instruments in Year 3, and now let's learn about brass and woodwind instruments.

The Brass Family

Maybe you would rather toot on a horn. Then you will join the *brass* section of the orchestra. You have a few brass instruments to choose from: trumpet, trombone, French horn and tuba.

Why do you think these are all called 'brass' instruments? It's because they are differently-shaped tubes usually made of the metal brass. Each one is played by blowing into a cup-shaped mouthpiece at one end. The shape and design of the tube takes that burst of air from the player's mouth and turns it into sound. Some instruments have keys that the musician can press, opening and closing valves to change the sound. Another one has a tube that slides longer and shorter to change the sound. Do you know which one that is? The *trombone*.

Long ago, *trumpets* weren't made with valves or fancy shapes. They were just metal tubes with a mouthpiece at one end and a big opening at the other. The sound that it made depended on the length of the tube, but a skilful player could blow it in different ways and produce a whole melody.

French Horn

Trumpet

Trombone

Tuba

Humphrey Lyttelton was a famous British jazz musician. Which brass instrument is he playing? The trumpet.

Humphrey Lyttelton was good friends with another great jazz musician, Louis Armstrong, whom we learnt about in Year 2.

The *French horn* is a long tube coiled into a circle. When the player blows into the mouthpiece, the air spirals around and around. French horn players have three ways to change the sound. They can change the shape of their mouths, called *embouchure* [om-boo-shoor] as they play. They can press keys to change the length of the tube and they can put one hand in the wide end, called the *bell*. Composer Wolfgang Amadeus Mozart wrote four different pieces in which the star instrument is the French horn. If you can listen to Mozart's *Horn Concertos*, you will hear the sound of a French horn playing alone. Once you recognise its sound, see if you can hear it even when it's playing with the other instruments of the orchestra.

The *tuba* is the largest instrument in the brass family. It's big and heavy, and the sounds it makes are big and low, deep and round. Once in a great while the tuba plays the melody, but most of the time it plays the lowest note in the harmony with an *oom-pa, oom-pa*.

You can read the story of William Tell on page 30. The Italian composer Gioacchino Rossini [jwa-KEE-no ro-SEE-nee] wrote an opera about him. An opera is like a play in which the actors sing rather than speak. Usually, an opera begins with an *overture*, or a bit played by the orchestra when there is no singing. The overture of Rossini's opera *William Tell* is famous. If you listen to it, you may find that you already know the closing tune. It is announced by two trumpets, joined by four horns and some drums before the strings start playing the distinctive rhythm. Can you imagine horses galloping across the mountains?

If you want to hear a whole group of different trumpets playing together, listen to *Sinfonietta* by Leoš Janáček [LAY-osh YANN-er-check]. Fourteen trumpets play festive fanfares at the beginning and the end.

The Woodwind Family

Do you like to whistle? Maybe you would like to join the *woodwind* section of our orchestra. You could play the flute or the piccolo, the clarinet or the oboe, the *cor anglais* [core on-glay] or the bassoon. They are all woodwinds.

Have you ever blown across the top of an empty glass bottle? Try it. You position your lips on the rim of the bottle, just so, and the wind from your mouth makes a breathy, hollow sound.

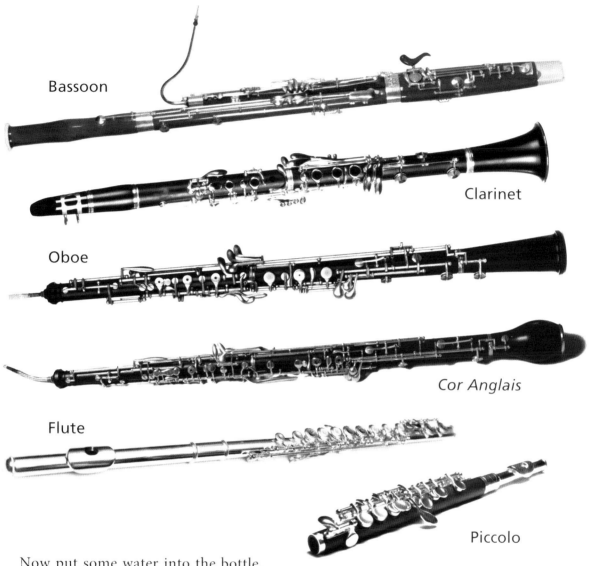

Bassoon

Clarinet

Oboe

Cor Anglais

Flute

Piccolo

Now put some water into the bottle, not enough to fill it. Blow across it again. What happens? Your bottle instrument changes pitch. Is it higher or lower? Pour some water out. What do you hear now?

Musicians who play the *flute* hold their mouths the same way you did. They blow over a hole on the top of their instruments. Just as your breath vibrated through the bottle and made a pleasant sound, theirs does, too. Flute players also press keys

This girl is playing the piccolo.

with their fingers to change pitch as they are playing. A *piccolo* works the same way, but it is smaller than a flute. In fact, the word 'piccolo' means 'little' in Italian. A piccolo's sound is higher in pitch than a flute's.

A Dreamy Flute Song

Do you know what a faun is? It's a creature that comes from ancient Greek mythology, half-man and half-goat. The French composer Claude Debussy [clode deb-oo-see] wrote a piece of music called *Prelude to the Afternoon of a Faun*. Maybe he was trying to write music that would carry us back to ancient times, when myths seemed real. Debussy made the flute an important instrument in his piece. He knew that even the ancient Greeks played music on flutes.

Other woodwinds are played differently from the flute and the piccolo. They are called *reed instruments*, because the mouthpieces of these instruments use 'reeds'. A *reed* is a thin, flexible piece of cane that vibrates when you blow on it or through a pair of them.

This was one of the first attempts to make a cor anglais. Compare it to the modern cor anglais and oboe you can see on page 207.

To understand better how a reed works, you can make your own one outdoors. Maybe you have done this before. Put a long, wide blade of grass flat and tight between your thumbs and blow on it. If you do it just right, you'll make a sound like a bird squawking. The sound comes when your breath makes the blade of grass vibrate. A reed in an instrument works like that blade of grass. The breath of the musician makes it vibrate, and that makes music.

Some examples of reed instruments from the woodwind family are the bassoon, clarinet, oboe and *cor anglais*. Each has a sound all of its own. The oboe plays high notes and can sound thoughtful. The lower-pitched bassoon can sound humorous. In between is the *cor anglais* which is like an oboe that has an angled crook to attach the reed to the instrument's body. You can hear its mysterious, exotic sound by listening to *The Swan of Tuonela* [TOO-a-nel-la] by Jean Sibelius [JARN si-BAIL-y-us]. The *cor anglais* represents a swan swimming in a legendary, circular river.

The *clarinet* is a very popular woodwind instrument. Clarinettists play in orchestras, bands and jazz groups. You can get to know the sound of the clarinet by listening to *Rhapsody in Blue* by the American composer George Gershwin. The piece starts with a solo clarinet, swooping famously up to a high note.

Now you have four families of instruments to choose from: the strings, the percussion, the brass and the woodwinds. Which will you play? Or would you rather stand at the front and conduct the orchestra?

These children are all part of an orchestra.

Composers and Their Music

One way to learn about music is to learn about different great composers. Knowing something about the lives of composers can help you hear new things in their music. We have already learnt a bit about Mozart, Vivaldi, Bach and Beethoven, and now we'll learn more about some other composers.

Have you read the two stories from *A Thousand and One Nights* starting on page 18? They were said to have been told by Scheherazade, the beautiful queen of Persia who made up stories night after night to save her life.

A Russian composer named Nikolai Rimsky-Korsakov [NI-ko-lie RIM-ski-KOR-sa-koff] was so enchanted by these stories that he wrote a *suite* (or a collection) of pieces of music called *Scheherazade*.

Rimsky-Korsakov's *Scheherazade* suite has four *movements*, which is a word used to name the parts within a larger piece of music. In each movement, we hear the voice of the storyteller as a melody played by a solo violin. Whenever we hear that theme, we think of Scheherazade spinning one of her fantastic tales.

As a young man, Rimsky-Korsakov served in the Russian navy and went to sea. He probably used those memories to compose the first movement of his suite, called 'The Sea and Sinbad's Ship'. At the very beginning, we hear a forceful theme that suggests the sultan demanding another tale. The solo violin answers, as if the clever queen has begun to tell her

The Russian dancer Marina Vezhnovets in the ballet of Scheherazade

tale. Next we hear a rocking and swelling rhythm, played by the strings. You can practically feel the waves! The music goes on and on, just like the sea, as Sinbad's ship sails over it.

Tchaikovsky: Music That Brings Strong Feeling

Peter Ilyich Tchaikovsky [IL-yich chy-KOFF-skee] was born in Russia in 1840. Even in his childhood, he had deep, tender feelings. After an evening of listening to a musical performance, he had trouble going to sleep. 'This music! This music!' he told his parents. 'It's here in my head and won't let me sleep!'

One day Tchaikovsky's music teacher gave him a short piece of music. 'Write variations on this piece,' his teacher said. He expected Tchaikovsky to write ten or twelve short pieces that sounded a little bit like the first. Tchaikovsky had so many musical ideas that, when he came to his next music class, he had written two hundred pieces!

Peter Ilyich Tchaikovsky in 1906

Tchaikovsky grew to be a man of strong fears and emotions. Some say that when he conducted an orchestra, he kept his eyes tight shut, afraid to see either the musicians or the audience. But perhaps he closed his eyes to hear the music better. Try it and see if it works for you.

Tchaikovsky composed music that brings out strong emotions in people who listen. Sometimes it sounds triumphant and happy. Sometimes it sounds dark and sad. Often it sounds happy and sad at the same time. Tchaikovsky also found ways to make his music exciting. One of his most famous pieces, the *1812 Overture*, conveys the feeling of winning a war. Tchaikovsky himself called it 'very loud and noisy'. During some performances, the percussion section fires real cannons, but without cannonballs!

Tchaikovsky composed many pieces of music for orchestras. He also composed three ballets, which are stories told through dance performed to music. You may already know Tchaikovsky's third ballet, called *The Nutcracker*. We saw a photo from *The Nutcracker* in Year 2. His second ballet tells the story of *The Sleeping Beauty*, a story you also know from Year 2. Tchaikovsky wrote his first ballet, *Swan Lake*, about another fairy tale. It's a story with magic, an evil wizard and true love, but not everyone lives happily ever after. Here is the story. Maybe you can listen to a recording of Tchaikovsky's ballet music, too.

The Story of *Swan Lake*

On the night before the grand ball in Prince Siegfried's palace, the prince's mother told her son he must choose a wife. But Siegfried preferred to go hunting. He grabbed his crossbow and set off into the forest. A flock of wild swans flew overhead.

As darkness fell, Siegfried came upon a mysterious lake. A line of swans glided silently toward him. He raised his crossbow to shoot.

The nearest swan rose from the water and transformed herself into a beautiful young woman.

'I am Odette, princess of the swans,' she said. 'An evil magician cast a spell on us. We are human from midnight to dawn, but by day we are swans, always under the power of the evil Von Rothbart.'

Siegfried asked if there was a way to break the spell and Odette answered: 'Only when someone falls in love with me and promises to stay faithful forever'. Siegfried knew he could make that promise. As their eyes met in a moment of true love, the air grew cold and an owl swooped down with a shriek.

'Von Rothbart!' cried Odette, and she became a swan again.

The next night, at the palace ball, all Siegfried could think about was the swan princess. Suddenly, two new guests arrived: a tall man in a swirling black cape and Odile, a beautiful young woman in a flowing black dress. Siegfried stared. Could it be? The swan princess? What he didn't know was that Von Rothbart had cast a spell on his own daughter, Odile, to make her look just like Odette. Just before midnight, Siegfried announced that he had found the girl he wished to marry. The caped man stepped forward.

'Do you truly love her?' he demanded.

'I do,' said Siegfried.

Prince Siegfried dances with Odette in the Swan Lake *ballet with Odette's companion swans behind them.*

A crash of thunder shook the castle. A bolt of lightning ripped the sky. Instantly, Odile changed into an ugly hag. Only then did Siegfried see the white swan, beating its wings at the window. What a mistake he had made!

He ran out into the storm. 'Odette!' he cried. He ran to the lake and found the swan maidens, huddled together on the shore, weeping. Standing apart, on a high rocky ledge, was his beloved Odette.

'Forgive me,' cried Siegfried. 'I was tricked by Von Rothbart. It's you whom I love.' They embraced, silently and for a long time.

'My dear prince,' said Odette, 'I cannot be yours, but I will not be Von Rothbart's. Remember, I will love you for all time.' Then she slipped from his arms and leapt into the dark water.

Without a pause, Siegfried leapt in after her. There was a splash, then the waters closed quietly over them both. A shrill cry pierced the night, like the scream of an owl dying. Von Rothbart's evil magic was destroyed by the love between Odette and Siegfried.

Edward Elgar is one of the greatest British composers.

Edward Elgar grew up in a large family above his father's music shop in Worcester. His father also tuned pianos and played the organ for a local church. Edward learnt to play many instruments, including the violin, piano and bassoon and he was famous locally for *improvising*, or making up music as he went along. When he left school, he went to work in his father's music shop where he was able to study all of the musical scores in his spare time. Because the family could not afford to pay for lessons, he taught himself about music. 'I read everything, played everything and heard everything I possibly could,' he said. He joined a *wind quintet*, which is five people playing woodwind and brass instruments. Every week he wrote a new piece for them to play.

When Elgar married, his wife, who was convinced that her husband was a genius, persuaded him that they must move to London so that he would become well known, but they struggled to support themselves and had to move back to Worcestershire two years later. Elgar always wanted to write a symphony but it took a long time before he thought he was ready. Before then, he wrote a piece called *Enigma Variations*. 'Enigma' means a puzzle. The 'variations' were musical portraits of his wife and friends. The 'enigma' was that nobody knew the 'theme', the piece that all the variations had in common. Elgar kept the secret all his life. When asked if he would reveal the theme, Elgar's usual answer was 'Never!'

Some of Elgar's ideas for a symphony turned into other pieces. He was particularly good at writing marches, with a military feel to them. Some he called 'Pomp and Circumstance'. Elgar's 'Pomp and Circumstance' became so popular that people tried adding words so that they could sing them. The most famous one is called 'Land of Hope and Glory' and it is sung every year at the Last Night of the Proms. King Edward VII recognised Elgar's work and made him a knight, so he became 'Sir Edward'.

If you listen to the fourth march, you can hear two main tunes, one quick and military,

the other more noble. It seems slower, but the beat is the same, just with more crotchets and fewer quavers. Can you hear as these tunes are shared between different groups of instruments? If you listen carefully to the cellos and trombones, can you hear a time when the second tune is played at the same time as the first? That is something that happens a lot in symphonies, which is what Sir Edward still wanted to write.

It is a tradition that 'Land of Hope and Glory' is sung every year at the Last Night of the Proms. The enthusiastic 'Promenaders' like to sing along!

Land of Hope and Glory

Land of Hope and Glory, Mother of the Free,
How shall we extol thee, who are born of thee?
Wider still, and wider, shall thy bounds be set;
God, who made thee mighty, make thee mightier yet!

The Planets Made Him a Star

This statue of Gustav Holst stands in his home town of Cheltenham.

Gustav Holst was born in 1874 in Cheltenham, where his father was a music teacher. As a boy, Gustav showed musical talent and learnt to play the violin and piano. Although the family was poor, Gustav's father borrowed enough money to send him to study at the Royal College of Music in London. While he was there, he started to play the trombone, as he suffered from cramp in his hands that made playing the piano painful. The young Holst was too poor to pay for train fares, so when he visited his family he used to walk the hundred miles to Cheltenham. He practised the trombone as he walked through fields, although sometimes the noise scared the sheep! He played well enough to earn a living playing in orchestras, so clearly the practice was worth it. Holst knew that he wanted to be a composer, but to support himself he began to teach at several schools in London, including St Paul's Girls' School in Hammersmith. His health was never very good, and friends would arrange for him to have holidays in warm countries. When he returned from one of these holidays, he found that a new music wing had been built at the school with a specially heated and soundproof room for him to compose in. He was so grateful that he wrote the *St Paul's Suite* to say thank-you.

He began to work on what would become his most famous and popular work, *The Planets Suite*. The seven movements of *The Planets* are given characters like the Greek and Roman gods who gave the planets their names. Holst wrote music sounding like a military march for Mars, 'the bringer of war'. The metre has five beats in each bar. Four beats is the usual, so it is harder to march in time to Mars. Jupiter is 'the bringer of jollity' and, like Elgar's 'Pomp and Circumstance', this music contains a tune to which people like to sing the words of a poem, 'I vow to thee my country'.

The Planets made Holst famous, but he didn't really want to be famous. He thought that a composer should live alone, thinking only of his music. He was pleased when one of his admirers, who wanted to be anonymous, gave him enough money to stop teaching and just think about his music for a while. He moved to Thaxted, in Norfolk, where he spent a year seeing nobody and living what he called 'the life of a real composer'. He wrote many more musical works, but nothing that would become as famous as *The Planets*. *The Planets* had made him a star!

Some Songs for Year 4

Here are the words for some favourite songs for Year 4 children. You may already know the music, but if you don't then see page 222 for some books and recordings that we recommend. You can listen to many of the songs online.

All Through the Night

Saying Welsh takes practice but you can always find a recording of this song to help you with pronouncing the words.

Original Welsh words by John Ceiriog Hughes

Holl amrantau'r sêr ddywedant

Ar hyd y nos.

Dyma'r ffordd i fro gogoniant

Ar hyd y nos.

Golau arall yw tywyllwch,

I arddangos gwir brydferthwch,

Teulu'r nefoedd mewn tawelwch

Ar hyd y nos.

English version by Harold Boulton

Sleep my child and peace attend thee,

All through the night;

Guardian angels God will lend thee,

All through the night;

Soft the drowsy hours are creeping,

Hill and dale in slumber steeping,

I my loving vigil keeping,

All through the night.

by William Douglas and Alicia Scott

You can guess the meaning from most of the words that are close enough to English, and a 'brae' is a hillside.

Maxwelton's braes are bonnie,

Where early fa's the dew,

'Twas there that Annie Laurie

Gi'ed me her promise true.

Gi'ed me her promise true –

Which ne'er forgot will be,

And for bonnie Annie Laurie

I'd lay me doun and dee.

Like 'Frère Jacques' which we read in Year 2, this song can be sung in a round with different people (or groups) starting to sing the song one line after another.

London's burning, London's burning!

Fetch the engines, fetch the engines!

Fire, Fire! Fire, Fire!

Pour on water, pour on water.

You can read about the Great Fire of London on page 165.

On Ilkley Moor Baht 'At

The words are in Yorkshire dialect. As we learnt in Year 3, rules in dialect are sometimes different from standard English. It will help to listen to a recording of people from Yorkshire singing it themselves. Here, an apostrophe (') usually means that an 'h' has been left out. Some words have modern English equivalents. 'Thou' and 'thee' are like 'you' and 'thy' is like 'your', speaking to one person whom you know well. Each verse only has one new line and you repeat the rest as we show below.

Where 'ast thou been since I saw thee? [Where have you been since I saw you?]
　　On Ilkley Moor baht 'at. 　　[On Ilkley Moor without a hat.]
Where 'ast thou been since I saw thee?
Where 'ast thou been since I saw thee?

　　On Ilkley Moor baht 'at.
　　On Ilkley Moor baht 'at.
　　On Ilkley Moor baht 'at.

Thou's been a-courting Mary Jane.

On Ilkley Moor baht 'at.

Thou's been a-courting Mary Jane.

Thou's been a-courting Mary Jane.

[You've been courting Mary Jane.]

On Ilkley Moor baht 'at.

On Ilkley Moor baht 'at.

On Ilkley Moor baht 'at.

Learn more about natural cycles on page 295.

Thou's going to catch thy death of cold…

[You're going to catch your death of cold.]

Then we shall 'ave to bury thee…

[Then we shall have to bury you.]

Then t' worms 'll come and eat thee up…

[Then the worms will come and eat you up.]

Then t' ducks 'll come
and eat up t' worms…

[Then the ducks will come
and eat up the worms.]

Then we shall come and eat up t' ducks…

[Then we shall come and eat up the ducks.]

Then we shall all 'ave etten thee.

[Then we shall all have eaten you.]

In Dublin's fair city,

Where the girls are so pretty,

I first set my eyes on sweet Molly Malone,

As she wheeled her wheel-barrow,

Through streets broad and narrow,

Crying, 'Cockles and mussels,
alive, alive, oh!'

'Alive, alive, oh,

Alive, alive, oh',

Crying 'Cockles and mussels,
alive, alive, oh!'

Alouette

French Canadian folk song

Alouette means 'lark' in French. The bird is dead and is being prepared for cooking. You can add extra verses by changing the head to another part of the bird as suggested below and repeating the earlier parts, a bit like 'Old MacDonald Had a Farm'.

In French:

Alouette, gentille Alouette,

Alouette, je te plumerai.

Je te plumerai la tête,

Je te plumerai la tête,

Et la tête, et la tête,

Alouette, Alouette! Ah!

Alouette, gentille Alouette,

Alouette, je te plumerai.

We sang 'Old MacDonald Had a Farm' in Year 1

In English:

Alouette, gentle Alouette,

Alouette, I will pluck you all.

I will pluck your feathered head,

I will pluck your feathered head,

And your head, and your head,

Alouette, Alouette! Ah!

Alouette, gentle Alouette,

Alouette, I will pluck you all.

…I will pluck your feathered neck,

I will pluck your feathered neck,

And your neck, and your neck,

And your head, and your head…

…I will pluck your feathered back,

I will pluck your feathered back,

And your back, and your back,

And your neck, and your neck,

And your head, and your head…

I will pluck your feathered wings,

I will pluck your feathered wings,

And your wings, and your wings,

And your back, and your back,

And your neck, and your neck,

And your head, and your head…

…I will pluck your feathered tail,

I will pluck your feathered tail,

And your tail, and your tail,

And your wings, and your wings,

And your back, and your back,

And your neck, and your neck,

And your head, and your head…

Scottish Folk Song

There was a man lived in the moon,
Lived in the moon, lived in the moon.
There was a man lived in the moon
And his name was Aiken Drum.

[chorus]

And he played upon a ladle,
A ladle, a ladle.
Played upon a ladle
And his name was Aiken Drum.

[repeat chorus]

And his hat was made of good
cream cheese,
Of good cream cheese,
of good cream cheese.
His hat was made of good cream cheese,
And his name was Aiken Drum.

[repeat chorus]

And his coat was made of good roast beef,
Of good roast beef, of good roast beef.
His coat was made of good roast beef
And his name was Aiken Drum.

[repeat chorus]

And his buttons made of penny loaves,
Of penny loaves, of penny loaves,
His buttons made of penny loaves
And his name was Aiken Drum.

[repeat chorus]

And his breeches made of haggis bags,
Of haggis bags, of haggis bags,
His breeches made of haggis bags
And his name was Aiken Drum.

[repeat chorus]

Learn more about the moon and astronomy on page 337.

Suggested Resources

Audio Recordings

Composer of the Week, BBC Radio 3 series (90 – 92 FM or digital radio): www.bbc.co.uk/podcasts/series/cotw/all

Horn Concertos by Mozart, performed by Barry Tuckwell (French horn) and the London Symphony Orchestra conducted by Peter Maag, from *Mozart Wind Concertos* (Double Decca) 2000

Prélude à l'après-midi d'un faune by Debussy, performed by the Royal Concertgebouw Orchestra conducted by Bernard Haitink, from *Debussy Orchestral Music* (Philips Duo) 1993

Rhapsody in Blue by Gershwin, performed by the London Symphony Orchestra directed by André Previn, from *Gershwin Rhapsody in Blue, Concerto in F, An American in Paris* (EMI Classics) 1998

Scheherazade by Rimsky-Korsakov, performed by the Kirov Orchestra conducted by Valery Gergiev (Decca) 2005

Sinfonietta by Janáček, performed by the Vienna Philharmonic Orchestra conducted by Sir Charles Mackerras, from *Janáček Sinfonietta, Taras Bulbas, Lachian Dances* (Double Decca) 1996

The Swan of Tuonela by Sibelius, performed by the Swiss Romande Orchestra conducted by Horst Stein, from *Finlandia* (Double Decca) 2004

William Tell Overture by Rossini, performed by the Chamber Orchestra of Europe conducted by Claudio Abbado, from *Rossini Overtures* (Decca) 2012

1812 Overture by Tchaikovsky, performed the Royal Philharmonic Orchestra conducted by Adrian Leaper, from *Tchaikovsky Festival* (Naxos) 1993

Books About Music

Children's Book of Music (Dorling Kindersley) 2010

Usborne Introduction to Music (Internet-linked) by Eileen O'Brien (Usborne) 2005

Stories from the Ballet by Geraldine McCaughrean (Orchard) 2011

Songbooks

Ta-ra-ra boom-de-ay by Beatrice Harrap and David Gadsby (A & C Black) 2001

The National Songbook 2 edited by Rachel Lindley (Novello) 2009

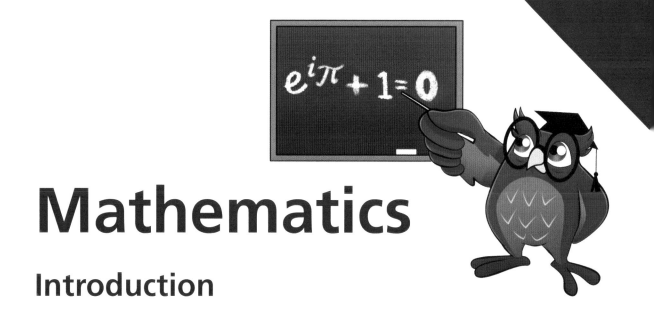

Mathematics

Introduction

Success in learning maths comes through practice, practice, practice: steady practice, thoughtful practice and practice with a variety of problems. Encourage your child to approach problems from different angles. Psychologists who have studied how maths is learnt explain that ability gained through practice is not different from mathematical understanding. Indeed, practice is the prerequisite for more advanced problem solving.

Although many adults feel anxious about their mathematical skills, it is important to encourage your child to explore mathematical concepts in fun ways, and to make practising maths fun. One effective way to practise with your child is to have him or her talk out loud while doing problems, explaining computational steps along the way. Your child's mental process becomes visible to you, and you can correct misunderstandings as they happen.

The best maths programmes incorporate the principle of incremental review: once a concept or skill is introduced, it is practised again in different ways, through exercises of gradually increasing difficulty. One result of this approach is that a child's arithmetic skills become automatic. Only when children achieve automatic command of basic facts – when they can tell you instantly what 9 plus 8 equals, for example – are their minds prepared to tackle more challenging problems. Maths learning programmes that offer both incremental review and varied opportunities for problem solving achieve the best results.

This chapter presents a brief outline of the maths skills and concepts that should be part of a good Year 4 education. We emphasise, however, that this outline does not constitute a complete maths programme, since it does not include as many practice problems as a child ought to do while learning this material. To learn maths thoroughly at the Year 4 level, children need to be shown these concepts and then encouraged to practise, practise, practise.

Numbers as far as Hundred Thousands

Thousands

In Years 1, 2 and 3 we have been learning how to build and recognise numbers. You can count to 1,000, so let's practise by counting in hundreds, like this: 100, 200, 300, 400, 500, 600, 700, 800, 900. What comes next? 1,000. Remember that 10 hundreds are the same as 1,000.

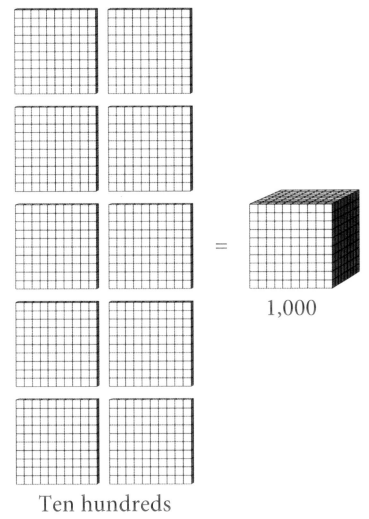

1,000

Ten hundreds

The number 1,000 has four digits. The place of a digit in a number affects its value. The village of Mevagissey in Cornwall is a small settlement with about 2,221 people living there. Let's look at the place values in this four-digit number.

thousands	hundreds	tens	ones
2	2	2	1

The 2 in the **thousands** place is 2,000.

The 2 in the *hundreds* place is 200.

The 2 in the **tens** place is 20.

The 1 in the *ones* place is 1.

You know how to write and add the sums of numbers written in expanded form. Add these numbers to find the number of people living in Mevagissey village:

The harbour of Mevagissey village

We learnt about different sizes of settlements in Year 3.

$$2,000 + 200 + 20 + 1 = \underline{\hphantom{xxx}}$$

You read 2,221 as 'two thousand, two hundred and twenty-one'.

Practise putting four-digit numbers into a place value chart. We've started the chart with 1,965, and you can continue to fill in the chart with 5,824 and 6,371:

	thousands	,	hundreds	tens	ones
1,965	1	,	9	6	5
5,824		,			
6,371		,			

Reading and Writing Four-Digit Numbers

In digits, the thousands are written 1,000, 2,000, 3,000, 4,000, 5,000, 6,000, 7,000, 8,000, 9,000. In words, the thousands are written one thousand, two thousand, three thousand, four thousand, five thousand, six thousand, seven thousand, eight thousand, nine thousand.

Learn to read any four-digit number, beginning with the thousands place. For example, 8,329 is read 'eight thousand, three hundred and twenty-nine'. How would you read 5,791? How would you read 2,015?

Learn to write any four-digit number in digits or in words. For example, in digits, two thousand, seven hundred and thirty-three is written 2,733. In words, 6,364 is written 'six thousand, three hundred and sixty-four'. Notice that you can put a comma between the thousands place and the hundreds place. This comma makes it easier to read large numbers.

If we were to fill in the place-value chart with some numbers we have learnt so far, it would look like this:

	thousands	,	*hundreds*	*tens*	*ones*
one					1
ten				1	0
one hundred			1	0	0
one thousand	1	,	0	0	0

The place-value chart can show numbers so big we couldn't fit the whole chart on the page. For now, let's learn two new place values: ten thousands and hundred thousands.

Ten Thousands and Hundred Thousands

The next two place values we will learn are the ten thousands place and the hundred thousands place. About 16,685 people live in the town of St Andrews in Scotland. Let's look at that number.

ten thousands	*thousands*	,	*hundreds*	*tens*	*ones*
1	6	,	6	8	5

The 1 in the *ten thousands* place is 10,000.

The 6 in the *thousands* place is 6,000.

The 6 in the *hundreds* place is 600.

The 8 in the *tens* place is 80.

The 5 in the *ones* place is 5.

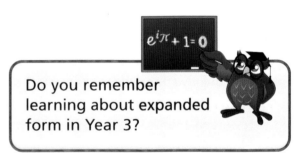

$e^{i\pi} + 1 = 0$

Do you remember learning about expanded form in Year 3?

The town of St Andrews

Now find the sum of these numbers that we have written in expanded form to find the number of people living in St Andrews:

$$10,000 + 6,000 + 600 + 80 + 5$$

= _____

You read 16,685 as 'sixteen thousand, six hundred and eighty-five'.

Belfast is a small city that is the capital of Northern Ireland. Let's learn about its population to see how many people live there.

hundred thousands	ten thousands	thousands	,	hundreds	tens	ones
2	6	8	,	3	2	3

The 2 in the *hundred thousands* place is 200,000.

The 6 in the *ten thousands* place is 60,000.

The 8 in the **thousands** place is 8,000.

The 3 in the *hundreds* place is 300.

The 2 in the **tens** place is 20.

The 3 in the *ones* place is 3.

Learn more about Northern Ireland on page 115.

Can you write 268,323 in expanded form?

_____ + _____ + _____ + _____ + _____ + _____ = _____

What does the sum add up to?

There are 268,323 people who live in the city of Belfast, which you read as 'two hundred and sixty-eight thousand, three hundred and twenty-three'.

Learn to read and write more five- and six-digit numbers. For example, you read 864,374 as 'eight hundred and sixty-four thousand, three hundred and seventy-four'.

The city of Belfast

227

You write six hundred thousand and eighty-four in digits as 600,084. You write 450,057 in words as 'four hundred and fifty thousand and fifty-seven'.

Do you see how this works? Now write down a few numbers above 100,000 and say them out loud. Also practise writing these large numbers in expanded form, then try writing numbers that are in expanded form in standard, unexpanded form.

Counting with Thousands

You count from a thousand to the next thousand by counting all 999 numbers in between. From 1,000 to 2,000, the numbers are 1,001, 1,002, 1,003, adding one more each time up to 1,999, and one more is 2,000.

It takes too long to count from any one thousand to the next. Practise counting in short stretches. Count from 4,994 until you reach the next thousand: 4,994, 4,995, 4,996, 4,997, 4,998, 4,999, 5,000. Or count backwards from 56,003 like this: 56,003, 56,002, 56,001, 56,000. What number is next? 55,999.

Can you count forwards from 7,989 to the next thousand and backwards from 23,010 to the nearest thousand?

Counting forwards is the same as adding 1 each time. Learn to add 1 quickly in your head to numbers, like this:

$$3,999 + 1 = 4,000$$
$$62,099 + 1 = 62,100$$
$$124,999 + 1 = 125,000$$

Counting backwards is the same as subtracting 1 each time. Learn to subtract 1 quickly in your head from numbers, like this:

$$3,000 - 1 = 2,999$$
$$94,260 - 1 = 94,259$$
$$300,000 - 1 = 299,999$$

You can also practise writing the numbers that come before and after a number. Here are the numbers that come before and after 76,609.

before   *after*

76,608 ← 76,609 → 76,610

Skip-Counting with Thousands

Learn to continue a line of numbers either forwards or backwards, counting in tens or in fives, or in even numbers or odd numbers. Here are some examples.

counting in tens:

forwards	7,210,	7,220,	7,230,	7,240
backwards	7,210,	7,200,	7,190,	7,180

counting in fives:

forwards	8,005,	8,010,	8,015,	8,020
backwards	8,005,	8,000,	7,995,	7,990

counting in odd numbers:

forwards	23,995,	23,997,	23,999,	24,001
backwards	23,995,	23,993,	23,991,	23,989

> Pick numbers in the thousands to practise skip-counting in fives and tens, and in either evens or odds. Practise going both forwards and backwards from each chosen number. Which numbers will you choose?

About how many stars do you think are in the night sky?

Rounding Numbers

Sometimes it is easier to say *about* how much something is instead of *exactly* how much it is. For instance, you might say that the night sky looks as if it contains 'about 4,000 stars', not '4,368 stars'. This is called *rounding numbers*. You round a number to show about how large it is.

> Read more about astronomy, the study of the night sky, on page 328.

In Year 3, we learnt about rounding numbers to the nearest ten. If the ones are less than five, you round down to the nearest ten. What is 54 rounded to the nearest ten? 50. If the ones are more than five, you round up to the nearest ten. What is 77 rounded to the nearest ten? 80. And do you remember the special rule for when a number is exactly between two numbers? When a number is exactly between two numbers, you round up to the greater number. So what is 35 rounded to the nearest ten? 40.

You can round a number to the nearest ten, hundred, thousand or hundred thousand. You round to these numbers in the same way. You can round to other numbers, too, but it usually makes it easier to round to numbers that have zeros as the last digits.

To round a number to the nearest hundred, you make it into the hundred that is closest. Take the number 246, for example, which is between 200 and 300. It is closer to 200. So 246 rounded to the nearest hundred is 200.

The number 289 is also between 200 and 300, but it is closer to 300. So 289 rounded to the nearest hundred is 300.

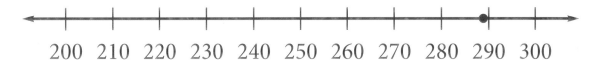

Round 362 to the nearest hundred. 362 is between 300 and 400. It is closer to 400, so 362 rounded to the nearest hundred is 400. Now what is 8,257 rounded to the nearest thousand? 8,257 is between 8,000 and 9,000. It is closer to 8,000. So 8,257 rounded to the nearest thousand is 8,000.

You do not always round numbers to the highest place value, because it depends on how close to your number you want to be. For example, there are 7,652 books in Lucas's school library. What is 7,652 rounded to the nearest ten? 7,650. Now what if you round it to the nearest hundred? 7,700. What is it rounded to the nearest thousand? It's 8,000.

Lucas at his school library

Comparing and Ordering Numbers

When you compare two numbers to see which is greater, always compare the digits in the largest place value first. That means you start from the left. Then compare the number in the next largest place value, and so on. As soon as you find that a number is greater in a place value, the entire number must be greater. Of course, any number that has thousands is greater than any number that just has hundreds. For example, 1,002 > 998. In the same way, 100,002 > 99,998.

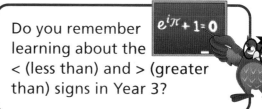

Do you remember learning about the < (less than) and > (greater than) signs in Year 3?

Let's look at an example that will help you see how to work out whether <, >, or = belongs between two large numbers. Our numbers are 4,827 and 4,627. If you think of them arranged by place values, you can set them up like this:

thousands	,	hundreds	tens	ones
4	,	8	2	7
4	,	6	2	7

↑ *The thousands are the same.*
↑ *The hundreds are different.*

First compare the thousands place. 4,000 = 4,000. The thousands are the same. So far the numbers seem equal. Then compare the hundreds place. 800 > 600. So 4,827 > 4,627.

Now compare 53,505 and 53,889.

ten thousands	thousands	,	hundreds	tens	ones
5	3	,	5	0	5
5	3	,	8	8	9

Are the numbers in the ten thousands place the same? Yes. What about the numbers in the thousands place? They are also the same. Are the numbers in the hundreds place the same? No, 500 < 800. So, 53,505 is less than 53,889.

Remember that you can order numbers from least to greatest. Try ordering the following numbers from least to greatest:

4,567   5,892   3,853   5,889

You would write: 3,853   4,567   5,889   5,892

You can also order numbers from greatest to least. These six numbers are ordered from greatest to least:

58,694   58,599   46,822   46,083   1,003   99

Try to order these numbers from least to greatest: 6,596   4,560   4,575   4,556
45,765   79,243   67,221

Now find numbers all over your house, at least six of them, and order them from greatest to least. (Hint: Try the last page-numbers of books, or the amount of energy listed on food packaging.)

Remember that a number statement that uses an equals sign is an *equation*. So, these are all equations:

$4 \times 7 = 28$ $221 = 221$ $548 + 22 = 570$

A number statement that uses the signs > or < is called an *inequality*. An inequality shows in what way numbers are *not* equal: a number is greater than or less than another. $4,827 < 4,900$ and $1,002 > 997$ are both inequalities.

Working with Numbers

Ordinal Numbers

Ordinal numbers give the place of something in an order. For example, June is the *sixth* month of the year. 'Sixth' is an ordinal number.

You may already know some ordinal numbers, like 'first' and 'tenth' and 'thirty-first'. The ordinal numbers continue in the same way to one hundredth: thirty-first, thirty-second, thirty-third, thirty-fourth, thirty-fifth, thirty-sixth, thirty-seventh, thirty-eighth, thirty-ninth, fortieth, forty-first, … , ninety-ninth, one hundredth.

You don't always have to write ordinal numbers out; sometimes they can be abbreviated. Here's a chart that gives you a few examples of the ways to abbreviate them.

Ordinal Number	Abbreviation	Ordinal Number	Abbreviation
first	1st	seventy-first	71st
second	2nd	seventy-second	72nd
third	3rd	seventy-third	73rd
fourth	4th	seventy-fourth	74th
fifth	5th	seventy-fifth	75th

All the ordinals that end in '-th' are abbreviated in the same way as 'fourth' and 'seventy-fourth'. For example, 'sixty-fifth' is 65th. 'Eighty-ninth' is 89th.

Using Number Lines

In Year 3 we started learning about *number lines*, which show numbers in order. A number line has arrows because the numbers on the line keep going on forever.

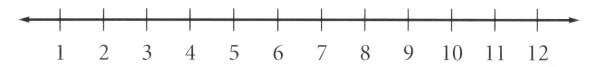

A number line can also show the larger numbers you've been learning about.

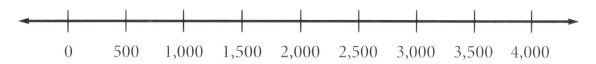

And a number line can also show negative numbers, which are below 0. Negative or minus numbers are the numbers to the left of zero on a number line.

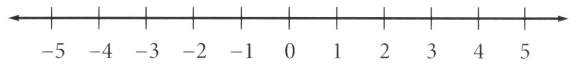

Positive numbers are the numbers to the right of zero on the number line. Zero is neither positive nor negative.

You can write positive numbers with or without a + sign: +2 = 2 ('positive two equals two'). You *must* write a minus sign with a negative number: −2 = minus 2 (also called 'negative 2').

Addition and Subtraction

Column Addition

In Year 3, we added numbers horizontally and vertically. Learn to add four or more numbers vertically in a column. Here is an example. Like before, begin by adding down the ones column first.

Add the ones
Regroup if necessary

Add the tens

tens ones

```
   2
  12
  19
  38
+ 64
-----
   3
```

$2 + 9 = 11$
$11 + 8 = 19$
$19 + 4 = 23$

$2 + 1 = 3$
$3 + 1 = 4$
$4 + 3 = 7$
$7 + 6 = 13$

tens ones

```
   2
  12
  19
  38
+ 64
-----
 133
```

To do addition vertically in columns, you often need to add combinations like $11 + 8 = 19$ or $19 + 4 = 23$ in your head. You also often have to regroup more than 1 ten. 23 ones is the same as 2 tens and 3 ones.

When you do a maths problem, you should always check your work. To check column addition, you add up from the bottom. Here's a check of the problem we just did.

Add the ones

Add the tens

tens ones

```
   2
  12
  19
  38
+ 64
-----
   3
```

$4 + 8 = 12$
$12 + 9 = 21$
$21 + 2 = 23$

$6 + 3 = 9$
$9 + 1 = 10$
$10 + 1 = 11$
$11 + 2 = 13$

tens ones

```
   2
  12
  19
  38
+ 64
-----
 133
```

Mental Addition

Remember that you can use brackets to group addends in different ways without changing the sum.

$$(8 + 2) + 3 = 13 \qquad 8 + (2 + 3) = 13$$

You can also add numbers in a different order without changing the sum.

$$2 + 3 = 5 \qquad 3 + 2 = 5$$

So, when you are adding many numbers together, you can group them, and then add them, in the easiest way. To find the sum of $8 + 6 + 2 + 9 + 4$ easily, group the pairs of numbers that add to 10, like this:

$$
\begin{aligned}
8 + 6 + 2 + 9 + 4 &= (8 + 2) + (6 + 4) \ + 9 \\
&= \quad 10 \quad + \quad 10 \quad + 9 \\
&= \quad 29
\end{aligned}
$$

When you are adding two-digit numbers in your head, look for two numbers that make an even ten. To add $28 + 35 + 12$ easily, group the numbers like this:

$$
\begin{aligned}
28 + 35 + 12 &= (28 + 12) + 35 \\
&= \quad 40 \quad + 35 \\
&= \quad 75
\end{aligned}
$$

More Mental Addition Techniques

We learnt in Year 3 that, when you are adding a number that ends in 9, you can make it an even ten and add ten in your head, and then subtract 1 from the final sum. For example, to add 37 and 29, you can think $29 = 30 - 1$.

Think: $37 + 29 = 37 + 30 - 1 = 67 - 1 = 66$

You can make an addend an even hundred and then subtract in the same way. To add 253 and 198, you can think $198 = 200 - 2$.

Think: $253 + 198 = 253 + 200 - 2$
$$= 453 - 2 = 451$$

When you are adding in your head, it is often easier to add a number in two parts. To find the sum of 84 and 28, you can think: $84 + 16$ makes an even hundred. So make 28 into $16 + 12$.

$$\text{Think: } 84 + 28 = 84 + 16 + 12 = 100 + 12 = 112$$

Here is another example.

$$\text{Think: } 365 + 411 = 365 + 400 + 11 = 765 + 11 = 776$$

Practise doing many mental addition problems, using these methods whenever they will help you.

Estimating Sums and Differences

You know how to round, or 'estimate', numbers to come quickly to an answer that is close to right. When you do not need to know an answer exactly, you can estimate addition problems to find out quickly what the approximate answer is. You can estimate the sums of two-digit numbers by rounding each number to the nearest ten, then adding. Here is an example.

$$
\begin{array}{ccc}
 & \textit{rounds to} & \\
29 & \longrightarrow & 30 \\
+\ 45 & \longrightarrow & +\ 50 \\
\hline
 & & 80 \\
\end{array}
$$

$29 + 45$ is about 80. Your answer is about 80, but how close is it really? Now try working it out exactly.

You can estimate the differences of two-digit numbers in the same way.

$$
\begin{array}{ccc}
 & \textit{rounds to} & \\
87 & \longrightarrow & 90 \\
-\ 41 & \longrightarrow & -\ 40 \\
\hline
 & & 50 \\
\end{array}
$$

$87 - 41$ is about 50. Again, try working it out exactly and check the difference.

In the same way, you can estimate the sums and differences of three-digit numbers by rounding to the nearest hundred, then adding or subtracting.

$$\begin{array}{rcl} & \textit{rounds to} & \\ 559 & \longrightarrow & 600 \\ +\,318 & \longrightarrow & +\,300 \\ \hline & & 900 \end{array}$$

$$\begin{array}{rcl} & \textit{rounds to} & \\ 419 & \longrightarrow & 400 \\ -\,187 & \longrightarrow & -\,200 \\ \hline & & 200 \end{array}$$

Practise adding and subtracting by estimating. Since you can add and subtract very quickly when you estimate, you can also use estimation as a quick way to check an answer. But estimation can only tell you if your answer is *about* right; it is not a sure way to check.

More Than One Operation

Sometimes you have to do more than one thing in a problem. For example, sometimes you have to add *and* multiply. These are each called *operations*. When there is more than one operation, always remember to solve the operation inside the brackets first. Here is an example.

$$7 \times (12 - 8) = 7 \times 4 = 28$$

Practise doing many problems with different kinds of operations. Here are some more examples.

$$(10 + 2) - (6 + 2) = 12 - 8 = 4$$
$$(43 - 38) \times (5 + 3) = 5 \times 8 = 40$$
$$(9 \times 4) + (6 \times 5) = 36 + 30 = 66$$
$$(36 \div 6) \div (4 - 1) = 6 \div 3 = 2$$

Practise writing >, <, or = in problems like these, which use more than one operation.

$$8 \times 6 < 82 - 31 \qquad 63 \div 9 > 3 \times 2 \qquad 21 + 11 = 4 \times 8$$

Remember that $8 \times 6 < 82 - 31$ and $63 \div 9 > 3 \times 2$ are inequalities. $21 + 11 = 4 \times 8$ is an equation, because both sides are equal.

Mental Subtraction

Here is a method to help you subtract numbers in your head. When you are subtracting a number that ends in 9, you can subtract an even ten instead, and then add 1.

For example, to take 19 away from 54, you can think: subtracting 19 is the same as subtracting 20, then adding 1.

$$\text{Think: } 54 - 19 = 54 - 20 + 1 = 34 + 1 = 35$$

You can make a number you are subtracting an even hundred in the same way. For example, to subtract 198 from 426, you can think: subtracting 198 is the same as subtracting 200, then adding 2.

$$\text{Think: } 426 - 198 = 426 - 200 + 2 = 226 + 2 = 228$$

When you are subtracting in your head, it is often easier to subtract a number by first taking away part of the number, then taking away the rest. For example, to subtract 23 from 48, you can first subtract 20, then subtract 3 more.

$$\text{Think: } 48 - 23 = (48 - 20) - 3 = 28 - 3 = 25$$

To solve 125 – 29, you can think: 125 – 25 makes an even hundred. So think of taking away 29 as first taking away 25, then taking away 4 more.

$$\text{Think: } 125 - 29 = (125 - 25) - 4 = 100 - 4 = 96$$

Practise doing many mental subtraction problems, using these methods whenever they will help you.

Sums and Differences of Four-Digit Numbers

Adding with Thousands

Sometimes when you add, you need to regroup hundreds as thousands. When you add vertically, always work from right to left. Let's find the sum of 2,635 and 3,728. To find this sum, add the ones, then the tens, then the hundreds, then the thousands.

```
 thousands
   hundreds
      tens
        ones

  2, 6 3 5
+ 3, 7 2 8
```

```
 thousands
   hundreds
      tens
        ones
  1   1
  2, 6 3 5
+ 3, 7 2 8
_____
  6, 3 6 3
```

In the same way you have learnt to regroup ones as tens, regroup when necessary as you move to the left. In this problem, you do not need to regroup tens as hundreds, but you do need to regroup hundreds as thousands (and also ones as tens, as you have done before). 6 hundreds plus 7 hundreds equals 13 hundreds. You regroup 13 hundreds as 1 thousand, 3 hundreds. Then you add the thousands. The sum equals 6,363.

Practise finding sums with three or more addends, as well as with two addends. Sometimes when you are adding four-digit numbers, you need to regroup thousands as ten thousands. You write 14 thousands as 1 ten thousand, 4 thousands. ▶

thousands
hundreds
tens
ones

```
  5, 6 2 7
  7, 4 8 2
       3 8
+    9 7 5
─────────
```

ten thousands
thousands
hundreds
tens
ones

```
1 2, 2 2
  5, 6 2 7
  7, 4 8 2
       3 8
+    9 7 5
─────────
1 4, 1 2 2
```

thousands
hundreds
tens
ones

```
  1,  1 1
  3, 5 8 4
     7 2 3
       1 9
+      2 5 0
─────────
  4, 5 7 6
```

◀ You often have to add numbers together that have a different number of digits. Given a problem like 3,584 + 723 + 19 + 250, practise writing the numbers in columns and then adding them. Be sure to keep the numbers in the correct place-value column.

In general, practise doing addition in columns until it is easy for you and you are very good at regrouping. Also practise estimating, to see if the sum is about right.

To estimate the sum of four-digit numbers, round to the nearest thousand.

rounds to

```
  5,334  ⟶    5,000
+ 2,926  ⟶  + 3,000
─────────    ───────
               8,000
```

5,334 + 2,926 is about 5,000 + 3,000, which equals 8,000. So you know that the sum of 5,334 and 2,926 should be about 8,000. When you actually add the two numbers, what do you get? Is it near 8,000?

Subtraction: Regrouping More Than Once

Sometimes when you subtract, you need to regroup more than once. When you subtract vertically, work from right to left.

Since you cannot take 9 from 4, regroup

Subtract the ones

Since you cannot take 8 tens from 1 ten, regroup again

Subtract the tens
Subtract the hundreds

```
                                      4 11           4 11
                   1 14              1 14           1 14
      5 2 4       5 2 4             5 2 4           5 2 4
    - 3 8 9     - 3 8 9           - 3 8 9         - 3 8 9
    ───────     ───────           ───────         ───────
                      5                3 5           1 3 5
```

Subtracting Across Zeros

Sometimes when you need to regroup, there is a zero in the next place. Then you need to regroup in a different way. Here is an example. Find the difference of 304 and 187.

```
  hundreds
     tens
        ones
    3 0 4
  - 1 8 7
  ───────
```

Subtract the ones. Since you cannot take 7 from 4, you need to regroup. But there are no tens to regroup. Change 3 hundreds to 2 hundreds and 10 tens. The 1 in front of the 0 in the tens column indicates a ten in that column. Now change the 10 tens to 9 tens and 10 ones.

```
  hundreds                      hundreds
     tens                          tens
        ones                          ones
       9
    2 10 14                       2 9 14
    3 0 4          OR            3 0 4
  - 1 8 7                      - 1 8 7
  ───────                      ───────
    1 1 7                        1 1 7
```

You can also think: change 30 tens to 29 tens and 10 ones, adding those to the 4 in the ones place.

Let's see on the next page how this process works when you have to subtract across several zeros. When subtracting four-digit numbers, first subtract the ones, then the tens, then the hundreds, then the thousands.

$$\begin{array}{r} 4,000 \\ -\ 2,896 \\ \hline \end{array}$$

Think: You need an extra ten for the ones place. Change 400 tens to 399 tens and add the extra ten to the ones place. Then subtract the ones, the tens, the hundreds and the thousands, column by column.

$$\begin{array}{r} 3\ \ 9\ 9\ 10 \\ 4,0\ 0\ 0 \\ -\ 2,8\ 9\ 6 \\ \hline \end{array} \qquad \begin{array}{r} 3\ \ 9\ 9\ 10 \\ 4,0\ 0\ 0 \\ -\ 2,8\ 9\ 6 \\ \hline 1,1\ 0\ 4 \end{array}$$

Four-Digit Subtraction

Practise subtracting with four-digit numbers until you can do it easily, especially across zeros. Practise writing a subtraction problem in columns and then subtracting. Here is an example. Find the difference between 3,037 and 1,682.

$$\begin{array}{r} 3,0\ 3\ 7 \\ -\ 1,6\ 8\ 2 \\ \hline \end{array} \quad \begin{array}{r} 3,0\ 3\ 7 \\ -\ 1,6\ 8\ 2 \\ \hline 5 \end{array} \quad \begin{array}{r} 2\ 9\ 13 \\ 3,0\ 3\ 7 \\ -\ 1,6\ 8\ 2 \\ \hline 5\ 5 \end{array} \quad \begin{array}{r} 2\ 9\ 13 \\ 3,0\ 3\ 7 \\ -\ 1,6\ 8\ 2 \\ \hline 3\ 5\ 5 \end{array} \quad \begin{array}{r} 2\ 9\ 13 \\ 3,0\ 3\ 7 \\ -\ 1,6\ 8\ 2 \\ \hline 1,3\ 5\ 5 \end{array}$$

Remember to check each subtraction problem by addition, like this:

$$\begin{array}{r} 1,3\ 5\ 5 \\ +\ 1,6\ 8\ 2 \\ \hline \end{array} \qquad \begin{array}{r} 1\ \ 1 \\ 1,3\ 5\ 5 \\ +\ 1,6\ 8\ 2 \\ \hline 3,0\ 3\ 7 \end{array}$$

You can also check to see if the difference of four-digit numbers is about right by estimating. Round each number to the nearest thousand and then subtract.

$$\begin{array}{r} 3,0\ 3\ 7 \\ -\ 1,6\ 8\ 2 \\ \hline \end{array} \xrightarrow{\text{rounds to}} \begin{array}{r} 3,0\ 0\ 0 \\ -\ 2,0\ 0\ 0 \\ \hline 1,0\ 0\ 0 \end{array}$$

3,037 − 1,682 is 1,355. What would this round to? 1,000.

Adding and Subtracting Amounts of Money

You add and subtract amounts of money the same way you add and subtract other numbers. Here are two examples.

Chris had been saving money for a very long time and had saved a total of £85.87. For his brother's birthday present, Chris bought a toy helicopter for £13.48. How much did Chris have left?

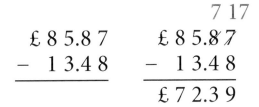

$$
\begin{array}{r}
£ 8\,5.8\,7 \\
-\ \ 1\,3.4\,8 \\
\hline
\end{array}
\qquad
\begin{array}{r}
^{7}\ ^{17} \\
£ 8\,5.\cancel{8}\,\cancel{7} \\
-\ \ 1\,3.4\,8 \\
\hline
£ 7\,2.3\,9
\end{array}
$$

At the shop, Anna's parents spent £51.68 on food, £6.80 on school supplies for Anna, £4.56 on flowers for Anna's granny and £12.84 on a new jumper for Anna. How much did they spend?

Do not forget to write the pound sign and the pence point in your answer.

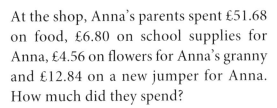

$$
\begin{array}{r}
£ 5\,1.6\,8 \\
6.8\,0 \\
4.5\,6 \\
+\ 1\,2.8\,4 \\
\hline
\end{array}
\qquad
\begin{array}{r}
1\ 2\ 1 \\
£ 5\,1.6\,8 \\
6.8\,0 \\
4.5\,6 \\
+\ 1\,2.8\,4 \\
\hline
£ 7\,5.8\,8
\end{array}
$$

More Mental Addition and Subtraction

You can add and subtract thousands the same way you add and subtract ones.

$$7 \quad + 2 \quad = 9 \qquad\qquad 60 \quad - 20 \quad = 40$$

$$7{,}000 + 2{,}000 = 9{,}000 \qquad 60{,}000 - 20{,}000 = 40{,}000$$

Learn to add and subtract thousands in your head in problems like these.

$$6{,}000 + \underline{} = 9{,}000 \qquad 54{,}000 - 24{,}000 = \underline{}$$

$$350{,}000 + \underline{} = 450{,}000$$

Also practise adding the amount it takes to reach the next thousand. This will help you learn place value.

$$9{,}990 + \underline{\hspace{2cm}} = 10{,}000$$

$$39{,}900 + \underline{\hspace{2cm}} = 40{,}000$$

$$59{,}980 + \underline{\hspace{2cm}} = 60{,}000$$

Multiplication

Multiplication Tables

In Year 2, you learnt the multiplication tables with 0, 1, 2, 5 and 10 as factors. In Year 3, you learnt the multiplication tables with 3, 4 and 8 as factors. Here are the rest of the multiplication tables to 10 with 6, 7 and 9 as factors.

6 as a *factor*	7 as a *factor*	9 as a *factor*
$0 \times 6 = 0$	$0 \times 7 = 0$	$0 \times 9 = 0$
$1 \times 6 = 6$	$1 \times 7 = 7$	$1 \times 9 = 9$
$2 \times 6 = 12$	$2 \times 7 = 14$	$2 \times 9 = 18$
$3 \times 6 = 18$	$3 \times 7 = 21$	$3 \times 9 = 27$
$4 \times 6 = 24$	$4 \times 7 = 28$	$4 \times 9 = 36$
$5 \times 6 = 30$	$5 \times 7 = 35$	$5 \times 9 = 45$
$6 \times 6 = 36$	$6 \times 7 = 42$	$6 \times 9 = 54$
$7 \times 6 = 42$	$7 \times 7 = 49$	$7 \times 9 = 63$
$8 \times 6 = 48$	$8 \times 7 = 56$	$8 \times 9 = 72$
$9 \times 6 = 54$	$9 \times 7 = 63$	$9 \times 9 = 81$
$10 \times 6 = 60$	$10 \times 7 = 70$	$10 \times 9 = 90$

Only the multiplication facts that are red are actually new. The others you already know. For example, if you know $9 \times 8 = 72$, then you know $8 \times 9 = 72$. Learn these facts so that you can say them easily. Also be able to give any product quickly, without making any mistakes. Remember that you can skip-count to get to the next fact in a table.

$8 \times 6 = 48$, so 9×6 is 6 more, or 54.

$7 \times 7 = 49$, so 8×7 is 7 more, or 56.

When you know all the multiplication facts well, practise filling in a table with all of them.

Do you remember filling in a smaller table in Year 3? Do you notice patterns in the answers you fill in?

x	1	2	3	4	5	6	7	8	9	10
1										
2								16		
3		6								
4								32		
5										
6										
7										
8										
9										
10										

Square Numbers and Square Roots

How many squares are there in each of these grids?

To find out, you can add the number of squares in each row.

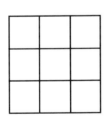 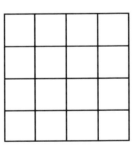 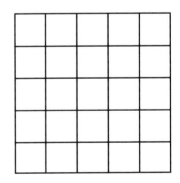

$$3 + 3 + 3 = 9 \qquad 4 + 4 + 4 + 4 = 16 \qquad 5 + 5 + 5 + 5 + 5 = 25$$

Or you can multiply the number of rows by the number of columns.

$$3 \times 3 = 9 \qquad 4 \times 4 = 16 \qquad 5 \times 5 = 25$$

The numbers 9, 16 and 25 are called *square* numbers. You can arrange them as squares, without any gaps, as wide as they are tall. A square number is the product of any number multiplied by itself. The number 3 is called a *square root* of 9, because 3 multiplied by itself equals 9. The number 4 is called a square root of 16, because 4 multiplied by itself equals 16. If you know how many little squares there are in a big square, the square root is the number of little squares along each side.

You can do square root problems in the other direction, too. What is a square root of 25? In other words, what number multiplied by itself equals 25? (The answer can be found in the grids we just looked at.)

The sign for square root looks like this: $\sqrt{}$

For example, $\sqrt{9} = 3$ and $\sqrt{16} = 4$

Find the square numbers

$7 \times 7 = \underline{\hspace{1cm}}$ $\qquad$ $9 \times 9 = \underline{\hspace{1cm}}$ $\qquad$ $10 \times 10 = \underline{\hspace{1cm}}$

Find the square roots

$\sqrt{64} = \underline{\hspace{1cm}}$ $\qquad$ $\sqrt{36} = \underline{\hspace{1cm}}$ $\qquad$ $\sqrt{100} = \underline{\hspace{1cm}}$

Now here's an interesting thing to try. If you fill in the square numbers on the practise table on the opposite page, what sort of line will the square numbers make on the table?

Review: Brackets and the Order of Operations

In Year 3, we learnt why brackets are important in maths to show you the order of completing different parts of a problem. Do you remember why that was?

In maths, brackets, which are also called parentheses, show you that you should solve what is inside the brackets first. It doesn't always make a difference. If you have a problem with several parts asking you only to add (like $7 + 8 + 3$) or only to multiply (like $5 \times 2 \times 4$) the order doesn't matter. The sum in the first problem is the same no matter the order in which you complete it. The same is true of the product in the second problem. Let's make sure:

Try $7 + 8 + 3$ in two different ways:

$(7 + 8) + 3 = \underline{\hspace{0.8cm}} + 3 = \underline{\hspace{0.8cm}}$ $\qquad$ $7 + (8 + 3) = 7 + \underline{\hspace{0.8cm}} = \underline{\hspace{0.8cm}}$

Now try $5 \times 2 \times 4$ in two different ways:

$(5 \times 2) \times 4 = \underline{\hspace{0.8cm}} \times 4 = \underline{\hspace{0.8cm}}$ $\qquad$ $5 \times (2 \times 4) = 5 \times \underline{\hspace{0.8cm}} = \underline{\hspace{0.8cm}}$

What answers did you find? For 7 + 8 + 3, was the sum 18 both times you solved the problem? For 5 × 2 × 4, was the product 40 both times?

We learnt in Year 3 that brackets are very important when you are adding some numbers and multiplying others in one problem because, if you don't solve the part in the brackets first, your answer will come out differently. For example, try this problem: 4 × 3 + 6. How do you know which way to solve it? Let's try it both ways:

$$(4 \times 3) + 6 = \underline{\hspace{1cm}} + 6 = \underline{\hspace{1cm}} \qquad 4 \times (3 + 6) = 4 \times \underline{\hspace{1cm}} = \underline{\hspace{1cm}}$$

Did you come up with 18 for the first way of solving the problem and 36 for the second way? Those are quite different answers! Now you see why brackets are so important. They show you which part of the problem to solve first so you know whether the answer should be 18 or 36.

Multiplying Visually and Vertically

If Jennie is having a party and wants each of the 16 people attending to have 3 balloons, how many balloons would she need to buy? One way to multiply 3 by 16 is to break 16 into smaller numbers. Graph paper can help show how this works. 3 × 16.

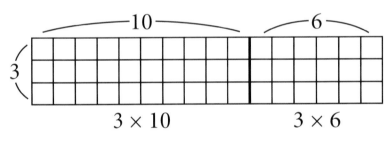

You can see from the picture that 3 × 16 is the same as (3 × 10) + (3 × 6) in expanded form. So you can multiply 3 × 16 like this:

$$3 \times 16 = (3 \times 10) + (3 \times 6) = 30 + 18 = 48$$

You can also write this multiplication problem vertically, like this:

$$\begin{array}{r} \overset{\text{tens ones}}{16} \\ \times\ 3 \\ \hline \end{array}$$

When you multiply vertically, you start with the ones and move to the left to multiply greater values. You write the first product underneath, then you multiply the bottom factor, 3 in this case, by the tens. Write that next product underneath the first product. Then add them together to find the total product. Let's go through it with the numbers now.

Multiply the ones

16
× 3
————
18

3 × 6 = 18

Multiply the tens

16
× 3
————
18
30

3 × 6 = 18
3 × 10 = 30

Add

16
× 3
————
18
+ 30
————
48

Notice how you write in the 0 to show that 3 × 10 is 3 tens, or 30, and not 3 ones.

Jennie needs to buy 48 balloons if she wants each of the 16 people to have 3.

Now let's multiply 8 × 26 in the same way. First draw the problem on graph paper in rows and columns. Then write it vertically and multiply. Notice that first you multiply 8 by the ones, then you multiply 8 by the tens.

Practise multiplying this way, making separate products for the ones and the tens, then adding.

26
× 8
————
48
+ 160
————
208

8 × 6 = 48
8 × 20 = 160

A Short Way to Multiply

Now let's go one step further and learn the short way to write multiplication. In this method, you write the products on the same line. Let's use 23 × 3 as an example.

First we write it vertically.

23
× 3
————

Next we multiply 3 by the 3 ones in 23. You know that 3 × 3 = 9.

23
× 3
————
9

Next we multiply 3 by the 2 tens in 23 and write the product on the same line.

23
× 3
————
69

Often when you multiply this way, you need to regroup. See what happens when you multiply 8 by 26 this way.

Multiply 8 by 6 ones. Now regroup 48 as 4 tens and 8 ones. Write the 8 ones down below, and carry the 4 to the top of the tens place.

$$\begin{array}{r} 4 \\ 26 \\ \times\ \ 8 \\ \hline 8 \end{array}$$

Next we multiply the 8 by the 2 in 26. Add the extra 4 tens to the product and write the answer on the same line.
(8 × 2) + 4 = 16 + 4 = 20

$$\begin{array}{r} 4 \\ 26 \\ \times\ \ 8 \\ \hline 208 \end{array}$$

Multiplying Tens, Hundreds and Thousands

It is easy to multiply tens, hundreds and thousands: use the multiplication facts you already know!

3 × 2 tens = 6 tens
3 × 20 = 60

$$\begin{array}{r} 20 \\ \times\ \ 3 \\ \hline 60 \end{array}$$

4 × 7 hundreds = 28 hundreds
4 × 700 = 2,800

$$\begin{array}{r} 700 \\ \times\ \ \ \ 4 \\ \hline 2,800 \end{array}$$

3 × 6 thousands = 18 thousands
3 × 6,000 = 18,000

$$\begin{array}{r} 6,000 \\ \times\ \ \ \ 3 \\ \hline 18,000 \end{array}$$

Practise solving problems like these quickly. Remember that you are multiplying tens, hundreds or thousands. Be sure to keep the right number of zeros in the product!

Multiplying Three-Digit and Four-Digit Numbers

You can multiply a three-digit number by a one-digit number by writing separate products for the ones, tens and hundreds. Then you can add the separate products.

$$
\begin{array}{r}
284 \\
\times \quad 7 \\
\hline
28 \\
560 \\
+\ 1{,}400 \\
\hline
1{,}988
\end{array}
$$

$$7 \times 4 = 28$$
$$7 \times 80 = 560$$
$$7 \times 200 = 1{,}400$$

The product of 7×284 is $1{,}988$.

Practise multiplying three-digit numbers this way. Then multiply a three-digit number the quick way, writing the products on one line.

Multiply 7 by the ones. *Regroup 28.*	*Multiply 7 by the tens.* *Add the 2 tens.* *Regroup 58 tens.*	*Multiply 7 by* *the hundreds.* *Add the 5 hundreds.*
2	5 2	5 2
2 8 4	2 8 4	2 8 4
$\times$ 7	$\times$ 7	$\times$ 7
8	8 8	1, 9 8 8

Here is an example where one of the digits in the number you are multiplying is 0. Remember that the product of any number and 0 is 0.

$$
\begin{array}{r}
4 \\
5\,0\,7 \\
\times \quad\quad 6 \\
\hline
3,0\,4\,2
\end{array}
$$

In this example, 6×0 tens $= 0$. You add 0 and the 4 tens you carried to the tens place.

Learn to multiply a four-digit number now. You multiply from right to left. First you multiply the ones, then the tens, then the hundreds, then the thousands. Often you have to regroup. Here is an example.

The process of regrouping, multiplying in the next place and then adding takes time to learn, and you need to practise it a lot. Practise multiplying one-digit numbers by two-digit, three-digit and four-digit numbers. You can make up your own numbers to multiply. Be sure to practise with numbers that have zeros in them.

$$
\begin{array}{r}
5 \quad\ 3 \\
1,7\,0\,4 \\
\times \quad\quad 8 \\
\hline
13,6\,3\,2
\end{array}
$$

Checking Multiplication

One good way to check multiplication is to estimate, to see if the product is about right.

When you are multiplying a two-digit number, find the two tens that the number is between. On page 247, you found that $8 \times 26 = 208$. To check this product, think: 26 is between 20 and 30. So 8×26 should be between 8×20 and 8×30. $8 \times 20 = 160$. $8 \times 30 = 240$. 208 is between 160 and 240.

You can write this check like this:

$$8 \times 20 < 8 \times 26 < 8 \times 30$$
$$160 < 208 < 240 ✔$$

A number statement like $8 \times 20 < 8 \times 26 < 8 \times 30$ is called a *double inequality* because there are two inequality signs.

When you are multiplying a three-digit number, check the product by finding the two hundreds that the number is between.

To check $6 \times 507 = 3,042$, you can think: 507 is between 500 and 600 (but much closer to 500).

$$6 \times 500 < 6 \times 507 < 6 \times 600$$
$$3,000 < 3,042 < 3,600 ✔$$

When you are multiplying a four-digit number, find the two thousands that it is between to check. Does $8 \times 1,704 = 13,632$?

$$8 \times 1,000 < 8 \times 1,704 < 8 \times 2,000$$
$$8,000 < 13,632 < 16,000 ✔$$

Check each multiplication problem by estimating in this way.

Another Way to Write Expanded Form

Remember that the expanded form of 7,836 is $7,000 + 800 + 30 + 6$. Now that you know how to multiply tens, hundreds and thousands, you can write the expanded form of a number in another way.

$$7,000 = 7 \times 1,000 \qquad 800 = 8 \times 100 \qquad 30 = 3 \times 10$$

So you can write 7,000 + 800 + 30 + 6 like this:

$$(7 \times 1{,}000) + (8 \times 100) + (3 \times 10) + 6$$

Practise writing numbers in this new expanded form. For example:

$$3{,}604 = (3 \times 1{,}000) + (6 \times 100) + 4$$
$$9{,}078 = (9 \times 1{,}000) + (7 \times 10) + 8$$

Solving Word Problems Using Multiplication

In word problems, the important step is deciding what mathematical problem you need to solve. Once you can write the problem in numbers, then you can solve it. Solve these word problems using multiplication:

1. At the beach, Andrea found 8 shells. Jeff found 5 times as many shells. How many shells did Jeff find?

2. Megan's red truck needs 15 litres of fuel to travel 100 km. How much fuel does she need to travel 700 km? (Hint: How many hundreds are there in 700?)

3. If the red truck travels 5 times faster than the bike and the bike travels 12 miles in an hour, how far will the truck travel in an hour?

Division

Division Tables

Now you can learn the division tables for the divisors 6, 7 and 9.

6 as a *divisor*	7 as a *divisor*	9 as a *divisor*
$0 \div 6 = 0$	$0 \div 7 = 0$	$0 \div 9 = 0$
$6 \div 6 = 1$	$7 \div 7 = 1$	$9 \div 9 = 1$
$12 \div 6 = 2$	$14 \div 7 = 2$	$18 \div 9 = 2$
$18 \div 6 = 3$	$21 \div 7 = 3$	$27 \div 9 = 3$
$24 \div 6 = 4$	$28 \div 7 = 4$	$36 \div 9 = 4$
$30 \div 6 = 5$	$35 \div 7 = 5$	$45 \div 9 = 5$
$36 \div 6 = 6$	$42 \div 7 = 6$	$54 \div 9 = 6$
$42 \div 6 = 7$	$49 \div 7 = 7$	$63 \div 9 = 7$
$48 \div 6 = 8$	$56 \div 7 = 8$	$72 \div 9 = 8$
$54 \div 6 = 9$	$63 \div 7 = 9$	$81 \div 9 = 9$
$60 \div 6 = 10$	$70 \div 7 = 10$	$90 \div 9 = 10$

Dividing Tens, Hundreds and Thousands

Sometimes you can divide tens, hundreds and thousands easily, using the division facts.

$$9 \div 3 = 3 \qquad 35 \div 7 = 5 \qquad 18 \div 6 = 3$$
$$90 \div 3 = 30 \qquad 3,500 \div 7 = 500 \qquad 18,000 \div 6 = 3,000$$

Notice how the quotient has the same number of zeros as the dividend? Practise doing problems like these in your head.

Two-Digit Quotients

Sometimes when you divide a two-digit number, the quotient has two digits. Divide 64 by 2. Remember, in division, you start with the highest place value in the dividend and move right. So in $2\overline{)64}$, we first divide the tens.

$$3$$
$$2\overline{)\,64}$$

Subtract 3×2 $-\,6$

Check $0 < 2$ 0

Subtract the product of 3×2. Make sure the remainder (0) is less than the divisor (2). Then bring down the 4 ones in 64. Divide the ones.

$$32$$
$$2\overline{)\,64}$$
$$-\,6\!\downarrow$$

Bring down the 4 04

Subtract 2×2 $-\,4$

Check $0 < 2$ 0

Make sure this next remainder (0 again in this problem) is less than the divisor (2).

You can tell that $64 \div 2$ will have a two-digit quotient because you can divide the 6 by 2. In the same way, $84 \div 5$ has a two-digit quotient because you can divide the 8 by 5. $47 \div 8$ has a one-digit quotient because you cannot divide 4 by 8. You need to divide 47 by 8 instead.

We started learning about remainders in Year 3. Here is a problem with a two-digit quotient and a remainder.

Divide the tens

$$1$$
$$5\overline{)\,84}$$

Subtract 5×1 $-\,5$

Check $3 < 5$ 3

Divide the ones

$$16 \text{ R}4$$
$$5\overline{)\,84}$$
$$-\,5\!\downarrow$$

Bring down the 4 34

Subtract 5×6 $-\,30$

Check $4 < 5$ 4

There is a remainder this time. Make sure it is less than the divisor. It is!

Checking Division

You check division by multiplying and adding the remainder, if there is one. Remember that multiplying by a number is the inverse of dividing by that number.

   Let's check our answers to the problems we did in the last section.

Division Problem:	Check by multiplying:	Division Problem:	Check by multiplying:

$$\begin{array}{r} 32 \\ 2\overline{)64} \\ -6\!\downarrow \\ \hline 04 \\ -4 \\ \hline 0 \end{array}$$

$$\begin{array}{r} 32 \quad \textit{quotient} \\ \times\ 2 \quad \textit{divisor} \\ \hline 64 \quad \textit{dividend} \end{array}$$

There is no remainder to add.

✔

$$\begin{array}{r} 16\ \text{R4} \\ 5\overline{)84} \\ -5\!\downarrow \\ \hline 34 \\ -30 \\ \hline 4 \end{array}$$

$$\begin{array}{r} 16 \quad \textit{quotient} \\ \times\ 5 \quad \textit{divisor} \\ \hline 80 \quad\ \ \textit{add} \\ +\ 4 \quad \textit{remainder} \\ \hline 84 \quad \textit{dividend} \end{array}$$

✔

When you check, you should end up with the number into which you first divided. Remember that this number is called the dividend. Check every division problem by multiplying, then adding the remainder if there is one, to get the dividend.

Dividing Three-Digit Numbers

Learn how to divide three-digit numbers by one-digit numbers.

First divide the hundreds

$$\begin{array}{r} 2 \\ 3\overline{)758} \\ -6 \\ \hline 1 \end{array}$$

Subtract 3 × 2
Check 1 < 3

Then divide the tens

$$\begin{array}{r} 25 \\ 3\overline{)758} \\ -6\!\downarrow \\ \hline 15 \\ -15 \\ \hline 0 \end{array}$$

Bring down the 5
Subtract 3 × 5
Check 0 < 3

Then divide the ones

$$\begin{array}{r} 252\,\text{R2} \\ 3\overline{)758} \\ -6 \\ \hline 15 \\ -15 \\ \hline 08 \\ -6 \\ \hline 2 \end{array}$$

Bring down the 8
Subtract 3 × 2
Check 2 < 3

Check by multiplying and adding

$$\begin{array}{r} 252 \\ \times\ 3 \\ \hline 756 \\ +\ 2 \\ \hline 758 \end{array}$$

252 *quotient*
× 3 *divisor*
756
+ 2 *add remainder*
758 *dividend* ✔

Sometimes there are not enough hundreds to begin by dividing hundreds. Then you need to think of the hundreds as tens, and divide the tens.

In the following example, divide the tens, since you cannot divide 6 hundreds by 8.

Think of 6 hundreds and 2 tens as 62 tens.

Divide the tens

$$\begin{array}{r} 7\ \ \ \\ 8\overline{)627} \\ -56\ \ \\ \hline 6\ \ \end{array}$$

Subtract 8 × 7
Check 6 < 8

Divide the ones

$$\begin{array}{r} 78\ R3 \\ 8\overline{)627} \\ -56\ \ \\ \hline 67\ \\ -64\ \\ \hline 3\ \end{array}$$

Bring down the 7
Subtract 8 × 8
Check 3 < 8

Check by multiplying and adding

78 *quotient*
× 8 *divisor*
624
+ 3 *add remainder*
627 *dividend* ✔

Learning long division takes lots of careful practice. Each time you divide and subtract, make sure the remainder is less than the divisor. When you have finished, multiply the dividend by the quotient and add the remainder to check.

Roman Numerals

The numerals we use most often – the digits 0, 1, 2, 3, 4, 5, 6, 7, 8, 9 – are called Arabic numerals because they were brought to Europe through contact with people from the area that was called Arabia. The ancient Romans used different symbols as their numerals. Even today you may come across Roman numerals on clocks, like this one, and to number the first pages of books. Check the first pages of this book!

Learn more about the ancient Romans on page 120.

Here are some of the symbols that the Romans used.

This Roman soldier is XXVIII years old.

I is 1

V is 5

X is 10

Those are all the symbols you need in order to write the numbers from 1 to 30. Here are the rules.

Rule 1

When a Roman numeral that is the same value or smaller comes after another numeral, you add the values together.

II = 1 + 1 = 2

XX = 10 + 10 = 20

XI = 10 + 1 = 11

Try to answer these:

III = _____ + _____ + _____ = _____

XII = _____ + _____ + _____ = _____

VIII = _____ + _____ + _____ + _____ = _____

Rule 2

When a Roman numeral of smaller value comes just before another, you subtract the smaller one from the larger one.

IV *Since I is less than V and comes before it, this is* 5 − 1 = 4

IX *Since I is less than X and comes before it, this is* 10 − 1 = 9

Here's a problem for you. What's this number?

XXIX

It's 10 + 10 + (10 − 1), or 29.

256

The Romans had just a few more symbols for their numbers:

L is 50

C is 100

D is 500

M is 1,000

These symbols, and the ones you learnt earlier, were the only number symbols they used and they could write thousands of numbers with them!

Parts of a Whole: Fractions and Decimals

Review: Recognising Fractions

Look over this list of fractions. We learnt these fractions in Years 2 and 3, and you should learn to recognise them quickly just the way you recognise the numbers 1 to 10.

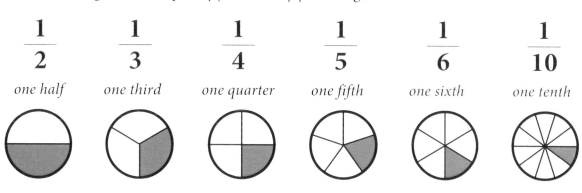

$\dfrac{1}{2}$	$\dfrac{1}{3}$	$\dfrac{1}{4}$	$\dfrac{1}{5}$	$\dfrac{1}{6}$	$\dfrac{1}{10}$
one half	*one third*	*one quarter*	*one fifth*	*one sixth*	*one tenth*

Numerator and Denominator

You know that a fraction represents a portion of a whole. It can be a part of one thing or a part of a group of things. The bottom number of a fraction, called the *denominator*, tells how many equal parts the whole was divided into. The top number of a fraction, called the *numerator*, tells how many of the equal parts you are talking about. For example, if you have an apple and you slice it in four quarters, you have made four equal portions. Each portion represents ¼, or one out of the four equal parts of the apple. Note that $\frac{1}{4}$ means the same as ¼.

$$\frac{4}{8}$$ In the fraction ⁴⁄₈, 4 is the numerator and 8 is the denominator.

In the fraction ⁹⁄₁₀, what is the numerator? What is the denominator? $$\frac{9}{10}$$

numerator $$\frac{3}{5}$$ *green paintbrushes*

denominator   *paintbrushes total*

⅗ of the paintbrushes are green.

Equivalent Fractions

Sometimes fractions with different numerators and denominators name the same amount. Fractions that name the same amount are called *equivalent* fractions.

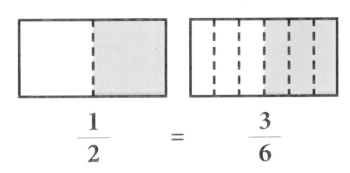

$$\frac{1}{2} = \frac{3}{6}$$

½ and ⁴⁄₈ are equivalent fractions: they name the same fraction of the rectangle.

Learn to recognise equivalent fractions. For example, from the pictures you should know that ½ = ³⁄₆ and ½ = ⁴⁄₈.

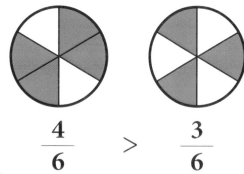

$$\frac{1}{2} = \frac{4}{8}$$

Comparing Fractions

Learn to compare fractions that have the same denominator by using the signs >, < and =.

⁴⁄₆ is greater than ³⁄₆. In ⁴⁄₆, there are 6 equal parts and you are talking about 4. In ³⁄₆, there are 6 equal parts and you are talking about only 3.

A rule of comparing fractions: when two fractions have the same denominator, the one with the greater numerator is the greater fraction.

$$\frac{4}{6} > \frac{3}{6}$$

Without using a picture, say whether the following fractions are greater than, less than or equal to each other:

$$\frac{5}{9} \underline{\quad} \frac{3}{9} \qquad \frac{2}{7} \underline{\quad} \frac{3}{7} \qquad \frac{1}{6} \underline{\quad} \frac{1}{6}$$

Mixed Numbers and Whole Numbers

1½ oranges

The numbers 0, 1, 2, 3, 4, ... are called the *whole numbers*. By calling them 'whole numbers', we mean that they are not fractions and that they name a full number.

A number like 1½ is called a *mixed number*. It has a part that is a whole number and a part that is a fraction. You read 1½ as 'one and a half'. When you read a mixed number, you always put an 'and' between its whole-number part and its fractional part. Here are some more mixed numbers:

$$2\frac{1}{4} \qquad 3\frac{1}{8} \qquad 6\frac{7}{9} \qquad 5\frac{1}{2} \qquad 3\frac{3}{4}$$

On a number line, 1½ is halfway between 1 and 2. It is 1 *plus* ½ more. In the same way, 1¾ is between 1 and 2, but it is closer to 2 because 1¾ > 1½. Similarly, 3½ is 3 plus ½, and it is halfway between 3 and 4 on a number line.

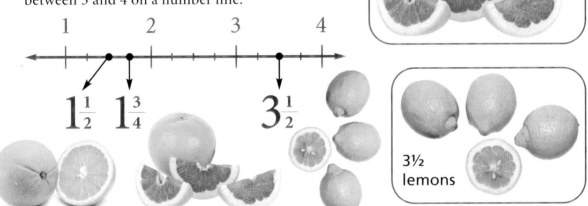

1¾
grapefruits

3½
lemons

You often use mixed numbers when you measure in centimetres and inches. You can see on this ruler that the centimetres are listed upside down and that there are little white marks to show the parts between each whole number. In the middle between each of the whole numbers showing centimetres, there is a taller line to show the half. On the top of this ruler you can see whole numbers that label the inches, with one tall line between each whole number to show ½ and also two medium lines that show ¼ and ¾, as well as smaller lines to show other fractions. Practise measuring to the nearest half centimetre, or to the nearest quarter and three-quarters of an inch using a ruler divided like this one.

Now can you draw some line segments? Try to draw one that is 4½ centimetres long and then one that is 5¾ inches long.

Decimals: Tenths

You can write the fraction ⅒ as the decimal 0.1

They mean the same thing: one tenth.

The dot to the right of the 0 is called a *decimal point*. The decimal point shows that the value of the digits to its right is anywhere between 0 and 1, like a fraction. A *decimal* is any number that uses places to the right of the decimal point to show part of a number. It is a different way of writing a fraction.

The first place to the right of the decimal point is the tenths place, so all of these fractions have 10 in the denominator.

You can write the mixed number 1⁷⁄₁₀ as the decimal 1.7. You could write the decimal 2.3 as the mixed number 2³⁄₁₀. How could you write the decimal 4.8?

ones	.	tenths
1	.	7
2	.	3
4	.	8

Decimals and Hundredths

The second place to the right of the decimal point is the hundredths place. The fraction ¹⁄₁₀₀ can also be written: 0.01 and they both mean the same thing: 'one hundredth'.

ones	.	tenths	hundredths	
0	.	0	1	$\frac{1}{100}$
2	.	4	7	$2\frac{47}{100}$
3	.	8	5	$3\frac{85}{100}$

Both 2.47 and 2⁴⁷⁄₁₀₀ mean 'two and forty-seven hundredths'. What do 3.85 and 3⁸⁵⁄₁₀₀ mean?

Notice that when there are both tenths and hundredths in a decimal, you read the tenths and hundredths together in terms of the hundredths. Also remember to put an 'and' between the whole-number part and the fractional part of a decimal, just as in mixed numbers.

Decimals and Fractions of 100

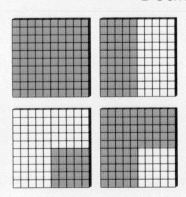

Each of these squares contains 100 smaller squares. The shaded areas can be represented by decimal numbers. The square at the top left, with all 100 squares shaded, is represented by 100 hundredths, or 1.00. The square at the top right, with 50 squares shaded, is represented by 50 hundredths, or 0.50. What proportion of the square at the top right is shaded? Half of it. It shows you that $0.50 = {}^{50}/_{100} = \frac{1}{2}$.

What can we say about the square at the bottom left? Of its 100 squares, how many are shaded? 25. The decimal number representing that proportion is 0.25. Those smaller squares make up one-quarter of the full square, showing how $0.25 = {}^{25}/_{100} = \frac{1}{4}$.

What about the square at the bottom right? How many smaller squares are shaded? 75. What proportion of the total is shaded? ¾. This shows that $0.75 = {}^{75}/_{100} = \frac{3}{4}$.

Multiplying and Dividing Amounts of Money

Now that you've learnt about decimals, you can multiply and divide amounts of money the same way you multiply and divide other numbers. Here are two examples.

Remember to write the pound sign and the pence point in your answer.

$$
\begin{array}{r}
3\,2 \\
£9.97 \\
\times \quad 4 \\
\hline
£39.88
\end{array}
$$

$$
\begin{array}{r}
£3.31 \\
5{\overline{)\,£16.55}} \\
-15 \downarrow \\
\hline
15 \\
-15 \downarrow \\
\hline
05 \\
-5 \\
\hline
0
\end{array}
$$

Word Problems

You have already done problems that ask you to add, subtract, multiply or divide. Sometimes you have to do two different operations in the same problem. These are called two-step word problems. Sometimes you do not need to know an exact answer for a word problem. You can estimate. Let's try a two-step word problem and an estimation word problem.

A Two-Step Word Problem

Lisa has saved up £28.50. For a school play, she buys 8 tickets to go with her friends. Each ticket costs her £2.39. How much money does she have left after buying them?

First you have to multiply, to find out how much the tickets cost her in total. You multiply amounts of money the same way you multiply other numbers. Include the pence point and the pound sign in the product when you have finished.

$$\begin{array}{r} {}^{3\ 7}\\ £2.39 \\ \times\qquad 8 \\ \hline £19.12 \end{array}$$

Then you have to subtract, to find out how much money she has left.

$$\begin{array}{r} {}^{1\ 18\ 4\ 10}\\ £\,2\,8\,.\,5\,0 \\ -\ 1\,9\,.\,1\,2 \\ \hline £\,9\,.\,3\,8 \end{array}$$

The money she began with
The cost of the tickets
The money she has left

If a ninth friend decides to come last-minute and Lisa buys him a ticket, too, how much would she have left? Solve this two-step word problem again to work it out.

An Estimation Problem

Kim has £20.00. She wants to buy a handbag for £13.49 and a bracelet for £8.98. Does she have enough money?

Estimate:

£8.98 *is about* £9.00

£13.49 *is about* £13.00

£ 9.00
+ 13.00
_____
£ 22.00

The handbag and the bracelet together cost about £22.00. So Kim does not have quite enough money to buy them both.

If your answer is close when you estimate, you need to work the problem out exactly. For example, if the cost of the handbag and the bracelet came to about £19.00 or £20.00, you would have to add up exactly how much they cost to answer the problem.

A Problem Where You Need to Guess

Dalmatian mollies cost 85p and goldfish cost 99p. Lewis buys some Dalmatian mollies and some goldfish, 5 in all. He pays £4.53. How many of each kind of fish does he buy?

You have to make a guess to start. Guess that he buys 2 Dalmatian mollies. Then he must buy 3 goldfish. How much will these cost?

$$(2 \times 85p) + (3 \times 99p) =$$
$$170p + 297p = 467p \ or \ £4.67$$

£4.67 is too much. By how much? £4.67 − £4.53 = 14p. As mollies are cheaper, having one more molly and one fewer goldfish will save 99p − 85p = 14p. So that means that Lewis has bought 3 Dalmatian mollies and 2 goldfish. Let's check.

$$(3 \times 85p) + (2 \times 99p) =$$
$$255p + 198p = 453p \ or \ £4.53$$

The second guess is correct. Lewis has bought 3 Dalmatian mollies and 2 goldfish.

Time, Dates and Graphs

Time to the Minute

Learn to tell time to the minute quickly. Remember that the minute hand moves from one number to the next in five minutes. On many clocks there is a short mark for each minute in between.

In one minute, the minute hand moves from one of these short marks to the next.

It is 9:20.

Now it is 9:21.

In the next picture, the minute hand is on the third mark between 1:45 and 1:50.

It is 1:48.

Practise writing time in minutes before and after an hour. Now can you tell what time it is, first on the hanging clock and then on the clock with Roman numerals?

Do you remember how many minutes there are in one hour? Yes, 60. To find how many minutes it is before the next hour, subtract how many minutes it is after the hour from 60. On the Roman numeral clock, it is 3:55, so it is 5 minutes before 4:00. If it is 8:38, how many minutes is it before 9:00?

$$\begin{array}{r} {}^{5}\cancel{6}\,{}^{10}\cancel{0} \\ -\ 3\ 8 \\ \hline 2\ 2 \end{array}$$

It is 22 minutes before 9:00.

Elapsed Time in Minutes

Learn to find how much time has elapsed in minutes. From 10:15 to 10:45 is 30 minutes, because 45 − 15 = 30.

To find how many minutes it is from 2:35 to 3:18, you do the problem in two steps. First find how many minutes it is from 2:35 to 3:00. 25 minutes, because 60 − 35 = 25. Then add 18 more minutes for the time from 3:00 to 3:18. 25 minutes + 18 minutes = 43 minutes. From 2:35 to 3:18 is 43 minutes.

24 Hours in a Day

You already know there are 24 hours in a day. Do you remember that in each day there are 12 AM hours and 12 PM hours? The AM hours are between 12 midnight and 12 noon. The PM hours are between 12 noon and 12 midnight.

Do you get up and get dressed closer to 7:30 AM or 7:30 PM?

Do you eat dinner closer to 6 AM or 6 PM?

The abbreviations 'AM' and 'PM' stand for the Latin phrases *ante meridiem* and *post meridiem*, which mean 'before noon' and 'after noon'.

Now what happens at exactly midnight and exactly noon — which is 12 AM and which is 12 PM? Lots of people confuse these, so to be clear it is best to say '12 midnight' and '12 noon' (or '12 midday').

We have learnt about the 12-hour clock but, to be very clear about what time it is, some people prefer to use a 24-hour clock. The 24-hour clock does not use AM and PM because it shows the time from 00:01 (or 12:01 AM) to 23:59 (or 11:59 PM). These two ways tell the same time, and they use the same numbers for half of the day. Look at the table to see.

What is 4 PM in 24-hour time? What is 9 PM?

In Year 3, we solved the following word problem using 12-hour time, but it is actually easier to solve now that you know 24-hour time. At 10:00 in the morning, Andrea's

12-hour time	24-hour time	12-hour time	24-hour time
12:00 MIDNIGHT	00:00	12:00 NOON	12:00
1:00 AM	1:00	1:00 PM	13:00
2:00 AM	2:00	2:00 PM	14:00
3:00 AM	3:00	3:00 PM	15:00
4:00 AM	4:00	4:00 PM	16:00
5:00 AM	5:00	5:00 PM	17:00
6:00 AM	6:00	6:00 PM	18:00
7:00 AM	7:00	7:00 PM	19:00
8:00 AM	8:00	8:00 PM	20:00
9:00 AM	9:00	9:00 PM	21:00
10:00 AM	10:00	10:00 PM	22:00
11:00 AM	11:00	11:00 PM	23:00

stomach starts to growl. She knows that she must wait until 1:00 in the afternoon before lunch will be served in the school canteen. How many hours will pass before she can eat lunch? To work this out, you can't just subtract 10 from 1 using time in AM and PM. First you think that from 10:00 to 12:00 is 2 hours, and from 12:00 to 1:00 is 1 hour. So, 1 + 2 = 3 hours before Andrea can eat lunch. Or, in 24-hour time, you can just subtract: 13:00 – 10:00 = 3 hours before lunchtime. Poor Andrea!

Working with the Calendar

Let's learn how to find a date that comes weeks before or after another date. Here's how.

Remember that a week has 7 days. One week before 12th May is 5th May, because 12 – 7 = 5. What is 2 weeks after 12th May? There are 14 days in 2 weeks, because 2 × 7 = 14. 12 + 14 = 26. So two weeks after 12th May is 26th May.

Learn to find the date one or two weeks before and after another date.

MAY

SUNDAY	MONDAY	TUESDAY	WEDNESDAY	THURSDAY	FRIDAY	SATURDAY
			1	2	3	4
5	6	7	8	9	10	11
12	13	14	15	16	17	18
19	20	21	22	23	24	25
26	27	28	29	30	31	

AUGUST

SUNDAY	MONDAY	TUESDAY	WEDNESDAY	THURSDAY	FRIDAY	SATURDAY
				1	2	3
4	5	6	7	8	9	10
11	12	13	14	15	16	17
18	19	20	21	22	23	24
25	26	27	28	29	30	31

You can also find out on which day of the week a date comes. Look at the calendar for August to work out these examples. If 10th August is a Saturday, 17th August, a week later, will also be a Saturday. What day of the week will be 10 days after Thursday the 15th? In 7 days, it will be Thursday again. Friday is the 8th day, Saturday the 9th day and Sunday the 10th. So 10 days after Thursday the 15th will be a Sunday (the 25th).

Writing Dates

You can write dates using words and numbers, or using only numbers.

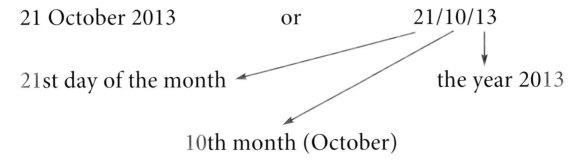

21 October 2013   or   21/10/13

21st day of the month   the year 2013

10th month (October)

Now write your birthday using words and numbers, and using only numbers. Can you write 15 May 2016 and 7 July 2020 in numbers only?

Reading and Writing Graphs

You know that a graph is a way of showing information in a diagram. There are different types of graphs. Learn to read *line graphs* and *bar graphs*. Let's review the bar graph first.

This bar graph shows how many of each kind of tree there are at the arboretum, rounded to the nearest ten. Each bar on the graph shows about how many trees of a certain kind there are. For example, there are about 50 chestnuts. About how many more oaks than chestnuts are there? 60 more oaks, because $110 - 50 = 60$.

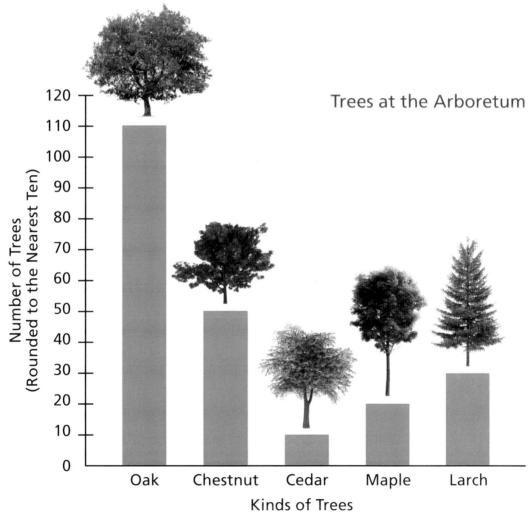

Trees at the Arboretum

269

You can make a graph, too. Here is a bar graph we made when we tossed a penny in the air twenty times and recorded how it fell each time. First we recorded how each toss fell using a tally.

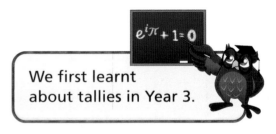

Nine tosses came up 'heads' with the image of the Queen showing, and eleven tosses came up 'tails' with the other side showing. Then we wrote the same information on a graph. For the number of heads that came up, we made one bar. For the number of tails that came up, we made a second bar.

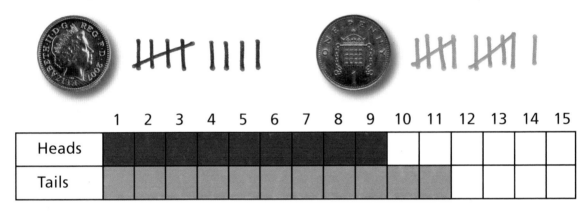

	1	2	3	4	5	6	7	8	9	10	11	12	13	14	15
Heads															
Tails															

Now you try it. Toss a penny into the air 20 or even 30 times, and use tallies to record how many times it comes up heads or tails. Then make your own graph.

Here is a line graph. You can use a line graph to show numbers in a different way.

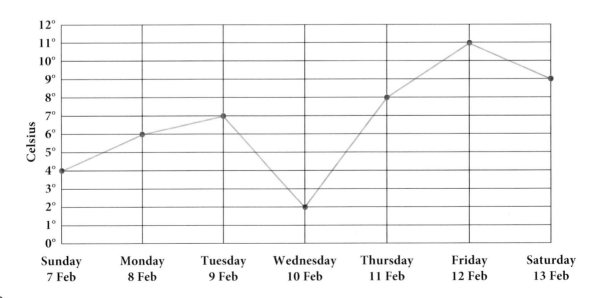

This line graph shows the daily maximum temperatures in London for the week of 7–13 February. Each point shows the highest temperature on that day. The line segments connect the points to show how the maximum temperature changed from day to day. The change in maximum temperature from Wednesday to Thursday was 6° C. How much warmer was the maximum temperature on Friday than on Sunday? 7° C, because 11 − 4 = 7.

A cold day in February on the Millennium Bridge

Geometry

Polygons

Remember these kinds of lines?

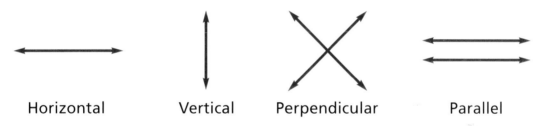

Horizontal   Vertical   Perpendicular   Parallel

Take a look at these figures. Can you see an important difference between the figures in the top row and the figures in the bottom row?

A *closed figure* is a figure that can be drawn with the same start and end point and does not require drawing over any part of the figure. This means there is a closed space inside the drawing. A closed figure can be formed with line segments, curves or a mixture of both.

Here is line segment TS or ST. If we put letter labels by the endpoints, we can use them to name the line segment.

S   T

A closed figure that is formed entirely by line segments is called a *polygon*. Triangles, rectangles and squares are polygons; circles are not polygons.

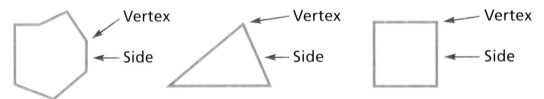

Vertex   Vertex   Vertex

Side   Side   Side

In a polygon, each side is a line segment. The point where two line segments meet is called a *vertex*. (The plural of 'vertex' is *vertices*.) Like all points, vertices are named by letters. You name a polygon by starting at one vertex and naming all the other vertices in order. Here are two examples.

Starting at point B, you could name this figure polygon BADC; you could also name it by naming the vertices in the other direction: polygon BCDA. Or you could start with any of the other points and name the vertices in order in either direction. Altogether there are eight possible names for this polygon. Can you write all of them?

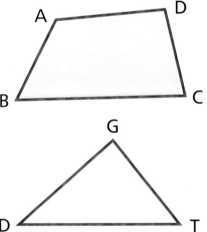

Here are the six possible names for the triangle on the right: triangle DGT, triangle DTG, triangle TGD, triangle TDG, triangle GTD, triangle GDT.

Having Fun with Polygons

Draw a polygon with any number of sides – let's say five. Now draw another polygon with five sides that looks very different. See how many polygons you can make with five sides.

Now do the same thing with a ten-sided polygon.

Angles

Whenever two sides of a polygon meet, they form an *angle*. Here's an example of an angle.

This polygon has four sides, four vertices and four angles.

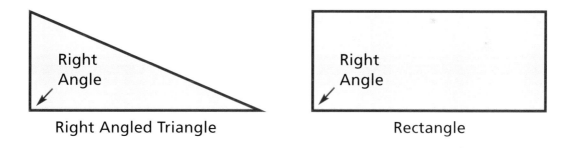

A *right angle* is an angle that forms a square corner.

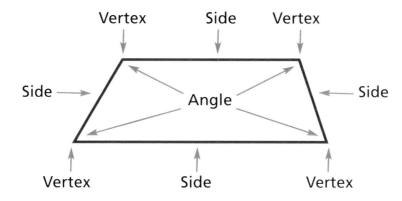

Right Angled Triangle   Rectangle

Squares and rectangles each have four right angles.

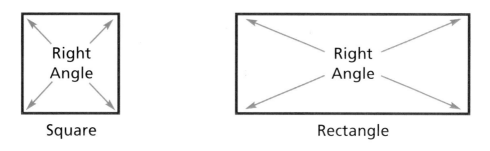

Square   Rectangle

Congruent and Symmetrical Figures

Two figures that are exactly the same shape and size are said to be *congruent*. Sometimes you have to turn one figure around or over to see if it is congruent with another.

These two triangles are congruent.

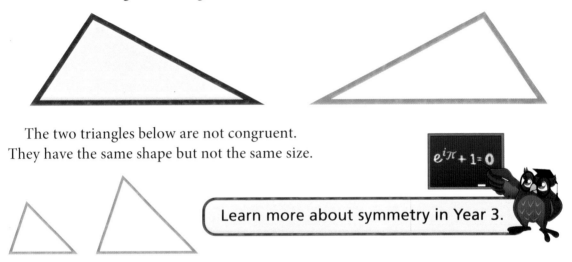

The two triangles below are not congruent. They have the same shape but not the same size.

$$e^{i\pi} + 1 = 0$$

Learn more about symmetry in Year 3.

What do you call a figure that can be folded in half and both halves match? The figure is said to be *symmetrical*. The fold line is called the *line of symmetry*. Sometimes figures have more than one line of symmetry. For example, a square has four lines of symmetry.

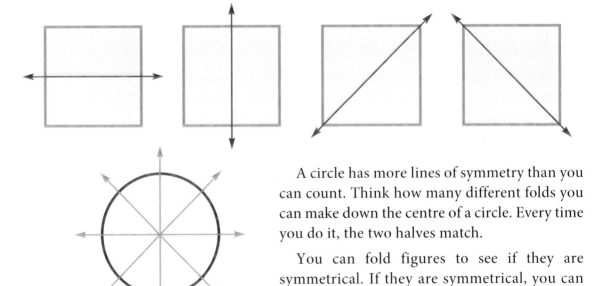

A circle has more lines of symmetry than you can count. Think how many different folds you can make down the centre of a circle. Every time you do it, the two halves match.

You can fold figures to see if they are symmetrical. If they are symmetrical, you can see how many lines of symmetry they have.

Make a Geometry Mobile

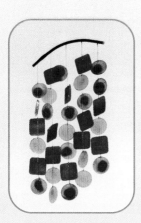

This mobile is made out of different glass shapes, and you can make your own geometry mobile out of craft paper. Start by drawing four or five symmetrical shapes out of different colours of craft paper. What sorts of symmetrical figures would you like to see on your mobile? All triangles, or an assortment of hearts, circles and diamonds?

Cut out your drawings of the figures, then use a hole punch or pierce a hole in each. Measure and cut lengths of string or thread that are 5, 10 and 12 centimetres long and tie the threads through the holes in your figures. You can use twigs or lolly sticks to hang the figures. The hard part is finding the right lengths for each string to make the pieces balance each other in a pattern you like.

Perimeter

The *perimeter* is the distance around a figure. To find the perimeter of a figure, add the lengths of its sides together.

Practise measuring the sides of polygons to the nearest centimetre or inch; then add the lengths together to find the perimeter of the polygon in centimetres or inches. Here is an example in centimetres.

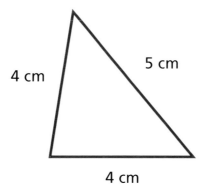

4 cm + 5 cm + 4 cm = 13 cm. The perimeter of the triangle is 13 cm.

Area

The *area* of a figure is the number of square units that cover its surface. A *square unit* has sides that are each one unit long. For example, this is a square centimetre ▶

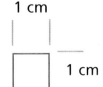

1 cm

1 cm

This rectangle has an area of 6 square centimetres. You write 6 square centimetres as 6 cm^2.

This polygon has an area of 11 square centimetres, or 11 cm^2.

Learn to find the area of a figure by counting square units. Make sure always to write your answer in square units, such as cm^2 or in^2.

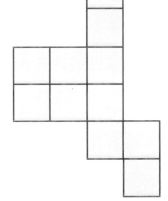

Solids

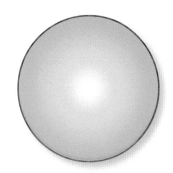

Three-dimensional objects are often called *solids*.

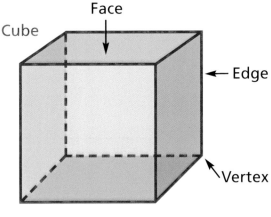

Cube

Face

Edge

Vertex

Some solids have curved surfaces, and some solids have flat surfaces. A flat surface on a solid is called a *face*. The line segment where two faces meet is called an *edge*. Edges come together at a vertex. The point of a cone is also a *vertex*. Learn to count the number of faces, edges and vertices on solids.

Now let's learn more about these solids: rectangular prism, pyramid and cylinder.

This *pyramid* has five sides: four triangles and one square, its base.

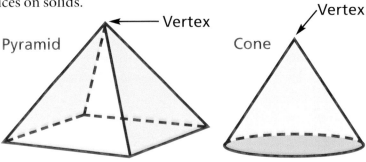

Pyramid

Vertex

Cone

Vertex

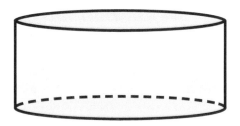

A *cylinder* has curved surfaces and flat surfaces.

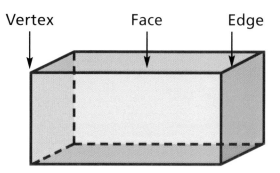

A *rectangular prism* has six sides that are rectangles, or it can have four sides that are rectangles and two ends that are squares. A *cube* is a special kind of rectangular prism in which all the sides are squares.

Measurement

Imperial and Metric Measures

In the UK, we use two systems of measurement: *imperial* and *metric*. You may already be familiar with both systems from your work in science in Year 2 and maths in Year 3. We have learnt about how to measure length and weight, and we have also talked about capacity (also called volume) which shows us how much something can hold.

Here are some of the units used to measure length, weight and capacity in each system. The abbreviation for each unit is in brackets.

Metric Measures		
Length	Weight	Capacity
millimetre (mm)	gram (g)	millilitre (ml)
centimetre (cm)	kilogram (kg)	litre (l)
metre (m)	tonne (t)	
kilometre (km)		

Imperial Measures

Length	Weight	Capacity
inch (in or ")	ounce (oz)	fluid ounce (fl oz)
foot (ft or ')	pound (lb)	pint (pt)
yard (yd)	stone (st)	gallon (gal)
mile	ton	

As the possible abbreviations for miles and tons are very similar to some metric abbreviations, it is safer to write them out in full. Happily, metric tonnes and imperial tons are very similar. A pound is shortened to lb because that is the abbreviation of the old Latin word for a pound.

Learn to change a measurement from one unit in a system to another. Here are some equations to show you how to change units in the Imperial system.

$$1 ft = 12 \text{ in} \qquad 1 \text{ lb} = 16 \text{ oz} \qquad 1 \text{ pt} = 20 \text{ fl oz}$$

$$1 \text{ yd} = 3 \text{ ft} \qquad 1 \text{ st} = 14 \text{ lb} \qquad 1 \text{ gal} = 8 \text{ pt}$$

Here are some examples of changes between units in a system.

Since 1 ft = 12 in, to find out how many inches are in 3 feet, you can add 12 in and 12 in and 12 in. 12 + 12 + 12 = 36, so 3 ft = 36 in. Now let's look at some examples.

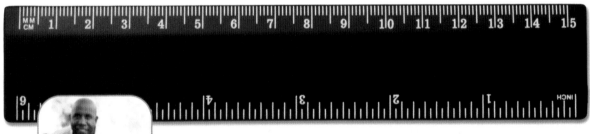

Martin and his dad ran 1,800 feet. To find out how many yards are in 1,800 feet, you can divide by 3, since 1 yd = 3 ft.

$$1,800 \div 3 = 600$$

$$1,800 \text{ ft} = 600 \text{ yd}$$

Martin beat his dad by 9 ft, or 3 yd.

This puppy weighs 4 lb. How much does it weigh in ounces? Since 1 lb = 16 oz, you can multiply.

$$
\begin{array}{r}
2 \\
16 \\
\times\ \ 4 \\
\hline
64\ \text{oz}
\end{array}
\qquad 4\ \text{lb} = 64\ \text{oz}
$$

You can find out how many pints are in 6 gallons of orange juice by multiplying.

$$1\ \text{gal} = 8\ \text{pt} \qquad 6 \times 8 = 48$$

$$6\ \text{gal} = 48\ \text{pt}$$

The imperial system gives us labels for some useful quantities, like pints of milk. In the metric system, it is a lot easier to change units because it is just like working with place value. Here are some equations for changing units in the metric system.

1 cm = 10 mm	1 kg = 1,000 g	1 l = 1,000 ml
1 m = 100 cm	1 tonne = 1,000 kg	1 km = 1,000 m

Each metre is 100 centimetres. So 5 metres are 500 centimetres, because $5 \times 100 = 500$. Each kilometre is 1,000 metres. So 6 kilometres are 6,000 metres, because $6 \times 1,000 = 6,000$. In the same way, 9 kg = 9,000 g. How many tonnes are 4,000 kg? Yes, 4. How many millilitres are in 62 l?

Measurement Word Problems

Learn how to solve problems that involve units of measurement. For example, Mrs Johnson has a kilogram of flour. She uses 570 grams to make two loaves of banana bread. She uses another 110 grams to make a batch of brownies. How many grams of flour does she use, and how many grams does she have left?

$$570 \text{ g} + 110 \text{ g} = \underline{\hspace{1cm}} \text{ g}$$

Mrs Johnson uses 680 grams of flour. She started with 1 kilogram of flour. 1 kg = 1,000 g.

$$
\begin{array}{r}
0\ \ 9\ 10 \\
\cancel{1}\,,\cancel{0}\ \cancel{0}\ 0\ \text{g} \\
-\ \ \ 6\ 8\ 0\ \text{g} \\
\hline
3\ 2\ 0\ \text{g}
\end{array}
$$

So Mrs Johnson has 320 grams of flour left.

In a relay race, there are three teams of five members each. Each team member had to sprint 200 m before passing the baton on to the next runner. How many kilometres did all of the team members run in total?

First, how many team members were running?

3 teams x 5 team members = _____ team members

Next, how far did the team members run altogether in metres? Write out how to solve this, then write it in expanded form to help you solve it.

15 team members x 200 m = (15 x 100) + (15 x 100)
= 1500 + 1500 = 3000 m

Wow! Altogether they ran 3,000 m or 3 km!

Practise problems like these, in which you first have to solve the problem in several steps and convert the unit of measurement. Be careful in measurement problems to remember which units you are working with. Always write the units you are working with in your answer.

Measure and Draw Line Segments

You've learnt about line segments. Now you can learn to measure the lengths of line segments in metric and imperial units.

To measure the line segment AB to the nearest quarter inch or half centimetre, line up one end of the segment with the 0 mark on your ruler. Look at the other end of the segment.

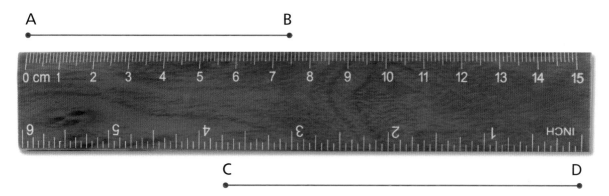

Line segment AB is 7½ cm long. Line segment CD is 3¾ in long.

Here are some line segments. Measure each to the nearest half centimetre and the closest quarter inch.

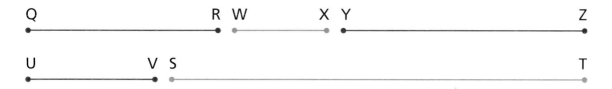

Now draw line segments of the following lengths.

4½ in	5½ cm	20 cm	7¼ in
10 cm	8¾ in	11½ in	5½ cm

Once you have mastered drawing those, now draw a line segment 5 mm long. See page 279 for help remembering how many millimetres are in a centimetre, then count the number of small lines between each centimetre on your ruler to help you.

Estimating Linear Measurements

When you are familiar with measuring centimetres and inches, as well as metres and feet, you can begin to estimate *linear* measurements. See the word 'line' in 'linear'? That's because linear measurements mean measuring on a straight line.

Measuring Ounces, Pounds, Grams and Kilograms

If you have scales to use, you can practise measuring weight at home or school. Some scales measure in grams and kilograms. Some measure in ounces, and some measure in pounds. What do your scales show?

Find five objects that feel as if they weigh different amounts. Weigh your objects and write a list of them with their weights, from lightest to heaviest.

Would you use metres or centimetres to measure this tortoise? Why would centimetres (or inches) work better for measuring the tortoise than metres (or yards or feet)? Estimate how many centimetres long this photograph of a tortoise is. Now estimate how many inches it is.

What about the chair you're sitting on? What unit would work best to tell how tall it is? Estimate the height of your chair's back. Then measure your chair and compare your answers.

Estimate and then measure five real objects of different sizes. Why did you choose each unit you used?

Measuring Weight

When you measure how heavy something is, you are measuring weight. In Year 3 we learnt how to use a balance to measure weight. Look at the balances in these pictures. When one side of the balance is lower than the other, which object weighs more?

Do the citrus fruits weigh less or more than 1 kg? Do the apples weigh less or more than 1 kg? Now look at the balances again. Which is heavier: the citrus fruits or the apples?

Measuring Capacity

There is a system of measurement used just for liquids (like milk, juice, water or paint). In the metric system, we use litres and millilitres. In the imperial system, we use fluid ounces, pints and gallons. A litre is a bit under the volume of two pints.

Use this table to help you answer the following questions.

Units of Measurement for Liquids

Metric	Imperial
1,000 millilitres = 1 litre	20 fluid ounces = 1 pint
	8 pints = 1 gallon

If you pour 1 gallon of milk into pint bottles, how many pint bottles will you fill?

8 pints equal 1 gallon. How many fluid ounces are in a gallon?

How many millilitres are in 3 litres?

Measuring Temperature

Do you remember the graph on page 270 that showed the daily maximum temperatures during a week in February? To describe the temperature, we used units called *degrees*, and we used a little circle to stand for that unit. The highest temperature we plotted on that graph was 11° C, and the lowest temperature was 2° C.

The metric system measures temperature in degrees Celsius, which we use in the UK. There is also another scale of measuring degrees, called Fahrenheit. When talking about temperatures, it is important to tell whether you are using Celsius or Fahrenheit. You use the initials of those words, C and F, to show which scale of measurement you are using.

What kind of weather is it when the thermometer looks like this? Can you read the temperature in degrees Celsius? In degrees Fahrenheit? It's about 18° C, or 64° F. Is it very hot, or very cold, or just right?

This thermometer in the snow shows temperatures using both scales of measurement. Let's use it to tell the temperature at which water freezes, in both Celsius and Fahrenheit.

A thermometer that measures temperature in degrees Celsius will read 0° C (zero degrees Celsius) when the temperature is just cold enough for water to freeze. At this same temperature – the freezing point of water – a thermometer that measures temperature in degrees Fahrenheit will read 32° F (thirty-two degrees Fahrenheit). The thermometer in the snow shows that it is about -1° C, or about 30° F, so it is below freezing.

We use negative numbers to talk about cold temperatures that are below freezing. On a winter day, a Celsius thermometer might read 10° C in the middle of the afternoon but, in the middle of the night, the temperature might go down to -2° C. This temperature can be described as 'minus two degrees Celsius', but people also say 'two degrees below zero Celsius'. That's cold!

Suggested Resources

Books

See Inside Maths by Alex Frith and Minna Lacey (Usborne) 2008

Mental Arithmetic, Books 1 and 2, by T R Goddard, J W Adams and R P Beaumont (Schofield & Sims) 1999, 2000

Junior Maths Book 2 by David Hillard (Galore Park) 2008

Practice in the Basic Skills, Books 3 and 4, by Derek Newton and David Smith (Collins) 2003

Maths on Target: Year 4 by Stephen Pearce (Elmwood) 2008

Be the Best at Maths by Rebecca Rissman (Raintree) 2013

Magnetic Tangrams: Explore the World of Tangram Pictures by Jon Tremaine (Barron's) 2009

Maths Dictionary by Carol Vorderman (Dorling Kindersley) 2009

Maths Made Easy: Times Tables, Ages 7-11, Key Stage 2 by Carol Vorderman (Dorling Kindersley) 2011

Online Resources

A Maths Dictionary for Kids by Jenny Eather:
www.amathsdictionaryforkids.com/dictionary.html

Mobile Apps

Arithmetic Wiz (The Rocket Studio) app for iPad or iPhone [free]

Crazy Tangram Puzzle of Animals (XiaoFang Li) app for iPad [free]

Division Wiz (The Rocket Studio) app for iPad or iPhone [free]

Multiplication + (The App Gate Inc.) app for iPad or iPhone [free]

Pizza Fractions: Beginning with Simple Fractions (Brian West) app for iPad or iPhone [free]

Tangram XL Free (Javier Alonso Gutierrez) app for iPad [free]

Science

Introduction

Children gain knowledge about the world by linking reading with observation and experience. They should be encouraged to view the world scientifically: to ask questions about nature; to seek answers through observation and study; to collect, count, measure and make observations.

As children amass information, their hypotheses may be based on intuition more than solid knowledge. Balancing a child's personal observations with well-expressed scientific fundamentals will guide his or her understanding in the right direction. Book learning also provides knowledge not likely to be gained by simple observations, such as the nature of the planets or the structure of a cell.

The topics that follow are consistent with those offered to children in countries that have had outstanding results from teaching science in the primary grades. We have also included biographies of people who have contributed to our advancement in science and who have researched some of the topics covered in this chapter. Our list of suggested resources at the end of the chapter can help you to take your child's investigations of science even further, and we also recommend the following to help your child to learn even more.

- You cannot go wrong starting with London's world-famous Science and Natural History Museums in Kensington, but they are not the only such places in the United Kingdom. They offer a wealth of online material which may prompt you to make a visit in person. The National Museum of Scotland in Edinburgh offers a wide range of interactive resources for exploring Science, and the Discovery Museum in Newcastle is also recommended. The Museum of the History of Science at Oxford is free but rather more serious in approach than the pricier At-Bristol Science Centre, which is interactive.

- A planetarium is a special domed theatre where views of the night sky and other pictures can be projected on the ceiling. There is a major planetarium at the Royal Observatory in Greenwich but more local ones are open at Chichester, Armagh, Stockton-on-Tees and elsewhere. The visitor centre at Jodrell Bank near Manchester is the ideal place to find out about the work of a radio telescope.

- The Royal Society has resources on its website that are designed for Key Stage 2. Go to invigorate.royalsociety.org and see many additional online resources listed at the end of this chapter.

- The Royal Institution Christmas lectures are broadcast on BBC television and there is a rich archive available online at www.richannel.org/christmas-lectures so you don't have to wait until Christmas to watch them. The lectures are so popular that there is a Wimbledon-style ballot to get tickets.

Classifying Animals

What Do They Have in Common?

A dolphin isn't much like a tiger, and you would never mistake a badger for a butterfly! Even though these creatures are very different, they all have something in common. They are all living creatures that move and breathe and have babies. They are all animals.

Now, name a kind of bird. Eagle, owl, robin, blue jay, flamingo, ostrich, macaw, duck – there are so many different kinds of birds. They come in different sizes and different colours. Some are dull brown and some are brightly coloured. But whatever their size or colour, they all have feathers and wings, and they all lay eggs. That is what makes them all birds.

Name a kind of insect. You have many to choose from: ants, bees, ladybirds, flies, crickets. Do you remember from Year 3 what insects have in common? All insects have six legs, three main body sections and a tough exoskeleton. No matter whether they are black or green, or whether they have dots or stripes, or whether they have wings or no wings – as long as they have six legs, three body sections and an exoskeleton then they are insects.

In Year 3 we learnt about Aristotle, who classified many living things.

Whenever you group things that have a lot in common, you are classifying. When we classify things, it helps us to understand and talk about them. Many living things can be classified as animals: horses, dogs, cats, monkeys, robins, flies, whales, jellyfish, worms and even you! But what about pine trees or rosebushes or blades of grass? They're not animals. They are plants.

When scientists want to classify the living things in the world, they begin by dividing things into these two very big groups: animals and plants. (They use other big groups as well, which you'll learn about in a later year.)

Does It Have a Backbone?

When we classify things, we often need to take a big group, such as animals, and break it into smaller groups. Scientists classify animals into two smaller groups by examining their skeletons. Reach your hand around behind you and run your fingers up and down the centre of your back. That long, bumpy ridge you feel is your backbone, which is also called your spine. It is made of a stack of small bones, each one called a vertebra [VUR-te-bra].

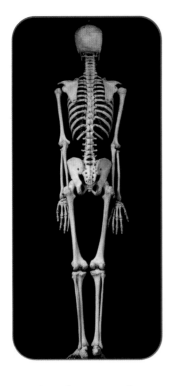

That is why animals with backbones are called vertebrates [VUR-teh-brayts].

◀ Where is the backbone on this skeleton?

You have a backbone. So do horses, dogs, cats, fish, birds and frogs. Many animals have backbones, but many do not. An animal that does not have a backbone is called an *invertebrate*, a word that means 'no backbone'. Can you think of an animal with no backbone? How about a little creature that droops like a noodle and slithers through the soil? That's right, an earthworm does not have a backbone. Neither does a moth, an oyster or a spider. They are all invertebrates.

Now you know how scientists divide animals into two big groups: invertebrates (which have no backbone) and vertebrates (which do have a backbone).

Classifying the Vertebrates

Now let's see how scientists divide the vertebrates into five smaller groups, called *classes*. The five classes of vertebrates are:

fish   amphibians   reptiles   birds   mammals

Let's learn about what makes a fish a fish, what makes a bird a bird and so on. As you learn about the different features of each class, try to name some animals in that class.

Fish

- Fish are cold-blooded.
- Fish live in water.
- Fish use gills to 'breathe' and take oxygen from the water.

Can you spot the red gills of this fish?

Cold-blooded and warm-blooded

Fish, amphibians and reptiles are *cold-blooded*. Birds and mammals are *warm-blooded*. What do we mean by cold-blooded and warm-blooded?

Snakes are cold-blooded animals, which means that their body temperature changes according to the temperature around them.

Some animals get the warmth they need from the air or water around them. When it's hot outside, their body temperatures rise. When it's cold, their body temperatures drop. These animals are called cold-blooded. It doesn't mean that their blood is always cold. It means their body temperatures go up or down depending on the temperature around them.

Other animals stay nearly the same temperature no matter whether the air around them is hot or cold. These animals are called warm-blooded. Mammals – like pandas – and birds are warm-blooded.

Are you cold-blooded or warm-blooded? On winter days, you might shiver with cold, and on hot summer days, you might feel like you're about to melt, but your body temperature normally stays steady around 37° Celsius. So that makes you warm-blooded.

- Most fish are covered with scales.
- Most fish hatch from eggs laid by the female outside her body.

- Goldfish, trout and sharks are different kinds of fish.

Amphibians

Tadpoles live underwater. When they grow into frogs, they live on land. In Year 3, we read about the lifecycle of frogs, which are amphibians.

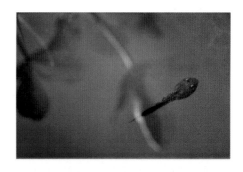

- Amphibians are cold-blooded.
- Amphibians live part of their lives in water and part on land. (The word amphibian means 'living in two places'.)
- When they are young, amphibians have gills to take oxygen from the water. When they grow up, most amphibians develop lungs that allow them to take oxygen from the air.
- Amphibians usually have moist skin with no scales.
- Frogs, toads and newts are amphibians.

Tadpoles grow into frogs.

Reptiles

- Reptiles are cold-blooded.
- Reptiles have dry, thick, scaly skin.
- Reptiles breathe with lungs.
- Reptiles hatch from eggs.
- Snakes, lizards, tortoises and turtles are reptiles.

The little tortoise is getting a ride.

Birds

- Birds are warm-blooded.
- Birds have feathers and wings.
- Most birds can fly.
- Birds breathe with lungs.
- Birds hatch from eggs. Most birds build nests in which to lay their eggs.
- Robins, parrots, chickens and eagles are birds.

Most birds feed their young until they are big enough to leave the nest and survive on their own.

Mammals

- Mammals are warm-blooded.
- Mammals have hair on their bodies.
- Mammals breathe with lungs.
- Baby mammals need care and feeding.
- Female mammals produce milk for their young. (Mammals are the only animals that do this.)
- Horses, cats, dogs, pigs, monkeys and humans are mammals.

Mother pigs produce milk for their piglets.

Most mammals live on land, although some mammals live in water. Whales and dolphins live in the water, but they are mammals and not fish. They breathe with lungs, not gills, and they need to come to the surface to breathe air.

Some mammals, like this humpback whale, swim deep underwater but swim up to the surface for air.

Ecology

Living Things Depend on Each Other

Close your eyes and imagine it's a cool summer day, and you're sitting by a little pond. Look around in your imagination. How many different living things are in this pond environment?

You might see a frog or a newt, ducks or a heron. You might see dragonflies skimming the surface of your imaginary pond. Hear that buzz? Is it a fly or a mosquito? Both of them can be found near a pond. If the water is clear and still, you might be able to see the fish that live underwater. If it's late in the day, you might notice some bats.

If you were walking at the edge of this pond, what living things would you hear and see? They all share the pond environment.

And don't forget all the plants. Plants are living things, too. Think how many plants live near, and even in, a pond. Little plants grow right up to the pond's edge, and some plants grow underwater.

There are also creatures, too small to see, living in the mud and in the water. All these living things depend on each other, and on the kind of world a pond setting provides. In other words, these plants and animals share the pond as their habitat.

A pond at Bourne Mill in Colchester.

This deer is also part of the pond's ecosystem.

In Year 2, we learnt about many different living things and their habitats – including the woodland, underground, desert and water habitats. Let's see how some of the creatures living in and near the pond's freshwater habitat depend on one another. Green bushes grow at the edge of the pond. The bushes absorb light from the sunshine. Their roots take in water and nutrients from the soil near the pond. The bushes use sunlight, water and nutrients to grow big and healthy.

A tadpole swims up and nibbles on one of the roots. But watch out, little tadpole! What's that coming up behind you? It's a hungry fish. Chomp! The fish eats the tadpole in one gulp.

A few months later the fish grows old and dies. Its body sinks to the bottom of the pond. Down under the water, tiny worms and *bacteria* – those creatures so tiny you can't see them – break down the dead fish's body as they use it for food. Nutrients from the decaying flesh and bones of the fish settle into the soil at the bottom of the pond. Those nutrients are absorbed by the roots of the bush growing at the water's edge. And so we're back where we started. This is one cycle in nature.

Look how many ways the living things of this pond depend on each other – and we haven't talked about how birds like herons catch fish to eat them, or how mammals like deer can come to drink water at the pond's edge! All these creatures, living together, are part of a cycle of nature.

Explore ponds online at
www.coreknowledge.org.uk/science.php

How Natural Cycles Work

The pond's cycle of nature depends on three groups of living things:

producers   consumers   decomposers

Producers make their own food. Can you name a kind of living thing that makes its own food? Not your parent in the kitchen, but something in nature that uses sunshine and water and nutrients from the soil? A plant produces its own food. Plants are producers. In our pond, the plants at the pond's edge are producers.

Can you trace the cycle of producers, consumers and decomposers in this pond?

All living things need energy to live, and all living things need food for energy. In our pond, the tadpole eats the plants. Then the fish eats the tadpole. The tadpole and the fish are *consumers*, since both of them consume (or eat) other living things. Are you a consumer? Yes, indeed. You eat plants and you may eat other animals. If you eat a chicken, lettuce and tomato sandwich, you are eating plants (the lettuce, tomato and the wheat in the bread) and an animal (the chicken). You and all the other animals in the world are consumers, because you consume food to get the energy you need.

When plants and animals die, they provide food for the *decomposers*. To 'decompose' means to break something down into smaller pieces. In the pond, the little worms and bacteria are decomposers because as they seek food to eat, they decompose the body of the dead fish and break it into smaller pieces. They eat some, but they drop some, too. Those pieces become part of the soil at the bottom of the pond.

You can see how producers, consumers and decomposers connect in a kind of natural cycle. Plants produce food. Animals eat plants, or they eat other animals that have eaten plants. When plants and animals die, decomposers break down their remains, leaving nutrients in the soil. Plants use those nutrients to produce their own food. And so, like a circle, this cycle of nature goes on and on.

Fossils

Have you ever made a sandcastle? Did you fill a bucket with wet sand and then turn it upside down to make a tower? You used the bucket as a mould. That tells you something about how fossils were made. They are made of rock, not just sand. The sandcastle lasts only until the sea comes in over it. A fossil lasts a very long time, millions of years in fact, but it takes a long time for the rock to form.

A fossil of a fish that lived many, many years ago.

Living things have soft parts, which decay quickly after they die, and hard parts, which last longer. You know that there are hard bones under your softer skin, muscles and blood vessels. If an ancient body is dug up it's usually just the skeleton and teeth that have survived. Similarly, the shells of snails and limpets last longer than the living creatures inside them. When these creatures die, sand and mud can cover the shell and start the long, slow process of turning into rock or stone. The shell is a mould, like the bucket for the sandcastle. In time, the sand and mud turn into rock that is formed around the shell and takes on its shape. This is a fossil. It is like a three-dimensional picture in stone of something that was alive before the rock formed.

Most fossils are small. Look on a pebbly beach (although some beaches are better than others). On beaches along the Jurassic Coast in Dorset you have a good chance of finding a stone with a print of a broken sea shell from long, long ago. You have a small chance of finding a whole shell fossil, a dinosaur bone or even a whole dinosaur! The animals are extinct but these fossils help us learn about them.

In Year 2 we first learnt about the dinosaurs and other animals that have become extinct.

Ammonites are seashells from animals that are extinct. If you found an ammonite like the one on the right, someone could cut it open and you'd see how beautiful it is inside, like you can see on the left.

Plants can become fossils too. Coal is a plant fossil, for example. Amber is particularly beautiful, formed when sticky resin went solid and eventually hardened into stone. Sometimes the resin caught an insect, which was then preserved for thousands and thousands of years.

What can you spot inside these pieces of amber?

Depending on Each Other

If one part of the cycle of nature changes, other parts may feel the change. This happened not long ago in the south-western United States, in Arizona. For centuries, wolves and deer had lived side by side in the forests in Arizona. The wolves, which are carnivores (meat eaters), killed and ate the deer. The deer, which are herbivores (plant eaters), ate moss, leaves, fruits and twigs. Then people moved in and began farming in that part of Arizona. The wolves started eating the cows and sheep on the farms. To protect their animals, the farmers killed the wolves. They kept on hunting the wolves until there were no wolves left.

When farmers killed wolves to protect their cows and sheep, they changed the balance of nature.

What do you think happened? Without the wolves to eat some of the deer, more deer lived. More and more deer went looking for food, and they ate all the green plants they could find. They even ate the very young trees. As the years passed, no trees grew big enough to make seeds from which new trees could grow. Finally, there were no plants left for the deer to eat. The forest was destroyed, and the deer began to starve.

People did not realise that the wolves were an important part of the natural cycle in their habitat. When this link disappeared, the balance of nature changed. Since then, people have brought wolves back to northern Arizona and set them free. The number of deer is decreasing, and the trees are beginning to grow again.

Wolves became extinct in the UK hundreds of years ago because farmers here also killed them to protect their livestock. Other animals in the UK that have become extinct include beavers and wild boar. When each of these animals has disappeared from its habitat, the ecosystem has changed.

A Web of Living Things

You have been learning about cycles of nature. You've read about producers, consumers and decomposers, and how they all depend on each other. You also read about what happens when part of a natural cycle changes.

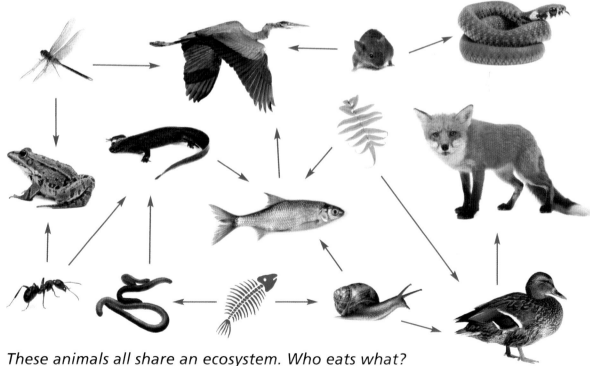

These animals all share an ecosystem. Who eats what?
See how many ways one kind of animal depends on another.

In learning about these things, you have been studying *ecology*. Ecology is the study of the relations between living things and their *environment* – the world around them. (The word 'environment' comes from a French word for 'all around'.)

In nature, living things depend on each other in an *ecosystem*, which is another word for 'environment'. The pond you have been thinking about is an ecosystem. It includes the pond itself, the stream that flows into it, and the surrounding woodland, as well as the community of creatures living in and near the pond, all affecting each other and depending on each other.

You can imagine an ecosystem as being something like a delicate, invisible web that holds life together for a group of living things. It changes whenever anything new comes into the web or anything old leaves it. If one or two strands of the web get damaged, the web might still hold together. But if too many strands are broken, that web changes its shape altogether. That is what happened in the Arizona ecosystem when the farmers got rid of the wolves, and what previously happened here in the UK.

As you can see from the example of the wolves, human beings are part of ecosystems, too. People are part of the world of nature, and we can do things to affect it. Let's look at some of the things people do to the environment.

Hold Your Breath!

Have you ever smelt the exhaust coming out of a lorry or bus? Have you ever seen thick smoke pouring from a factory's chimney?

Exhaust and smoke often contain harmful chemicals that pollute the air. To *pollute* means to make something dirty or impure or unsafe.

Cars, lorries and some buses are one cause of air pollution. Their engines burn fuel, usually some petrol or diesel oil. From their exhaust pipes these vehicles put out harmful emissions. (*Emissions* are what cars and other vehicles put in the air as a result of burning

Smoke from this factory pollutes the air.

fuel in their engines.) Now imagine a city full of cars, lorries and buses, every one of them burning fuel and releasing emissions. When city air gets so dirty that the sky starts looking brown, it is called *smog*, a word made from the two words 'smoke' and 'fog'. If people breathe in too much smog, it can damage their lungs. When London experienced bad smog in the 1950s, the law was changed to stop people burning so much fuel with bad emissions, especially coal for heating. We don't ever want our cities to get that bad again.

Factories can also pollute the air with their smoke and emissions. There are now laws in place to regulate pollution coming from factories.

Should You Drink the Water?

Litter pollutes the environment, too.

Go to a sink, turn on the tap and out comes a nice clear stream of water. Do you know where that water comes from? People get most of their water from lakes, rivers and water under the ground. If you live in the countryside, your water may come from an underground well. This water is often very pure because it has passed through layers of sand and soil and rock that help to filter out particles and leave the water clean and clear.

Cities often get their water from rivers and lakes. The city engineers use man-made filters to clean it. Then they add small amounts of chemicals, such as chlorine, to kill germs. (You've probably smelt chlorine in the water of a swimming pool.)

Of course, we only want to drink water that is clean and pure. But water can get polluted. Whenever people litter and don't put their rubbish in the bins, then this litter can be swept by rain into rivers and lakes so that it pollutes the water and makes the water dangerous to drink.

In the past, factories could pollute water by dumping chemicals and waste products into lakes and rivers. Now there are careful limits in the UK about how much is safe. Sometimes farmers put chemicals, such as fertilizers and pesticides, into the soil, and then the rain washes these chemicals into nearby rivers, lakes and underground water supplies.

Too much of these chemicals and other particles would pollute the water and make it harmful for people and other animals to drink.

In Year 3 we learnt about the water cycle. If water evaporates into polluted air, the water that comes down as rain and flows into rivers and lakes can also become polluted by the air. That's another reason why it's not safe to drink water straight from rivers and lakes.

The Human Body:
The Skeletal and Muscular Systems

Muscle and Bone

Imagine that you're eating a nice turkey drumstick. (Or, if you're a vegetarian, imagine someone else eating that drumstick!) The drumstick has skin, muscle and bone. When you eat the meat, do you know what you're eating? You are eating muscle.

Do you know what part of a chicken the drumstick is? It's the lower leg. Now touch your own lower leg, which is also called your *calf*, between your knee and your ankle. Your calf has skin, muscle and bone, too. You can see and touch the skin. You can feel your muscles when you flex your foot. You can also feel the hard bone of your shin.

There are two big bones in your lower leg, called the *tibia* and the *fibula*. The bone you feel along your shin is the tibia, the larger of the two lower leg bones. The fibula is deeper inside your muscle.

See all the muscles in this picture?
Can you feel any of them in your own body?

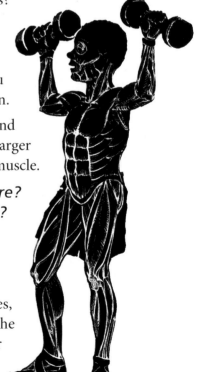

Bones and Connections

Most of your body is soft and squishy, but not your bones, which are very hard. Your bones give your body its shape, the way a stiff clothes hanger gives shape to a floppy shirt. Your bones also protect the soft organs inside your body.

Is your skeleton inside or out?

In Year 3 we learnt that insects have an *exoskeleton*, which means that their bodies are made of a tough outer layer surrounding softer insides. Human beings have an *endoskeleton*, which means that their soft skin and muscles surround the hard bones inside their bodies.

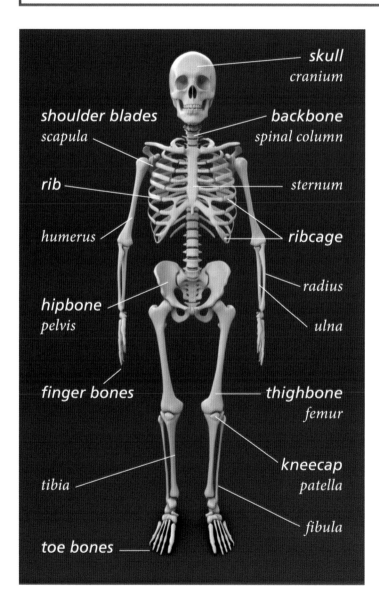

skull
cranium

shoulder blades
scapula

backbone
spinal column

rib

sternum

humerus

ribcage

radius

hipbone
pelvis

ulna

finger bones

thighbone
femur

tibia

kneecap
patella

fibula

toe bones

All your bones put together make up your skeleton. From head to toe, an adult's skeleton is made up of 206 bones. That's a lot of bones!

Bones come in many shapes and sizes. The biggest bone in your body is your thighbone, also called your *femur* [FEE-mer]. The smallest bone in your body is a tiny little bone inside your ear, called the *stirrup*. It's about the size of a grain of rice!

Lift your arm and bend it. Your arm bends at your elbow. Your elbow is a *joint*. A joint is a place where your bones come together. At each joint, the bones are connected by strong, stretchy tissue, like big rubber bands, called *ligaments*. Joints make it possible for you to bend, twist, run, chew, kick a ball, touch your toes and hold a pencil. Can you point to some other joints in your body?

Touch the tip of your nose. That tough stuff you feel is called *cartilage*. In some places in your body, such as in your knee, cartilage keeps bones from rubbing together. When you were born, your skeleton was made of cartilage. But as you grew up, hard bone replaced the soft cartilage.

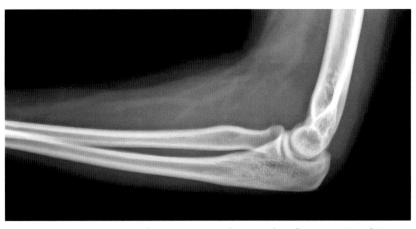

Can you see in this X-ray where the bones in this person's arm come together to bend at the elbow?

Let's learn about your most important bones.

The Skull

The bones in your head are called your *skull*. Your skull surrounds and protects one of the most important organs in your body, your brain. The top part of your skull is called the *cranium*. It is made up of eight bones that fit tightly together to act like a helmet around your brain.

The Spinal Column

Run your hand gently down the centre of a friend's back and feel how bumpy it is. Those bumps are your twenty-four vertebrae, stacked on top of one another. Stretchy ligaments join the vertebrae into a long, flexible chain of bones called the *spinal column*, the spine or the backbone. A thick pad of cartilage provides a cushion between each vertebra.

When someone tells you to stand up straight, you straighten your spinal column. Your spinal column helps hold up your head and upper body. Your spine can bend forward, back and sideways. It can swivel in both directions. All of these movements are possible because of the way the bones, ligaments and cartilage join.

The Ribs

Start just under your armpits and run your fingers along your sides. Do you feel ribs? Your ribs connect with cartilage to a hard bone in the centre of your chest called the *sternum*, or breastbone. From your sternum, your ribs curve around and connect to your spinal column in your back. You have twelve ribs on each side of your body and together they form your *rib cage*. Your rib cage is a strong yet flexible set of bones that protects your lungs, heart and stomach.

The Scapula

How many ways can you move your arms? You can point down to the ground. You can lift your arms above your head. You can swing your arms forward and back. Your arms can move in all these directions because of the way they are attached to your body at the shoulder bone, or *scapula* [SKAP-yoo-luh]. The word 'scapula' comes from the Latin word for 'shovel'. Your scapula looks a bit like the blade of a shovel. It's a big, flat, triangular bone that joins the arm to the spine. People often call the scapula the shoulder blade.

The Pelvis

When you sit down, stand up, walk or run, you are moving your pelvis. The *pelvis* is a set of bones at your hips. Your legs connect to your upper body at the pelvis. The word 'pelvis' comes from the Latin word for 'basin' or 'sink'. If you look at the pelvis on a skeleton, you can see why that name fits. The bones that make up the pelvis come together in a shape like a big bowl. The bowl shape of the pelvis protects your intestines and other digestive organs. When a baby is growing inside a mother's body, the mother's pelvis cradles the baby until birth.

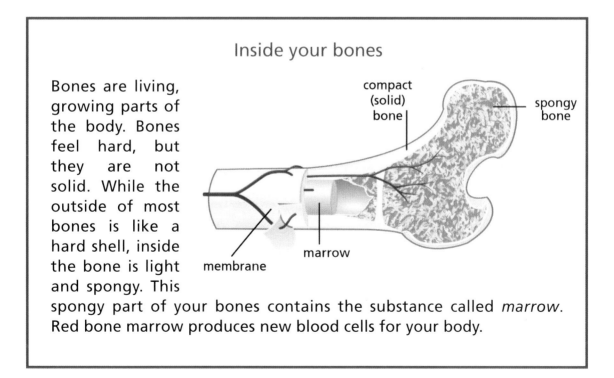

Inside your bones

Bones are living, growing parts of the body. Bones feel hard, but they are not solid. While the outside of most bones is like a hard shell, inside the bone is light and spongy. This spongy part of your bones contains the substance called *marrow*. Red bone marrow produces new blood cells for your body.

compact (solid) bone

spongy bone

marrow

membrane

Will You Sign My Cast?

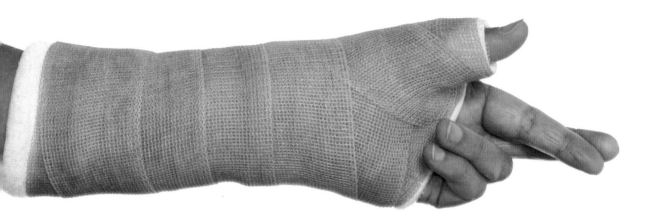

Sometimes bones break, but they do grow back together. To examine a broken bone, a doctor looks at a special kind of picture taken with an X-ray machine. X-ray machines use a sort of invisible light, called *X-rays*, that can travel through muscle but not bone. This creates a picture that shows the bones inside your body.

Here's an X-ray image of a boy's arm after he broke it. To help it heal, his doctor carefully lined up the broken pieces of bone. Then she put a cast around his arm. He had to wear the cast for six weeks to hold the bone in place and protect it while new bone cells were growing.

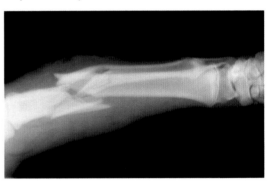

This X-ray shows a broken arm.

Many Muscles

Let's pretend that you're a powerful Olympic athlete. Now, show me your muscles – stand up, stretch out your arms, then bend them at the elbow as you curl your fists towards your head.

When you do that, you are tightening the muscles on the upper part of each arm, called the *biceps* [BUY-seps]. So you've shown me two of your muscles. But did you know you have about 650 muscles in your body?

You use hundreds of different muscles when you play tennis or any other sport. Exercise helps keep your muscles strong.

Some muscles, such as the ones in your ears, are as tiny as a thread. Other muscles, such as the hamstring muscles in the back of your leg, are thick and wide. Where do you think your biggest muscle is? It's called the *gluteus maximus* [GLOO-tee-us MAX-i-mus], and it's the muscle you sit down on (your bottom).

You use your muscles when you walk, run, jump, swim, skate, ride a bicycle, play tennis or football. Every time you move, you use your muscles.

Even when you're not exercising, you use muscles. When you read, your neck muscles hold your head up and your eye muscles move your gaze across the page. When you smile, you use about fifteen different face muscles. When you frown, you use more than forty different face muscles. So smile – it's easier than frowning!

When you move, your muscles work in pairs. When you bend your arm, you tighten your biceps, while another muscle on the lower part of your arm, called the *triceps*, relaxes. Can you point to the biceps and triceps in this picture? Can you feel them in your arm?

When you stretch your arm out straight again, the opposite occurs: the biceps relaxes and the triceps tightens. That's how many muscles work in your body. When one pulls tight, a companion muscle relaxes.

See how, when you bend your arm, your biceps muscle tightens. When you straighten your arm, your biceps muscle relaxes and your triceps muscle tightens. Try it.

Voluntary and Involuntary Muscles

When you tighten your biceps, you use *voluntary* muscles. Voluntary muscles are the ones you can control. You can choose whether to make a header, kick a ball or raise your hand or sit down. Whenever you do these things, you are using voluntary muscles.

But your body also depends on many muscles that move whether or not you want them to. These are called involuntary muscles. For example, your heart is an *involuntary* muscle. It keeps on pumping blood without your telling it when to do so. Involuntary muscles in your intestines work automatically to help you digest the food you eat. Involuntary muscles work all the time, whether you're awake or asleep, and whether or not you think about them.

This boy is using voluntary muscles to jump for the header, as well as other involuntary muscles inside his body.

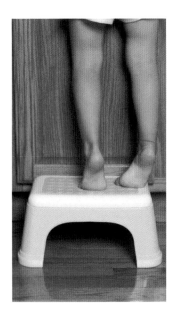

Connecting Muscles and Bones

Muscles make you move by pulling on the bones of your skeleton. To do this, the muscles must be attached to the bones. Throughout your body, strong fibres called *tendons* connect muscles to bones.

Your largest and strongest tendon is called the *Achilles* [a-KIL-eez] *tendon*. It connects your calf muscle to your heel bone. It's easy to find your Achilles tendon. Gently pinch the back of your foot, just above your heel. Do you feel something like a strong, tough rope? Wag your foot up and down and feel how the Achilles tendon stretches and relaxes.

The Achilles tendon stretches from the calf to the heel.

Why is it called the Achilles tendon? A myth from ancient Greece tells of a boy named Achilles who was destined to become a great warrior. When he was a baby, his mother dipped him in the river Styx. She believed its water would protect him from all harm. But when she dipped him, one part of his body never touched the water – his heel, by which his mother was holding him upside down in the river.

Read more myths from Ancient Greece starting on page 52.

Achilles grew up to become the mightiest and most feared warrior in the Trojan War. It seemed that no sword, spear or arrow could harm him. But when a poisoned arrow pierced his heel, he died. Today people still use the phrase 'Achilles' heel' to refer to a person's special weakness.

The Human Body:
The Brain and Nervous System

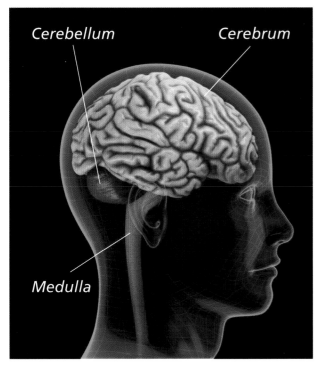

The human brain has three main parts.

Your Powerful Brain

Inside your body there's an organ that you use to think, talk, listen, look, hear, smell, taste, dream, feel, make decisions and remember. Sounds like a computer, phone, camera, television and scrapbook all rolled into one, doesn't it? It's your brain, which connects with your nerves to do all of these things.

Your brain is in charge of everything you do. It's like the prime minister of your body. It keeps your heart beating. It makes sense of the information coming to it from your sensory organs – your eyes, ears, nose, tongue, and skin. It sends orders all over your body. It stores information in memory,

309

such as the aroma of orange peel, your best friend's favourite colour or the way to solve the maths problems you learnt last week.

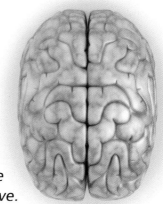

A curious fact

A groove runs down the middle of your cerebrum and divides it into two halves: right and left. Here's an interesting fact: the right half of your cerebrum controls the left half of your body, while the left half of your cerebrum controls the right half of your body.

This model shows the two halves of the cerebrum from above.

The human brain is a pinkish-grey, wrinkled, spongy organ. An adult's brain weighs about three pounds. The brain is divided into three main parts, which you can see in the picture on the last page. The *cerebrum* [seh-REE-brum] is by far the biggest section, about nine-tenths of your brain. Most brain activity takes place in the outer layer of the cerebrum, called the *cerebral cortex*. It's full of deep, wiggly grooves. Different parts of the cerebrum do different things. Some parts understand speech, other parts store memories, others control how hungry you feel, others control eye movements, and so on.

Deep in the back of your brain lies the *cerebellum* [ser-ee-BELL-um]. It coordinates your balance and movements. When you first ride a bicycle, for example, you have to concentrate really hard. Soon you learn to balance and move your body easily, without even thinking about what you're doing. When that happens, your cerebellum is in control.

The *medulla* [me-DULL-lah] or brain stem, lies even deeper than the cerebellum. It controls involuntary body functions. What are some involuntary body functions you can think of? Did you think of your heartbeat, breathing or digestion?

You've Got Nerves

You've probably seen telephone lines running from pole to pole, carrying messages back and forth from homes and businesses the world over. If you imagine your brain as your central communications headquarters, then you can think of your nerves as the wires running throughout your body.

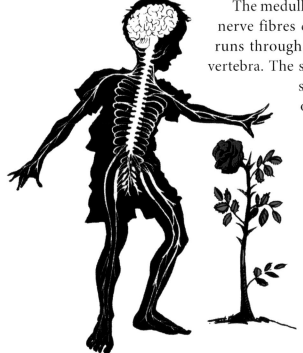

The medulla connects your brain to a thick bundle of nerve fibres called your *spinal cord*. The spinal cord runs through your backbone, through a hole in each vertebra. The spinal cord connects to many nerves that stretch throughout your body, branching out to your legs, arms, toes and fingers.

Your nerves carry messages back and forth to and from your brain. How does this work? Let's see what happens in the nervous system when you lean down towards a rose. First your eyes send signals along special nerves to the brain. Your brain recognises the image of a flower, then compares the image with others in your memory and recalls that this kind of flower often has a pleasant smell. Your brain sends signals through your spinal cord and nerves to many muscles, giving the orders that make you bend closer to the flower. Your brain then sends a message to breathe in deeply. The scent of the rose comes into your nose, then signals of that scent travel through nerves to your brain. Ah, the sweet smell of a beautiful rose!

What signals might be travelling through this boy's nervous system?

Reflex Responses

Imagine that you've just sniffed that lovely rose. You reach to bring the flower closer to you when suddenly a sharp thorn pricks your thumb. Without thinking, you jerk your hand away.

When this happens, it is called a *reflex action*. Reflex actions happen almost instantly, without the brain's sending a message to perform the action. When you touched the sharp thorn, a signal of pain raced from your finger to your spinal cord, which then sent back an immediate command to your muscles, saying, 'Get back!' Your body didn't wait for your brain to receive the pain message and respond to it. Instead, your reflexes took over and saved you from feeling even more pain. Your reflexes will work the same way if, for example, you accidentally touch something hot, such as a dish that's just been taken out of the oven.

Has a doctor ever tested your reflexes? Try this. Sit in a chair and cross one leg loosely over the other. Ask someone to give you a gentle tap just below the kneecap. If the tap comes gently in just the right place, your leg will kick out automatically. You didn't have to think about it – it's a reflex.

When is the last time you sneezed? That was a reflex, too, as is blinking.

A doctor may use a soft rubber hammer near your knee to test your reflexes.

Light and Vision

Fast and Straight

You walk into a dark room, flick on the light switch and, *presto*, the room instantly fills with light. It seems to happen all at once. That's because light travels fast – *amazingly* fast! The speed of light is 186,000 miles *per second*. Light travels so fast that in the time it takes you to blink your eyes three times, light could travel to the moon and back!

Rays of light travel in straight lines. You can see this by making shadows. In a darkened room, shine a desk lamp or flashlight at a wall. Now hold this book in front of the light. What happens? The light doesn't bend or curve around the book. Instead, the book blocks the rays of light, which are travelling in straight lines. That's why you see the shadow of your book on the wall. You can also make shadow figures using your hands. See how many different figures you can come up with!

Your book or hand does not let light pass through it because it is *opaque* [oh-PAKE]. Opaque materials block light. A wooden door is opaque. So is a metal can. Can you name some other things that are opaque?

Can you make a shadow figure like this using one hand? Your hand blocks the rays of light and casts a shadow.

Some materials are the opposite of opaque: they are *transparent*. Transparent materials are clear. You can see through them. They let light pass through almost unchanged. Glass and water are transparent.

You can only see these fish because both the glass bowl and the water are transparent.

Mirrors Flat and Curved

When you need to look your best, you wash your face, comb your hair, then look at your reflection in a mirror, right?

A mirror *reflects* light, which means that the light that hits it bounces back. How does this happen? First the light passes through the transparent glass part of a mirror. The back of the glass is coated with a special silver paint. When the light hits the silver surface, it bounces back through the glass. Shine a torch at a mirror, and you can see how almost all the light is reflected.

The mirrors that hang on the walls at home or school are flat mirrors. A flat mirror is also called a *plane* mirror (like in maths, where plane figures are flat, two-dimensional shapes). When you look in a plane mirror, you see a reflection that looks almost exactly like yourself. But even though you see a clear image of your smiling face, the image is reversed. If you hold this book up to a mirror, the writing will look backwards. But if you hold backwards writing up to a mirror, you can read it! Use a mirror to read this secret message:

Can you write your name like this?

Some mirrors are made with curved glass. Mirrors that curve inwards are called *concave*. (To help remember this name, think of a 'cave' as something hollow.) The inner surface of a shiny spoon can work as a concave mirror, because the surface curves inwards. Concave mirrors make objects appear larger than they are. This also happens with some car rear-view mirrors.

Mirrors that curve outwards are called *convex*. Have you ever seen your face reflected in a shiny ball, like a Christmas tree ornament? The surface of the ornament curves

Have you ever seen yourself in funfair mirrors?
These ones make this street look quite funny!

outwards, so it works as a convex mirror. It collects light rays from a wider area and reflects them to your eyes as a smaller image. Objects reflected in a convex mirror look smaller than they really are.

Funfair mirrors can make people look very tall, very short or like they have some very strange shapes. How do these mirrors work? The reflection you see is made of light rays, bouncing back to your eyes. Funhouse mirrors are curved – concave and convex shapes – so they bounce light rays back in odd directions.

Lenses

Put an apple in a bowl of water. What do you see? From the side, like in this picture, the part of the apple that's underwater looks a lot larger than the part above the surface, doesn't it? Why? What do you see when looking from the top?

This apple floating in a bowl of water looks a bit odd because the light rays speed up and change course just a bit as they move between the water and the air.

Whenever you see something, you are seeing light rays bouncing off it. The light travels from the apple, through the water and the glass, then through the air before it reaches your eyes. Transparent materials allow light to pass through, like we saw with the fish in the glass fishbowl of water on page 313. But light moves less quickly through transparent materials than through air. So, water and glass slow light down much more than air, which you can see particularly well when your apple is half-in and half-out of the water. The light rays change course just a little when they move from water to glass, then from glass to air. It is called *refraction*. Light leaving the water is bent closer to the surface.

Those slight changes in the course of the light rays travelling between the apple and your eyes make the partly-submerged apple look crooked and misshapen.

Now try putting a pencil in a straight-sided glass that is half full of water. What do you see? Does it also look crooked when seen from the side? When looking from above, things in water appear shallower than they really are.

The top of the water is flat but the area where it touches the glass is curved. A curved, refracting surface is a kind of *lens*.

What's heat haze?

Sometimes on an extremely hot day you can see 'heat haze'. This is when some air gets hotter or more humid than the rest and changes the speed of light. Light rays get bent as they pass through and things beyond the haze look distorted or 'hazy'. It doesn't often become hot enough for this to happen in the UK, but perhaps you can see heat haze if you are abroad in Spain, America or other hot countries in summer!

Lenses, lenses everywhere! Can you name each of these things with lenses?

Sometimes we want to change the path of light rays coming from the things we are viewing in order to see them better. For that, we use things called lenses. If you have looked through a magnifying glass or binoculars, or if you wear glasses, then you have looked through lenses.

A lens is a curved piece of transparent material, usually glass or plastic. We say that a lens 'bends the light', but actually, the curve of the lens makes the light rays change course. That's how a magnifying glass works. When you hold a magnifying glass at the right distance from a book, the words come into focus and look bigger. The light rays coming from the page of the book have travelled through the lens glass and changed course slightly to appear larger to your eyes. They look as if they have come from a larger book.

> We looked at pictures taken through microscopes and learnt about Antonj van Leeuwenhoek's in Year 3, and we'll look at pictures taken through telescopes on pages 341 and 344.

Lenses can make things look bigger or smaller. Have you ever looked through a pair of binoculars? Binoculars use lenses to make faraway things look bigger. But what happens when you look through binoculars the wrong way around? They make things appear smaller.

Because of lenses, we can see the world better than we ever could with only our eyes. Lenses in telescopes help us see things far away, as far away as the moon, planets and stars. Lenses in microscopes help us see tiny things close-up, including things we cannot see with our eyes alone, such as the cells in our body or the little creatures that live in a drop of pond water.

Now go back to the pencil in the glass of water. Without the water, the pencil in the glass looks ordinary. It's not the glass that is changing its appearance. Add the water and the pencil, seen from the side, looks thicker in the part that is underwater. The water acts as the lens. Now take the pencil out and hold it behind the glass of water. Does that change how it looks? You might move the pencil left and see it appear to move right. But tip the water away and the glass is no longer a lens.

Hunt for old windows

But aren't windows made of glass? Why don't windows bend the light and make things look funny? The two sides of a window, the inside and outside, are parallel. (Do you remember parallel lines from Year 3?) Light entering the glass from the air gets bent but it gets straightened again as it leaves. Some very old windows aren't perfectly parallel. What you see through them gets distorted. See if you can find some of these windows near where you live in old or historic buildings!

What Colour Is Light?

What colour is sunlight? You might think it has no colour at all, but scientists call the light that comes from the sun *white light*. What's amazing is that the white light of sunshine is actually made up of all the colours in the rainbow!

You can prove it if you have a *prism*, which is a wedge-shaped piece of clear glass. If you hold the prism near a sunny window, the light will shine through and make a rainbowlike band of colours. When light goes through a prism, the glass slows it down and changes its course. We say the light is *refracted*. The prism bends the rays of light, but the rays of each colour bend differently so we can see all of the colours coming out the other side of the prism, like in this picture. Red bends the least and violet bends the most. This shows that, even though light may appear to be white or colourless, light is really made up of all colours.

A prism separates white light into the spectrum of colours: red, orange, yellow, green, blue, indigo and violet.

How Your Eyes See

Close your eyes and what do you see? Nothing, of course! But why? You might say, 'Because my eyes are closed, silly!' Or you could answer: 'Because no light is coming into my eyes.'

You see things because light bounces off them, and then this light enters your eyes. Another way of saying this is that things reflect light, and we see the reflected light. But that's just the beginning. Let's find out what happens when you see.

Look at the picture of the eyeball and its parts. Rays of light first pass through your *cornea* [KOR-nee-uh], a transparent covering on the outside of your eye. (Remember, 'transparent' means 'clear' or 'see-through', like glass.) Next the light goes through the *pupil*, which is a

Somewhere over the rainbow

Is there a pot of gold at the end of a rainbow? Rainbows are so unusual and beautiful that you almost want to believe the magical stories about them. When you see a rainbow in the sky, you see sunlight reflected off water droplets in the sky. The droplets work like prisms to refract the sunlight and separate it into a combination of colours called the *spectrum*. The colours of the spectrum always appear in the same order: red, orange, yellow, green, blue, indigo and violet. You can use a funny sentence to help you remember that order: Richard Of York Gave Battle In Vain. The first letters of each word spell ROYGBIV, which reminds us of the order of the colours in a rainbow. On a sunny day, you can make a little rainbow by turning on a hose and putting your thumb over the end to make the water come out as a mist. When the light bounces off the droplets of mist, you should see your own little rainbow.

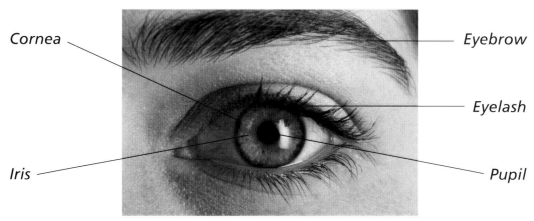

The parts of an eye.

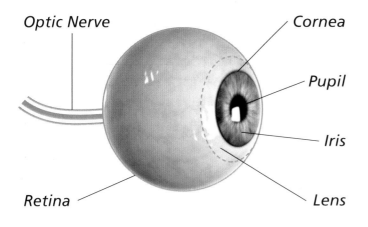

Optic Nerve

Cornea

Pupil

Iris

Retina

Lens

A cross-section of the eyeball.

hole in the middle of the iris. The *iris*, the coloured part of your eye, helps the pupil open and close. On a bright sunny day, the iris makes the pupil grow smaller to let in less light. In a dark room, such as a theatre, the iris makes the pupil grow wider to let in more light. (By the way, the iris is an involuntary muscle – it works without your thinking about it.)

Look deep into my iris

The iris, the colourful part of your eye, gets its name from Iris, the goddess of the rainbow in ancient Greek mythology. Look at your eyes in a mirror. What colour are they? Brown, blue, green? The parts of your eye that you can see make up only a small portion of the entire eyeball. Much of the eye is inside the skull, protected behind hard bone.

The pupil opens and closes to let more or less light into the eye, responding to the amount of light coming into it. Which picture shows the eye on a bright, sunny day? Which shows the eye in a dark room?

Want to see your iris at work? Go into the bathroom and turn the light on. Look at your eyes in the mirror and see how small the pupil is (the black circle in the centre of your eye). Now turn the light off and count slowly to 20. Flick the light back on and – quick! – look at your pupils. They grew larger in the dark, because of the work of the iris muscle.

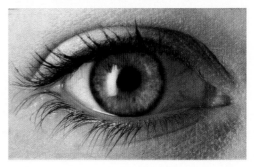

After light rays pass through the iris, they go through the lens. Muscles attached to the lens change its shape just a little bit, to help the lens focus. The lens focuses the light rays onto the surface at the back of the eyeball, called the *retina* [RET-in-ah].

Inside the retina, light rays change into electrical signals. These signals travel along the optic nerve to your brain. The brain makes sense of the signals and recognises the image as, for example, a tree, cat, car or the letters on this page. It all happens so fast you don't even notice. All you do is open your eyes and see.

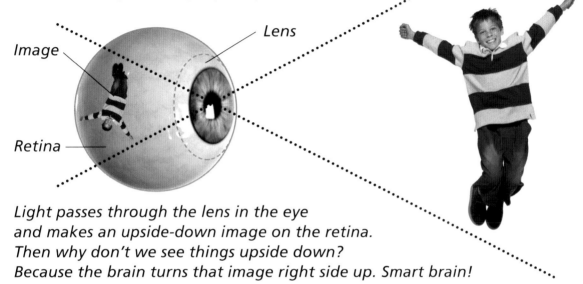

Light passes through the lens in the eye
and makes an upside-down image on the retina.
Then why don't we see things upside down?
Because the brain turns that image right side up. Smart brain!

Getting in focus

In some people's eyes, the lenses don't change and focus as well as they should. Those are the people who need glasses. A person who can see things close-up but needs glasses to focus on things far away is called *near-sighted*. A person who can see things far away but needs glasses to focus on things close-by – in order to read, for example – is called *far-sighted*. Glasses made of differently shaped lenses correct each of those seeing problems.

There are even glasses designed to help people see both far away and close-up. They are called *bifocals*. Can you guess why? Here's a hint: The prefix 'bi-' means 'two'. Bifocal glasses are made from two differently shaped lenses. They help a person's eyes focus in two different ways, to see close-up and to see far away.

Sound and Hearing

Good Vibrations

An alarm clock rings, a dog barks, a voice calls: 'Time to get up.' Every day is full of familiar sounds. But what exactly is sound?

Sound is caused by a back-and-forth movement called *vibration*. Try this. Close your lips and hum. While you're humming, feel your throat under your chin. Do you feel a tingling? It is caused by something moving back and forth very fast. When you hum, the vocal cords in your throat are vibrating back and forth, which makes the air around them vibrate. These vibrations of air strike your eardrums and make them vibrate, to create the sound you hear.

Here's a way you can see how sound makes the air vibrate. Stretch a piece of cling film over the surface of a bowl and fasten it tightly with a rubber band. Sprinkle a few grains of dry rice, salt or sugar on the film. Now take a big pan, hold it near the bowl and strike it with a spoon a few times. Do you see the grains jump when you hit the pan? That is because the pan is vibrating, which causes the air and then the plastic to vibrate. We call the vibrating air sound waves. When you hit the pan, sound waves travel through the air and cause the plastic to vibrate, which in turn makes the grains jump.

Sound waves move out from a vibrating object in all directions, making the air move back and forth in a way that we can't see. Sounds compress and decompress the air, pushing and then relaxing, making invisible vibrations. Those back-and-forth vibrations spread out from the source that made them, getting weaker as they get farther away. That's why you hear your friend standing right next to you more clearly than you hear someone calling from across the street.

What Does Sound Travel Through?

Sound can travel through all kinds of matter: through gases, through liquids and through solids. Every time you speak, you prove that sound travels through gases, since the sound of your voice is travelling through air, which is made of gases like oxygen. Lightly touch your fingertips to the side of a speaker when the sound is coming out. Try it with an iPod stereo speaker, television or radio. Do you feel the vibrations?

Can you think of an example that proves sound travels through liquid? Have you ever heard someone's voice underwater in a swimming pool? It sounded funny, but you could hear it. That sound was travelling through a liquid. Some animals, like whales and

Humpback whales sing and communicate underwater because sound can travel through liquid.

dolphins, depend upon sound that travels through the water. Whales sing underwater and can hear each other from more than a mile away.

At first, you might not think that sound travels through solids, since we build walls to keep out sounds. But in your room, sometimes you hear laughter or talking from the room next door, don't you?

Try this. Drum your fingers on a table. Now rest your ear right on the table's surface and drum your fingers on it again. Doesn't it sound louder? That's because the sound is travelling through the solid table.

Voices from a distance

Our word 'telephone' comes from two old Greek words: *tele*, which means 'at a distance' and *phone*, which means 'sound'.

You can make your own telephone that will let you hear a friend's voice at a distance. You'll need two paper or plastic cups, two paper clips and about five metres of string or strong thread. Have an adult help you poke a small hole in the bottom of each cup. Stick one end of the string into each hole, and knot it tightly around a paper clip. You take one cup and your friend takes the other. Walk apart from one another until the string stretches out straight and tight. Now when you whisper or talk into your 'telephone', your friend should be able to hear you through it.

How does this work? Remember, sound can travel through solids. When you talk into the cup, you make it vibrate. The vibrating cup makes the string vibrate. The vibrating string makes the bottom of the other cup vibrate. Those vibrations go into your friend's ear, and that's when your friend hears the sound of your voice.

The Speed of Sound

Remember how fast light travels? Faster than anything else – an amazing 186,000 miles per second. That's about 300,000 kilometres per second, or about 300 million metres per second! Sound travels much more slowly than light. In warm air, sound travels at about 340 metres per second, or about 770 miles per hour. Of course, that's still very fast compared to a car going 70 miles per hour on the motorway! But there are jet aeroplanes that can fly as fast as the speed of sound. We say that they 'break the sound barrier'. In 2012 the first man jumped and fell faster than the speed of sound. He survived because he had a special space suit and parachute.

Here's an example that shows how light travels faster than sound. During a thunderstorm, a crash of thunder and a bolt of lightning happen at the same time.

Twice the speed of sound

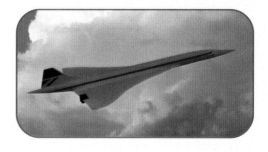

In 1962, British and French designers began a plan to take people as fast as possible around the world. They chose to build a supersonic airliner, which they called the Concorde. The sleek shape, sound and name of Concorde became very popular and easily recognisable, and often people would pause what they were doing to watch one fly by.

What made a Concorde special? It was very, very fast. It could travel faster than sound, twice as fast in fact. It could travel faster than the Earth spins, so passengers going west would arrive in New York earlier in the day than when they set off in London. They seemed to be travelling back in time! The flight took about three hours, which was under half the time that it took an ordinary aeroplane. It helped that the Concorde was stylish too, with graceful curves to help it move through the air.

The last Concorde passenger flight was in 2003. Why did it stop? Mostly because to go so fast meant burning such a lot of fuel. Since there weren't many of this type of aeroplane, looking after them was also expensive. The remaining Concordes are now in museums.

When you're far away, though, you see the lightning before you hear the thunder. Why? Because the light travelled much, much faster to your eyes than the sound did to your ears. How far away? Since sound travels through air at 340 metres per second, three seconds is about a kilometre and five seconds is about a mile.

Loud and Quiet

If you're listening to digital radio and your favourite song comes on, you might say, 'Turn it up!' and increase the volume.

When you turn up the volume, you are making the sound louder. A scientist might say that you are increasing the sound's intensity. How far away you can hear a sound depends on its intensity. A quiet sound, like a whisper, doesn't travel very far. But a really loud sound can travel for hundreds of miles. More than a hundred years ago, when a volcano exploded on the island of Krakatoa, the sound could be heard in Australia, almost three thousand miles away!

How would you arrange the sounds below in order of intensity, from quietest to loudest?

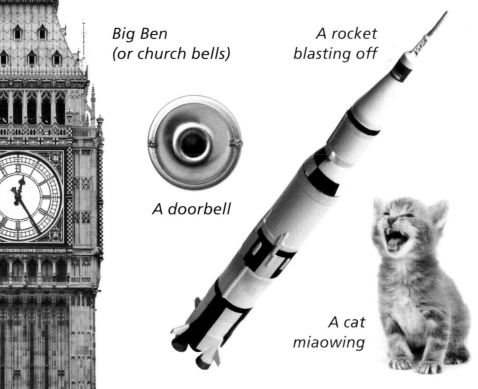

Big Ben
(or church bells)

A rocket
blasting off

A doorbell

A cat
miaowing

High and Low

Pretend that you're an opera star. Sing the highest note you can sing. Now sing the lowest. When we describe how high or low sound is, we are talking about the sound's pitch. A bird singing makes a high-pitched sound. A dog growling makes a low-pitched sound. Think of a flute and a tuba. Which instrument makes high-pitched sounds? Which makes low-pitched sounds?

How high is the highest note you can sing?

When you sing a high note, your vocal cords vibrate very fast, hundreds of times a second. When you sing a low note, your vocal cords vibrate more slowly. Faster vibrations make a sound with a higher pitch. Slower vibrations make a sound with a lower pitch.

See more about high and low pitches in the Music chapter.

Try this. Take a large rubber band and loop it around a drawer knob. Pull it tight and pluck it. Now loosen it and pluck it again. Can you hear the difference? When it's pulled tight, the rubber band makes a higher-pitched sound. Is the rubber band vibrating faster when it's loose or when it's pulled tight?

Your noisemaker: the larynx

You carry a noisemaker around with you wherever you go. It's called your *larynx* [LA-rinks], or voice box, and it's in your throat. When you felt your throat and hummed, you were feeling the vibration of your larynx.

How does your body make a sound? Air travels from your lungs and past your vocal cords, which stretch open and shut like two thick rubber bands inside your larynx. You use muscles to relax or tighten your vocal cords, which changes the pitch of your voice from low to high. You use your tongue, teeth and lips to form words.

How the Ear Works

Eardrum: handle with care

The eardrum is a delicate, airtight seal. Never poke anything long or sharp into your ear, because it could damage your eardrum. Extremely loud sounds can damage the eardrum, too. If sounds are loud enough to feel uncomfortable, it's time to move somewhere quieter or turn the volume down. Damaged eardrums are hard to heal. Without healthy eardrums, you won't hear well.

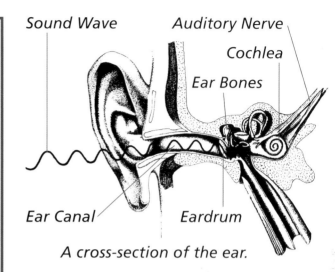

A cross-section of the ear.

Let's find out what happens when sound waves enter your ears.

If you look at someone's head, you see the *outer ear*. The outer ear is made of cartilage. Nature has cleverly designed the outer ear to catch and direct sound waves through an opening into the ear canal.

The vibrations travel through the air inside the ear canal to the eardrum. Like a drum, the eardrum is made of thin tissue stretched tightly across an opening.

Read how the dwarf Sindri used an anvil on page 51.

Each of your eardrums is only about as big as the fingernail on your little finger. Sound waves enter the ear and make the eardrum vibrate.

Next, those vibrations travel through three bones deep inside the ear. They're called the *hammer*, *anvil* and *stirrup*. These are the tiniest bones in your body. They get their names from their shapes. The hammer looks like a tiny hammer. The anvil looks like an anvil, the heavy iron surface that a blacksmith uses. And the stirrup is shaped like a stirrup, the metal loop below a horse's saddle for the rider's foot.

Vibrations are passed from the hammer to the anvil to the stirrup, and then on to the *cochlea* [COC-lee-uh]. The cochlea is a spiral. Can you find it in the picture? Does its shape remind you of a certain animal? ('Cochlea' comes from the Latin word for 'snail'.)

The cochlea is filled with liquid, which vibrates as sound enters. When the liquid vibrates, it shakes tiny hairs inside the cochlea. The hairs are connected to nerves that send signals to a big nerve called the auditory nerve. The auditory nerve carries the signals to the brain and – *ta-dah!* – you hear the sound.

Astronomy

The Universe: Big and Getting Bigger!

On a clear night, go outside and look up at the sky. What do you see? Is the Moon shining? Are the stars twinkling?

There you are, a single small person on this planet called Earth, looking up into the vastness of space. It seems to go on forever. But for every star you see, there are billions more you can't see. On and on the universe goes, stretching out in all directions, farther and bigger than anyone can imagine.

We call the science of outer space, planets and stars astronomy. That word comes from the Greek word *astron*, which means 'star'.

The stars in the universe are grouped into huge *galaxies*, which are groups of stars that are held together by gravity (we'll learn more about gravity later in this chapter). Some galaxies, like ours, are spirals, like paper windmills. Others look like oozing blobs of light.

Read more starting on page 354 about Caroline Herschel and Isaac Newton, after whom these space observatories were named.

Our Sun is only a single star among the billions of stars that make up the galaxy we live in, which is called the Milky Way. Why is it called the Milky Way? On a dark, moonless night, away from cities, you can sometimes see a fuzzy, milky-white stripe running across the sky. That white stripe is made up of the billions of stars in the Milky Way.

The Andromeda Galaxy, taken by the European Space Agency's Herschel and XMM-Newton space observatories.

Beyond the Milky Way, there are billions more stars in the galaxies that are our closest neighbours. One of our close neighbours is the Andromeda galaxy, but don't expect to travel there soon. Even though Andromeda is closer to us than most other galaxies, it is 2½ million light-years away. That means that light travelling from Andromeda to Earth takes 2½ million years to arrive! We are looking far, far back into Andromeda's history. If anything were watching us now from there, it would be seeing the earth as people started making tools out of stone.

Beyond Andromeda, there are still billions more galaxies. Astronomers – the scientists who study outer space – have made an amazing discovery. All these billions of galaxies are flying out and away from each other. In other words, the universe is *getting bigger*!

When astronomers observed how galaxies seem to be flying away from each other, they came up with a *theory* – an idea or an explanation, based what they had found out – for how the universe began. Their idea is called the Big Bang theory. Scientists will use this explanation until a better one replaces it. About 14 billion years ago all the matter in the universe was packed into a super-dense ball. No one knows exactly what it was or why it happened, but something caused this ball to explode with a big bang. The explosion sent chunks of matter flying out into space. Eventually, this matter became the stars, planets and everything else in our universe.

Just think! All matter came from that super-dense ball that exploded billions of years ago. And since you are made of matter, that means you are made of the stuff of stars!

How Do We Learn About Outer Space?

Astronomers learn about distant planets, stars and galaxies by looking through powerful telescopes, made of lenses and mirrors that let the human eye focus on objects far, far away. As soon as the first telescopes were invented, in the 1600s, people began to observe the stars and planets more closely. What they learnt also taught them a lot about this planet of ours called Earth.

The observatory at La Palma in the Canary Islands is set faraway from bright lights and high on a hilltop so it will be above many of the clouds.

The biggest telescopes need to be in special buildings in faraway places, where city lights don't make it hard to see out into the night sky. The Royal Observatory at Greenwich outside London is a historic observatory but, as the city grew bigger, it

Read about some important, pioneering astronomers starting on page 352.

became harder to view the stars from there. Other observatories around the world in the Canary Islands and in Hawaii have better luck seeing the night sky with their faraway locations and good weather.

Today's astronomers also use another kind of telescope, called a *radio telescope*. That doesn't mean they listen to radio programmes from far away. Remember X-rays for looking at bones? Radio waves are another sort of invisible light. Faint signals from distant stars can be detected with a big, reflective dish and special equipment. They gather information that might not be seen through telescope lenses.

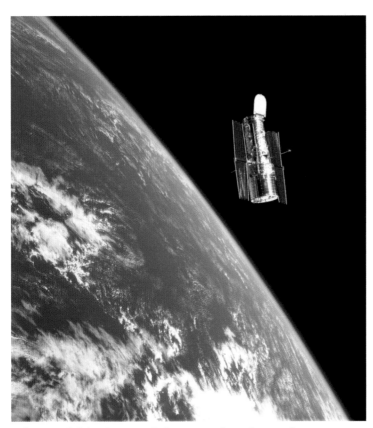

The Hubble Space Telescope has been important in helping us learn more about astronomy.

The first person in space was a Russian, Yuri Gagarin, whose rocket took him into orbit in 1961. The Americans Neil Armstrong and Buzz Aldrin were the first people ever to set foot on the moon (see the photo on page 339), and several other American astronauts also travelled to the moon between 1969 and 1972. They made everybody think differently about how much people are able to achieve.

NASA, the American space agency, built a reusable spacecraft called the *Space Shuttle*. Astronauts could land it like an aeroplane rather than parachute into the ocean. From 1981 to 2011 it flew many missions to deliver scientific equipment or work on satellites. In 1990, the Space Shuttle put the Hubble Space Telescope into orbit about 370 miles above the Earth. Up there, it is outside the Earth's atmosphere which could bend the light like the water in the glass experiment on page 309. The Hubble Space Telescope is about as big as a bus. It weighs as much as two adult elephants, or about twelve tonnes! It uses a concave mirror three metres across to collect light from faraway stars, then radios information about that light back to Earth. It provides us with many beautiful pictures of space.

There are useful experiments that can be done in the weightless conditions of orbit. To let people live in space for many weeks on end, countries have worked together to build space stations. The International Space Station crosses the sky most days. If you can track it with binoculars you may be able to make out its outline.

Two shuttle missions ended disastrously when all the astronauts died. Their job is dangerous and requires bravery as well as fitness and scientific skill. It also takes a long time. Travel to Mars takes months. No food grows there, so astronauts would either have to take all their food with them or work out a way of growing it. They would also need enough air and water to last, again unless they could make their own. Planning to live on Mars would be like planning to live underwater or in the frozen Antarctic, only harder and with less chance of coming home.

Since robots and machines are capable of sending back pictures and information, astronomers also learn a great deal from *unmanned space probes*. These spacecraft carry cameras, computers and scientific instruments far into space. They send radio signals back to Earth. Sometimes astronomers turn those signals into pictures, like postcards sent from outer space!

Space Shuttle Endeavour launched in 2008 and carried astronauts to work on the International Space Station.

One mission was called Galileo after the Italian scientist you'll read about on page 353. This spacecraft started to orbit Jupiter in 1995 after a voyage of six years from Earth starting on board a shuttle. It dropped a probe to the surface of the planet and flew as close as it could to the moons. Much of what we know about the huge volcanoes on the moon Io and what may be an ice-covered ocean on Europa came from this mission.

In 2006, the spacecraft *Venus Express* reached its target planet and has sent back pictures and information, suggesting volcanoes, lightning and hurricanes on or above Venus's surface. It does not sound like an easy place to live.

An image from the Galileo mission of active volcanic plumes on Jupiter's moon Io.

The Curiosity rover.

During 2012, the Curiosity mission landed a rover on Mars. The landing was so successful that the *rover*, like a robot car filled with scientific instruments and cameras, was able to drive about on the surface, finding out about Mars's rocks, soil and atmosphere.

Voyager 2 left Earth in 1977. It passed close to Jupiter, Saturn, Uranus and Neptune and is still going. After photographing the planets and their moons, it is now concentrating on small particles even farther away in space.

Our Solar System

When we say 'solar system', what do we mean? We mean all the planets, moons and other heavenly bodies that circle around our Sun. 'Solar' comes from the Latin word 'sol', which means 'sun'. 'System' means a group of things that move and interact with each other. So the 'solar system' is the group of planets that move in circles around our Sun.

Hundreds of years ago, people believed that the Sun, the stars and the other planets circled Earth. It made sense. We saw everything crossing the sky every night. A Greek astronomer called Aristarchus suggested that Earth circled the Sun, but his idea didn't catch on. Then, in the 1500s, a Polish

Read more about Copernicus and his ideas on page 352.

astronomer named Nicolaus Copernicus [ko-PERN-ick-uss] argued that the Sun appeared to move across the sky because the earth was spinning right round every day. The planets were in a system with the Sun, not the Earth, in the middle – a solar system. Not many people believed Copernicus during his lifetime, but today no one would argue with him.

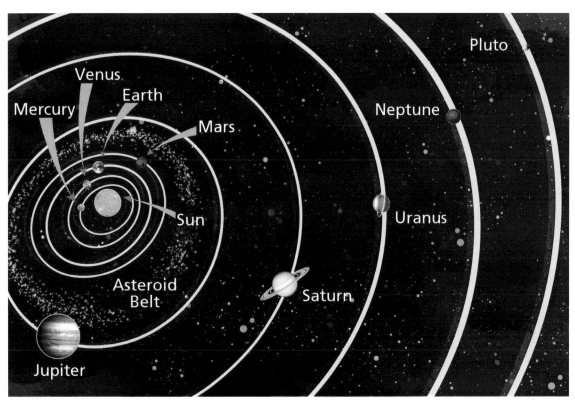

Our solar system

The Sun is a star like other stars you see at night. The Sun looks bigger and brighter than other stars because it is closer to us. Even though it's the closest star, the Sun is still 93 million miles from Earth.

You know that light travels fast. When you turn on a light, think how fast its light reaches your eyes. For the Sun's light to travel 93 million miles to reach us here on Earth, it takes about eight minutes.

How big is Earth compared to the Sun? Look at this picture. Very occasionally the planet Venus appears in front of the Sun, which you can see as the black dot on the sun in this picture. Venus is about the same size as Earth, but Venus is three to four times closer to the Sun than the Earth. Look how small Venus looks compared to the Sun!

The Sun with the black dot of Venus passing in front.

Like other stars, the Sun is a giant ball of churning, glowing, exploding gas. On a very hot day on Earth, the temperature might reach 40 degrees Celsius. The surface of the Sun is about 5,500 degrees Celsius, and astronomers believe that the deep core inside the Sun might be almost 16 million degrees!

The natural world depends upon the energy that comes from the Sun. Without the light and heat we get from the Sun, life on Earth simply wouldn't exist. But don't worry. The Sun isn't going away. It's been around for billions of years and will still be around billions of years from now.

Planets in Motion: Orbit and Rotation

Around the Sun travel the planets: Mercury, Venus, Earth, Mars, Jupiter, Saturn, Uranus, Neptune and Pluto. We started learning a bit about the planets in Year 2, and also how some people call Pluto a dwarf planet because it is so small. More planets are still being discovered in the universe, so astronomers are thinking of new ways to decide what counts as a planet. The word 'planet' comes from an old Greek word that means 'wanderer'. But the planets do not wander aimlessly around the solar system. They travel around the Sun in fixed paths called *orbits*, which are shown by the oval pale blue lines you can see in the image of the solar system on page 333.

As the planets orbit (go around) the Sun, they also rotate. That means they spin around like a top. Like the other planets, Earth both orbits the Sun and rotates. We say that Earth rotates around an axis, which is an imaginary line running through the planet from the North Pole to the South Pole.

*The earth spins around an invisible axis, shown here
by the yellow line that looks like a toothpick.*

If you were to spend a day keeping track of the position of the Sun in the sky, it might appear as though the Sun were moving. Get up early one morning and observe where you see the Sun. A few hours later Earth has rotated so that it looks as though the Sun has moved to a different place in the sky. But really, the Sun isn't moving. It only appears to move because Earth is rotating on its axis. When evening comes, observe where the Sun sets. It always sets in the west and rises in the east. We talk about the Sun 'rising' and 'setting' because that's what the Sun appears to do. But remember: it only looks that way. Earth is moving, not the Sun.

It takes a day for Earth to make one complete spin around its axis. When the place where you live is turned towards the Sun, it is day for you, while it is night for people on the opposite side of Earth. As Earth continues to rotate, the place where you live turns away from the Sun, and it becomes night for you.

The Earth doesn't stand straight up and down on its axis as it spins. It tilts slightly, as you can see in the picture, and this tilt causes the different seasons. When we have summer, our part of Earth is tilting toward the Sun. The tilt means that sunlight shines more directly on us, bringing warm weather. When we have winter, our part of Earth is tilting away from the Sun. This position makes the sunlight shine less directly on us. The areas tilted away from the Sun receive less sunlight. Winter is cold because we receive less heat from the Sun.

In Year 2 we did an experiment with a globe and a lamp to understand what makes day and night.

335

*People living in different hemispheres experience winter
and summer in different times of the year. Can you see why?*

Try this with a globe (or a ball you can mark with a North Pole and South Pole) and a desk lamp. Shine the desk lamp at the equator. Holding the globe at the poles, tilt the top (north) slightly toward the lamp. That's summer for the continents in the Northern Hemisphere, like Europe and North America, when they receive sunshine more directly. Now tilt the top of the globe slightly away from the lamp. This makes the continents in the Southern Hemisphere, like Africa and Australia, receive more direct sunshine. Did you know that when people in Europe are enjoying sunny summer days, people in New Zealand are shivering because it's the middle of winter? Now you know why.

Do you know how long it takes for Earth to make one complete orbit around the Sun? In other words, do you know how long it takes Earth to go around the Sun and come back to where it started? It takes one year (365 days) for Earth to orbit the Sun.

Happy leap year

Actually, it takes Earth 365¼ days to make one complete orbit around the Sun. To make up for those quarter days, we have a leap year every fourth year, when the month of February has 29 days instead of 28. That extra day makes up for four quarter days.

Earth's Satellite: The Moon

Earth orbits the Sun. And what orbits Earth? The Moon. Another way of saying this is that the Moon is a *satellite* of Earth. You may think of a satellite as a device that gets blasted into space by a rocket and then orbits Earth, sending down radio signals and scientific measurements. That's one kind of satellite. In astronomy, the word 'satellite' can mean any heavenly body that orbits another. The word 'satellite' comes from the Latin for 'attendant', meaning someone who waits on an important person.

On some nights, you might look up at the sky and say, 'Look, the Moon is shining so brightly!' The Moon may look bright, but it does not make its own light, as the Sun does. The Moon reflects the light cast on it by the Sun.

Moon shapes

Ask a friend to hold a ball up in the air. Have another friend stand a few feet away and shine a torch at it. Now look at the ball. See how one side is lit up and the other is darker, in shadow? The Moon has a lit-up and a shadowy side, just like the Earth.

Find a position to stand where you see half a lit-up ball and half a ball in shadow. That's a way to think about what you're seeing when the half-moon appears in the sky.

Can you find the position to stand to see a crescent of light? That's what you're seeing when the crescent moon appears.

There are nights when no moon appears in the sky at all, even if the sky is clear. That's the time we call the new moon. Of course, the Moon is out there, but you can't see it. In fact, when there's a new moon, the Moon is overhead during the day, but the bright sunlight makes it impossible to see from Earth. Find it on the diagram on page 338.

The Moon appears to change shape, but the Moon doesn't actually change. What does happen? The Moon reflects the light of the Sun. Depending on the position of the Moon and Sun to our eyes, we on Earth see all, part or none of the Moon. With your finger, trace how the Sun's light travels from the Sun to the Moon and then to Earth, where we see it.

Over the course of a month, the Moon may look as if it is changing shape and size, but what changes is the way the Moon reflects sunlight to our eyes on Earth. It takes 29 days

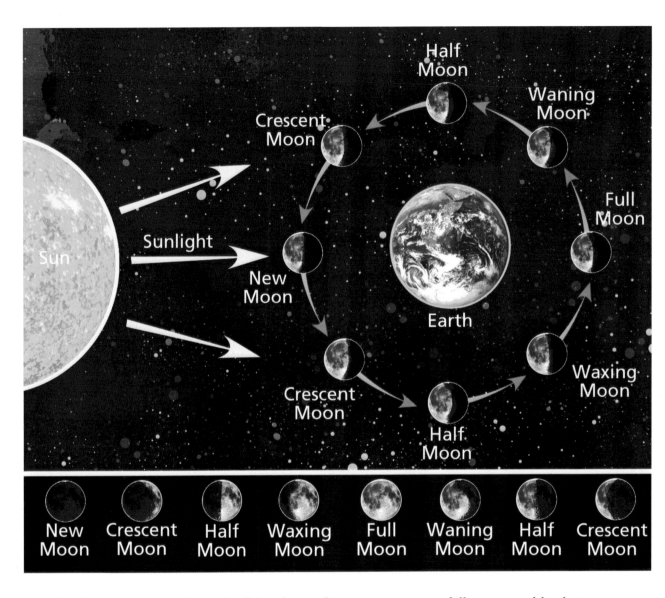

for the Moon to go through all its *phases*, from new moon to full moon and back to new moon again. When more of the Moon is becoming visible each night, we say the Moon is *waxing*. When less of the Moon is becoming visible each night, we say it is *waning*. It's fun to pay attention to the Moon every night for a few weeks, to notice how it waxes and wanes.

What is the Moon made of? Not green cheese! The Moon is mostly a big ball of rock. There is no atmosphere on the Moon – no air, no water, no clouds, no rain. Nothing grows on the Moon. All you can see on the lunar landscape are rocks and moon dust. (Remember from Year 3 that 'lunar' is a word for anything that has to do with the Moon. It comes from 'luna', the Latin word for the Moon.)

When you were little, did you ever look up at night and see the face of 'the Man in the Moon'? It is fun to imagine a face there, even though what you are seeing are huge mountains and craters on the surface.

Human beings have visited the Moon and walked on its surface. On 20 July, 1969, Neil Armstrong on the Apollo 11 space mission became the first person to set foot on the Moon. As he stepped from his spacecraft onto the Moon's surface, he said, 'That's one small step for a man, one giant leap for mankind.' (The 'a' wasn't heard in the recording of these famous words, but audio analysis shows that Armstrong really said 'a man'.)

Apollo 11 astronauts 'Buzz' Aldrin and Neil Armstrong left footprints (and a flag) on the Moon.

The Force of Gravity

What keeps the Moon orbiting around Earth instead of floating off into space? *Gravity.* Gravity is a force between bits of matter, attracting every bit to the centre of the Earth or other celestial bodies.

Gravity is the force that keeps your feet on the ground. You may not feel it, but gravity affects you all the time. When you throw a ball up into the air, what happens? No matter how high you throw the ball, it always comes back down. The gravitational force between the Earth and the ball pulls the ball down to the ground. If it were not for the pull of gravity, the ball would just keep going up. In fact, without gravity, if you jumped, you would keep moving out into space!

Black holes

Astronomers have found some places in the universe where the force of gravity is so strong that it captures everything that comes near it. These super-dense places pull in everything – nothing can escape. Their pulling power is so strong that not even light can escape from them, which is why astronomers call these places *black holes*.

Earth's gravity pulls on the Moon, the Moon's gravity pulls on Earth. The moon is moving fast enough not to fall down and hit the Earth but not so fast that it disappears off into space. Those forces keep the Moon in orbit around Earth. In the same way, the Sun's gravity pulls on Earth and the other planets and keeps them in their orbits around the Sun.

The power of the pull of gravity between objects depends on two things: how far apart the objects are and the *mass* of each object – that is, how much matter each object contains. Objects that are close together and objects that have lots of mass attract each other strongly. Things that are far apart and things with small mass attract only weakly.

Let's think about what these rules mean. If you were on the Moon, you could jump much higher than you can when you are on Earth. You could jump high, like when you're on a trampoline. Why? Since the Moon is much smaller than Earth

Gravity is the force of attraction that makes this ball fall back down to Earth.

and contains much less matter than Earth, its gravitational pull is weaker than Earth's. With gravity pulling more weakly, you can jump higher. You would even weigh less on the Moon – only about one-sixth of what you weigh here on Earth. Can you work out, then, how much you would weigh on the Moon? Divide your weight by six to find out!

Although the Moon has less gravity than Earth, its gravity still affects us. The gravity of the Moon (with just a little help from the gravity of the Sun) pulls on the waters of the oceans here on Earth. That gravitational pull causes the tides, which are the regular patterns by which the ocean's water level rises and falls.

If you've spent a day at the beach, you've probably noticed the difference between low tide and high tide. At low tide, you can play on a broad, sandy beach. But when high tide comes, the ocean's water level rises and covers part of the beach, leaving less room for you to play. So if your sandcastle gets washed out by the tide, blame the Man in the Moon!

Do you remember what we learnt about the tides in Year 2? Now you know more.

When Day Becomes Night: A Solar Eclipse

As the Moon orbits Earth, it sometimes moves right between Earth and the Sun. Then the Moon blocks our view of the Sun and casts a shadow on Earth. And when that happens, we on Earth see a *solar eclipse*.

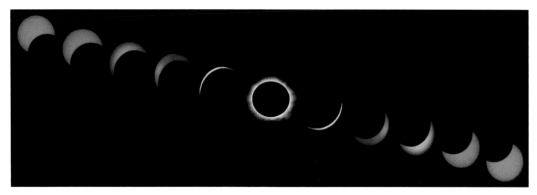

This picture of a solar eclipse was taken over several minutes when the Moon passed between the Sun and the Earth and blocked our view of the yellow ball of the Sun.

As a solar eclipse begins, it looks as if a dark disc is creeping slowly across the face of the Sun. The disc – which is the Moon – seems just as big as the Sun, but that's because the Moon is so much closer to Earth than the Sun. As more and more of the Moon blocks the light of the Sun, day seems to turn to night, no matter what time it is. The sky darkens. Stars become visible.

A solar eclipse lasts only a few minutes. The Moon moves out of its position between the Earth and the Sun. The sky brightens. Hundreds of years ago, before people understood about the solar system, they were terrified by solar eclipses. They didn't understand why the Sun seemed to be getting darker in the middle of the day.

Now, when Earth moves between the Moon and the Sun, what do you think will happen? Remember that the Moon does not make its own light. It just reflects the light of the Sun. If Earth blocks sunlight from reaching the Moon, Earth will cast a shadow on the Moon so it will become invisible for just a little bit. When that happens, it's called a *lunar eclipse*.

Protect your eyes!

Even when you're studying the Sun, **never** look directly at it, either with your eyes alone or through binoculars or a telescope. You could damage your eyes or even blind yourself. If you happen to be somewhere where you can see a solar eclipse, here's a simple way to view it safely. Poke a little hole in an index card. Hold it about a metre above a white piece of paper. A little image of the sun will be projected by the hole onto the paper. Alternatively buy a plastic viewing filter from an astronomical society like the British Astronomical Association for a few pounds.

The Inner Planets

Let's take a quick tour of the solar system. We'll visit all nine planets, but let's start with the four planets closest to the Sun – Mercury, Venus, Earth and Mars. These four are often called the inner planets.

Mercury

The closest planet to the Sun, Mercury, was named after the Roman god Mercury, the swift and speedy messenger of the gods. The name fits because it is the fastest moving planet; compared to Earth, Mercury orbits the Sun much more quickly. A year on Mercury – one complete orbit around the Sun – takes only 88 of our Earth days.

A photo of Mercury taken by Messenger

In 1974, *Mariner 10* was the first spacecraft to fly by Mercury and send back pictures of its surface. We learnt that Mercury gets very hot and very cold – over 400 degrees Celsius when facing the Sun and down to 160 degrees Celsius below zero when facing away from the Sun. NASA's *Messenger* spacecraft began orbiting Mercury in 2011 and continues to send back many pictures of its rocks, craters and valleys to help us learn more about this planet.

Venus

The second planet from the Sun, Venus, gets its name from the ancient Roman goddess of love and beauty, perhaps because it appears to shine so brightly and beautifully in the sky. In the morning or the evening, you can often see Venus. It has been nicknamed the 'morning star' and 'evening star' because you can see it, brighter than any star, just above the horizon at dawn or dusk. But Venus isn't a star. It's a planet. Thick clouds always cover Venus. Those clouds reflect sunlight, making the planet look bright.

Venus is a hot, yellowish planet.

Earth

As you sit at school or lie in your bed, it's hard to think of Earth as a huge, round planet spinning on its axis and orbiting the Sun. But like the other planets in our solar system, Earth is always moving in relation to the Sun. It moves in a nearly round path, speeding around the Sun at more than sixty thousand miles per hour!

*Astronauts in outer space can look back towards Earth and see
the lights of cities as well as the outlines of continents.*

If you were an astronaut looking back at Earth from your spacecraft, you would see a blue, green and white ball. What do you think the white is? Clouds, lots of clouds. And the blue is water, lots of water. Nearly three-quarters of Earth is covered with water. All that water is one of the main reasons there is life on Earth. The green is land.

As far as we know now, Earth is the only planet with life on it. But with all those billions of other galaxies out there, you can't help but wonder.

Mars

This image was taken by the Curiosity *rover on Mars.*

The fourth planet from the Sun is Mars, named after the Roman god of war. Sometimes you can see Mars in the night sky, even without a telescope. Mars is nicknamed the 'red planet' because of its orange-red colour. That colour comes from the large amount of iron compounds, like rust, in the planet's rocky surface.

For many years, people thought that, among all the other planets in the solar system besides Earth, Mars was the one most likely to have life. In 1976, two Viking space probes landed on the surface of Mars and found no life. The Viking probes sent back pictures of a bare, rocky, dusty planet. A more ambitious mission led by NASA, called Curiosity, sent many pictures back from Mars in 2012. See a picture taken by the *Curiosity* rover on page 344.

The Asteroid Belt

Between Mars and Jupiter, the fifth planet from the Sun, is the *asteroid belt*, which is made up of thousands of chunks of rock and metal that are orbiting the Sun. Some asteroids are as small as a rugby ball. Others are as big as a mountain. The biggest asteroid, called Ceres, is 600 miles across. That is one quarter of our Moon's diameter!

Where did the asteroids come from? Scientists think they are bits and pieces left over from when the solar system was first formed that didn't join up enough to become planets.

Sometimes asteroids change orbit and some have orbits that cross those of the inner planets. Some scientists think that one such asteroid, 8 miles or so across, might have hit Earth about 65 million years ago, creating enormous waves, fires and a thick cloud of dust that blocked out the sunlight for years. These scientists think that this terrible disaster wiped out much of the life on our planet, including the dinosaurs.

The Outer Planets

Now you have learnt about the four inner planets in the solar system. Can you name them again? The inner planets are all solid and rocky. But when we move to the outer planets, we find that four of them are made mostly of liquid and gas. These four, called the gas giants, are Jupiter, Saturn, Uranus and Neptune. After them comes the best known 'dwarf' or minor planet, tiny Pluto.

Jupiter

Jupiter, the largest planet in our solar system, was named after the Roman king of the gods. Jupiter is over a thousand times larger than Earth. Jupiter is mostly made of hydrogen, in

The Juno *spacecraft left Earth in 2011 and should arrive at Jupiter in 2016 to study this planet.*

liquid form inside the planet and as gas on its surface. Strong winds swirl that gas into colourful clouds of red, orange, yellow and brown.

Imagine looking up and seeing many moons in the sky. Galileo, the great Italian astronomer who lived around 1600, looked through a telescope and discovered four moons around Jupiter. If you can hold a pair of binoculars steady, you could see them for yourself. Since then, astronomers have found twelve more moons and many smaller orbiting rocks. In the 1990s, a space probe travelled toward Jupiter. It was called the *Galileo* – can you guess why? In 1995, *Galileo* reached Jupiter. In 1999, it flew past one of Jupiter's moons, called Io, and sent back amazing pictures like the one on page 332. We're looking forward to seeing more pictures and learning much more about Jupiter when the *Juno* spacecraft arrives there in 2016.

Saturn

Saturn, the second largest planet in our solar system, was named after the Roman god of the harvest. This planet looks different from all the rest because of its spectacular rings. Astronomers know that the rings are made of ice, dust and rock, but they aren't sure where all that stuff came from. Some

Saturn has easily recognisable rings.

think the rings may be the remains of a moon that shattered long ago. As of now, 53 moons still orbit Saturn, but astronomers continue to find new, small moons.

Uranus

The farther we get into outer space, the less we know about the planets. Uranus, the seventh planet from the Sun, was named after the father of all the Greek gods. Uranus has rings as well, but they are much fainter than Saturn's. Until 1986, only five moons were known to circle Uranus. Then the *Voyager 2* spacecraft flew by and sent back information showing ten more moons around the planet.

Can you spot the blue moon Ariel and its shadow as it passes in front of the blue-green planet Uranus?

Neptune

The last of the four gas giants, Neptune, is the eighth planet from the Sun. It was named after the Roman god of the sea. This planet is so far away that it takes about 165 Earth years to complete one orbit around the Sun. We learnt a lot about Neptune when the *Voyager 2* spacecraft flew by the planet in 1989. It also showed us that Neptune is a frozen and stormy planet, bluish in colour, with the strongest winds in the solar system, travelling up to twelve hundred miles per hour!

The Hubble Space Telescope took this photo of Neptune.

Pluto

Far out in the dark, cold reaches of space, you'll find the smallest planet of our solar system, Pluto, named after the Roman god of the underworld. Most of the time, Pluto is the farthest planet from the Sun. Sometimes its orbit crosses inside the orbit of Neptune – but not again until the twenty-third century. Mark that on your calendar about 200 years from now!

Only the most powerful telescopes on Earth can see Pluto. Astronomers did not even discover this small planet until 1930. In 1978, astronomers found one moon around Pluto and named it Charon, after the man in Greek mythology who took souls to the underworld. In 1992, astronomers found a belt of small, icy objects the same sort of

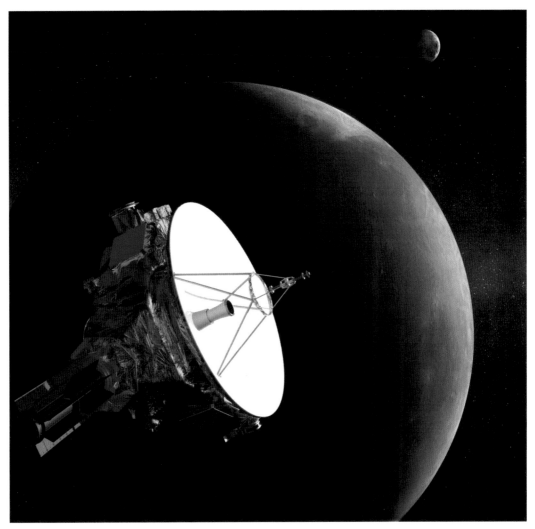

An artist shows how the New Horizons spacecraft will take photos to help us learn about Pluto and its moons.

distance from the sun as Pluto and called it the Kuiper [KIE-pah] belt. Because it is not even the biggest in that region, astronomers started to call Pluto a 'dwarf planet' in 2006. Ceres, the biggest asteroid, and Eris, the largest known object in the Kuiper belt, were awarded the same title. The definition may change again in the future because, like major planets, Pluto is big and round and orbits the sun.

In 2006, the *New Horizons* spacecraft left Earth headed towards Pluto. It is scheduled to arrive in 2015. This mission will be the first to travel to Pluto and will let us learn much more about it.

A solar system model

You can make a model of the solar system. It will give you an idea of just how spread out it all is. Our scale will be tiny. We'll make our planets bigger, so you can see and touch them, but really we are thinking about the distances of planets from the Sun.

You need nine beads, some pipe cleaners, some polyester sewing thread (or string) and some scissors to cut them. Stand a stick or a pole up in the ground. A cricket stump is ideal. It stands for the sun so the planets can orbit it.

Inner planets

You know that four planets are much nearer the Sun than the others. We will model them with pipe cleaners. You have four inner planets, so you need four pipe cleaners and four beads.

The distances from the centre are:

Mercury 4 cm ● Venus 7 cm ● Earth 10 cm ● Mars 15 cm

Curl one end of a pipe cleaner around the stump or pole, then, with a ruler, measure a straight section the right distance from the pole. Bend the other end upwards, through the middle of a bead and bend the tip over to stop the bead falling off. You may have to join two pipe cleaners together for Mars, if one is too short.

Outer planets

The five planets of the outer solar system need to be a lot further away.

We'll now use the sewing thread for the five outer planets. Tie a bead to the end, measure the correct distance, allowing some extra for tying up, then tie the other end around the central pole. You probably need to be outside for this part. The distances are:

Jupiter 50 cm ● Saturn 1 m ● Uranus 1.9 m ● Neptune 3 m ● Pluto 3.9 m

Orbits

Now do you see how big the solar system really is? The Sun is a long way from the Earth. It is so far away that, although it is far bigger than the Earth, the Sun looks small in the sky. And yet the distance to Neptune is many times further again.

When you have made the model, try making some planets start to orbit. Hold the bead that represents your chosen planet and move anti-clockwise around the pole for the Sun. Try to keep the pipe cleaner or the thread straight and watch out for tangles. Think about how to keep the other threads out of the way while a planet is orbiting. The orbit is just like a thread keeping our planets the right distances from the Sun. Earth's orbit is bigger than Venus's orbit, Jupiter's orbit is even bigger and Pluto's orbit is even bigger than that. This gives us an idea of how big the solar system is.

Dirty Snowballs and Shooting Stars

Chunks of matter called comets and meteors are hurtling through space. Astronomers think that, like asteroids, these heavenly bodies may be left over from the beginnings of the solar system.

Comets are sometimes called dirty snowballs because they're made of ice, rock and dust. When a comet passes near the Sun, the Sun's rays melt some of the ice, which causes a huge tail of gas and dust to form. The tail of a comet can stretch out for hundreds of thousands of miles!

Halley's Comet in 1986

Millions of comets orbit the Sun. Sometimes a comet that passed close enough to Earth for people to see will come back hundreds of years later and be visible again. The English astronomer Edmund Halley predicted that a big comet, seen in 1531 and 1607, would return in 1758. He was right, and scientists named the comet after him. Halley's comet last came into view in 1986. It takes about 76 years for it to return to Earth's view. You can look forward to seeing it in the year 2061. There are many other comets, too, like Comet Lovejoy which was seen in 2011.

Comets don't appear very often, but on many nights you might be able to see something bright streak across the night sky. These shooting stars, as they're often called, are not really stars at all. They are *meteors*, bits of matter that soar through space and sometimes cross the path of Earth. When a meteor falls through Earth's atmosphere at a super-fast speed, it gets so hot that it burns up and makes the fiery streak you might see in the sky.

Scientists estimate that several hundred million meteors enter Earth's atmosphere every day! Most burn up and never reach the ground. A meteor that made it to the ground is called a meteorite.

Most meteorites are made of iron and rock. Scientists are very eager to collect and study all the meteorites they can find. What might these scientists be hoping to find?

By joining the stars like in this outline, you can see the Great Bear and other constellations in the night sky.

Constellations:
Shapes in the Stars

Long ago, when the earliest humans looked up into the night sky, what thoughts do you think passed through their minds? As they stared at the stars, they began to see shapes and patterns – bears and lions, maidens and heroes. These 'join the dots' pictures that people have imagined in the stars are called *constellations*. They have names like Leo (the Lion), Taurus (the Bull) and Orion (a legendary hunter).

One star pattern you can easily see is called the Plough, which looks like a blade with a long handle. The Plough is part of the constellation called Ursa Major, or the Great Bear. Since the Earth travels along its orbit and moves through space during the year, constellations appear to be flipped when you view them at different times of the year.

Read the legend 'The Hunting of the Great Bear' to learn more about this constellation on page 44.

You can use the Plough's stars to find which way is north. Find the two stars furthest from the handle. Let your eyes follow an imaginary line starting at the bottom star, going through the top one, then keep going. The first bright star you see, brighter than any others around, is Polaris, or the Pole Star. Polaris is part of another constellation. It's the brightest star in the Little Bear. You need a clear, dark night to see any of the others.

Stars and constellations were important to sailors, who used them to determine compass directions. You can do that, too. When you look at the Pole Star, you are facing north. Once you know where north is, you can find your way south, east or west.

The Lives of Famous Scientists

Nicolaus Copernicus

Today we know the real reason why the Sun seems to go around Earth every day. It's because Earth spins on its axis, and the view of the Sun from any one point of Earth changes as it spins. It's Earth that moves.

But five hundred years ago, people believed that Earth was still and the Sun moved around it. Nicolaus Copernicus [nick-o-LOUSS co-PER-ni-cus] was brave enough to question that belief.

Copernicus was born in Poland in 1473. He studied astronomy at a Polish university. Then, wanting to learn more, he travelled to Italy. If you can find Poland and Italy on a map, you will see that he had to cross the Alps to make that journey. Some say he and his brother walked the whole way across the Alps, just to get to Italy to study. In the Italian city of Bologna [buh-LON-ya], he studied not only astronomy but also medicine and law.

When he travelled home to Poland, Copernicus's work kept him from studying astronomy all the time. He was a priest in a cathedral and he also helped run the government in the part of the country where he lived. No matter what work he did, though, he kept thinking about and studying the planets in every minute of free time.

Nicolaus Copernicus

Copernicus wrote down his proofs for why Earth must revolve around the Sun. Pope Clement VII heard about them and his court asked for a copy to read. Friends told Copernicus he should publish his ideas in a book so that more people could read them. But Copernicus was not ready. He knew that rumours about his ideas were upsetting some people, who didn't want to change their minds about the importance of Earth in the universe.

Finally, a younger man named Rheticus came to work with Copernicus on a book. The book was called *De Revolutionibus Orbium Coelestium*, which is Latin for 'About the Revolutions of the Planets in the Sky'. Copernicus waited so long to write and publish his book that not long after he received a printed copy in his hands, he died, at the age of 70. Now we consider that book to be the vital step to our understanding that Earth and the other planets in our solar system travel around the Sun.

Galileo Galilei

Galileo Galilei

Scientists are always trying to discover new things. Two aspects of this are difficult. One is making the discovery in the first place. The other is persuading other people to change what they think and agree with your new idea.

The story of Galileo Galilei is about a man who made many discoveries but had trouble persuading other people that he was right. He was born in 1564 in Pisa and while quite young he became Professor of Mathematics there. The town is famous for its beautiful leaning tower, which was where Galileo conducted one of his experiments.

Experiments are a big part of how scientists persuade other people of the truth of their ideas. You try something out and predict what the result will be. Better still, you can repeat the test and get other people to try it out for themselves, with the same results.

Does something heavy fall faster than something light? Galileo climbed the tower and dropped a big weight and a small weight off the top at the same time. Let's hope he checked first that no one was standing underneath! He dropped the weights at the same time and

353

they hit the ground at the same time. Was that what you expected? It was not what Aristotle taught would happen. Although Aristotle was a great thinker, he was not right about everything. Despite Galileo's demonstration, some teachers at the university still wanted Aristotle to be always right, so Galileo lost his job there.

See a photo of the 'leaning tower of Pisa' on page 183.

Happily, Galileo knew some people with influence. They helped him get a job in Padua in Italy, where he learnt about the telescope. He designed his own that was even better than those traditionally used, and he could even see

We read about Aristotle in Year 3.

mountains on the face of the Moon and the moons of Jupiter. Seeing that the moons were circling another planet convinced Galileo of the truth of Copernicus's theory: the Earth was not the centre of the universe.

In 1610 Galileo moved back to live near Pisa, but he still had enemies there. They tried to make trouble for him with the Church by altering one of his letters in which he explained why Copernicus's theory did not go against what the Bible said. The trouble-makers succeeded. The Catholic Church declared that Copernicus was wrong.

Galileo still had friends in high places. One of his friends became Pope Urban VIII, head of the Roman Catholic Church, in 1623. For now, Galileo was welcome to discuss Copernicus's theory, so long as he remembered to call his work a 'hypothesis', meaning that other explanations were still possible. This worked nicely until 1630, when Galileo wrote a book stating that the Sun was at the centre of the solar system and that the Earth orbited it. The Pope then turned on Galileo and he was made to say that Copernicus's theory was wrong (although it wasn't).

Galileo was forced to move to outside Florence, where he was not allowed out of his house. Still, his later life was fairly comfortable. He had time to put his writings in order and publish them in different countries. In the year that Galileo died, Isaac Newton was born in England, and he was able to build upon some of Galileo's ideas.

Isaac Newton: Discoverer of Gravity

Isaac Newton is one of the most famous scientists, and he lived from 1643–1727. The first story everyone hears about Isaac Newton is that he was sitting in a garden under a tree when an apple fell on his head. You or I might have thought 'Ouch!', or eaten

Isaac Newton

the apple or saved it to go in a pie. Newton thought more deeply than that. He started wondering why it fell down – not up – or even why it fell at all.

At first it seems obvious. All our lives everything we've seen fall has fallen down. It's altogether harder to work out what makes things start falling.

No, the apple didn't really hit his head. It's a good story, though, and he did get ideas when he watched an apple fall. It occurred to him that the same gravity that pulled the apple to earth might also be pulling the Moon around the Earth in circles.

Isaac Newton studied just about anything he could. His greatest book was called *Mathematical Principles of Natural Philosophy*. Natural philosophy means wanting to know about how things are, which includes all of science. A lot of what you have learnt about light came from Newton's experiments. He found that a prism could split light into different colours, and he built an improved telescope using a curved mirror instead of lenses.

It wasn't easy being a genius. Newton was born after his father died. He grew up in a Lincolnshire village called Woolsthorpe, where his mother wanted him to be a farmer. He studied at Cambridge University, where he needed to work as a college servant to pay his way. When Cambridge was afflicted by the Great Plague, he retreated to Woolsthorpe and made some great discoveries there, including the theory of gravity. Who would ever imagine you could learn so much from an apple?

Anyone who has tried to understand a ball bouncing or an athlete running owes a lot to Isaac Newton. He worked out the laws of how objects move that work in all known cases until they move so quickly they are close to the speed of light, or are so small that nothing can measure them. His theories were the best that science could offer for two and a half centuries.

Learn more about the Great Plague on page 164.

One of Newton's friends was Edmond Halley [HAL-ee] the observer of the comet, but Newton made enemies too. He argued with Astronomer Royal, John Flamsteed, over when to publish a book on astronomy, and he reacted badly to criticism from Robert Hooke, another scientist in the Royal Society. The worst argument of his life was over mathematics with Gottfried Leibniz [GOTT-freed LIBE-nits] because both men had a similar idea around the same time, and each wanted to claim the discovery as his own.

Even if the people he quarrelled with disliked him, many more people have every reason to be grateful to Isaac Newton. His book *Mathematical Principles* contained so many central scientific ideas, expressed so very clearly, that they have set our standard for scientific discovery ever since.

Caroline Herschel

Caroline Herschel

Caroline Herschel was born in 1750 in Hanover, which is now in Germany. As her mother did not think that girls should be educated, she was forced to do little else except housework for many of her early years. However, Caroline was very curious and desperately wanted to learn. Although her father had never gone to school to receive a formal education, he did his best to teach her what he knew. When Caroline was a child, a comet passed over Hanover. Her father took her out to view it and then helped her learn about the constellations. A *comet* is an object in space that is made of dust and gas and, since it travels around the Sun, it can only be viewed during specific times when it is passing overhead in the sky. Learn more on page 350.

Caroline's father was a musician who played the oboe, and her four brothers all learnt to be musicians as well. One of her brothers, William Herschel, became an organ player who moved to

See a picture of an oboe in the Year 2 book and read more about woodwind instruments on page 207.

Bath, and Caroline later moved to England to join him. Caroline helped her brother and, in return, William taught her how to be a singer. Caroline began to give singing performances in Bath and Bristol.

William was also very interested in learning about mathematics and astronomy. He taught Caroline mathematics and English, and she learnt about astronomy as she helped him with his hobby of making telescopes in his free time. Soon the pair began to spend every spare moment focusing on astronomy: they made telescopes, observed the night sky and made mathematical calculations using the information they recorded from their observations. These were a bit like the missing number problems you solved, and they figured out the missing numbers to learn how far different planets and stars were from Earth using other numbers they knew.

In 1781, William made a big discovery! He found a new planet in our solar system – Uranus. King George III began to pay William to conduct research about astronomy, and William and Caroline gave up their work in music to work on astronomy. William and Caroline both made observations of the night sky, but Caroline's own research was often put to one side as she helped William with his observations at night and, during the day, she made mathematical calculations for him to understand the information he collected. Caroline knew her maths very well and was able to complete the equations accurately.

Whenever she could, Caroline made her own observations and, in 1786, she discovered her first comet! Since it was very rare for women to be scientists at that time, Caroline became well-known and journalists wrote articles about her discovery. When King George III heard the news, he began to pay her to work as William's assistant.

Over the next eleven years, Caroline discovered eight new comets while also working as William's assistant. After that, she started a new project of correcting the official star catalogue, which contains information on all the stars we know about. In 1798, Caroline sent her new catalogue to the Royal Society, which included 560 stars that hadn't been included before.

After sending this large catalogue to the Royal Society, Caroline continued to help William with his work and she also began to share all that she knew with her young nephew, John Herschel. Caroline taught John mathematics and astronomy, amongst other subjects, and he followed in his father's and his aunt's footsteps as a successful astronomer and mathematician. Caroline was now well-known for her work and she was invited several times to the Royal Observatory by members of the Royal Family.

Caroline Herschel discovered the Wizard Nebula in 1787.

Later, after William died, Caroline moved back to Hanover. She researched nebulae, which are clouds of dust or gas that are between stars. She made a catalogue of 2,500 nebulae to help not only John with his research but also many, many different astronomers who read her work. In 1828, the Royal Astronomical Society awarded its gold medal to Caroline for her research on nebulae. Years after she died, a minor planet was named Lucretia after Caroline Lucretia Herschel to honour her work in astronomy.

Alexander Graham Bell

Even as a boy, Alexander Graham Bell was fascinated by sound. 'How do the vocal cords make noise?' he asked. 'How does the ear hear?' He and his brother dissected the larynx of a sheep, then built a machine of tin and rubber, designing it to work like the sheep's vocal cords. When they blew through the machine, it made a noise.

Bell was born in 1847 in the United States. His father and his grandfather were teachers who taught students who could not speak or hear. Many of their students had been deaf all their lives. Bell's father and grandfather invented 'visible speech', which showed deaf people how to move their mouths to pronounce different letters.

Alexander Graham Bell demonstrated his invention – the first telephone.

The young Bell learnt that when air vibrations come into the ear, we hear sounds. A friend of his father's had demonstrated that principle to him by scattering sand on top of a drum, then playing the violin nearby – just like the experiment we tried on page 316. Vibrations from the violin made the drumhead vibrate. The sand, in turn, vibrated and shifted around.

In those days, around 1860, people had two ways to communicate over long distances. They could write letters or use the telegraph, which had been invented by Samuel Morse in 1840. The telegraph worked by sending electrical pulses through long wires. By following a code, now called Morse code, the pulses spelled out words.

Alexander Bell wondered whether wires could carry more complicated signals. Could they carry the sounds of the human voice? In an electrical shop in Boston, Bell and another inventor named Thomas Watson began building machines to test the idea.

Bell designed a machine with two parts that worked like the voice box and the ear, connected by electrical wire. One part of the machine, the transmitter, turned sounds into electricity and sent them through the wire. The other part, the receiver, turned the electrical signals back into sound.

In March 1876, the invention finally worked. Alexander Graham Bell spoke into the transmitter: 'Mr Watson! Come here – I want to see you!' Thomas Watson, 20 metres away in the next room, heard the words quite clearly.

In June 1876, Bell showed his invention at America's Centennial Exhibition in Philadelphia. The emperor of Brazil was there. He held the receiver to his ear, and from the far end of the hall, Alexander Graham Bell spoke into the transmitter, reciting words from Shakespeare's play *Hamlet*: 'To be, or not to be: that is the question.'

For his new invention, Bell received the Centennial Prize. Later that year, Bell and Watson attached their instruments to telegraph wires and spoke to each other between Boston and Cambridge, Massachusetts, two miles apart. It didn't take very long before people wanted telephones. Within a year, hundreds of households in Boston were connected by telephone wires.

Throughout the rest of his life, Alexander Graham Bell continued experimenting. He worked on early versions of phonograph records, air conditioners and X-ray machines. He even designed a circular kite. But he will always be remembered for his most important invention: the telephone.

Suggested Resources

Books

General

Ultimate Book of Science (Oxford Children's) 2010

Animals and Reptiles

Encyclopedia of Animals (Dorling Kindersley) 2006

A Colony of Ants and Other Insect Groups by Anna Claybourne (Raintree) 2013

Everything You Need to Know About Animals by Nicola Davies (Kingfisher) 2013

The Kingfisher Science Encyclopedia by Clive Gifford, Peter Mellet, Martin Redfern, *et al.* (Kingfisher) 2005

Big Book of Awesome Animals by Lynn Huggins-Cooper (QED) 2009

A Rookery of Penguins and Other Bird Groups by Jilly Hunt (Raintree) 2013

Interesting Invertebrates by Heidi Moore (Capstone Global) 2011

Classification of Animals by Casey Rand (Raintree) 2010

Look Inside a Pond by Louise Spilsbury (Raintree) 2013

Discover Science: Reptiles by Belinda Weber (Kingfisher) 2011

Ecology

Eyewitness: Ecology by Brian Lane (Dorling Kindersley) 2005

Ecosystems (Planet Earth) by Jim Pipe (TickTock) 2008

Fossils

The Fossil Girl: Mary Anning's Dinosaur Discovery by Catherine Brighton (Frances Lincoln) 2006

Discover Science: Rocks and Fossils by Chris Pellant (Kingfisher) 2011

How Does a Bone Become a Fossil by Melissa Stewart (Raintree) 2010

Human Body

Human Body: A Children's Encyclopedia (Dorling Kindersley) 2012

Let's Grow: Muscles and Bones: A Cross-Curricular Song by Suzy Davies (A & C Black) 2005

Understanding Your Muscles and Bones by Rebecca Treays (Usborne) 1997

Body: An Amazing Tour of Human Anatomy by Robert Winston (Dorling Kindersley) 2005

Astronomy

The Kingfisher Space Encyclopedia (Kingfisher) 2012

Inside Stars (Inside Series) by Andra Serlin Abramson, Mordecai-Mark Mac Low (American Museum of Natural History) 2011

Eyewitness: Astronomy by Kristen Lippincott (Dorling Kindersley) 2008

Eyewitness: Space Exploration by Carole Slott (Dorling Kindersley) 2009

Mobile Apps

GoSkyWatch Planetarium (GoSoftWorks) app for iPad [free]

Planets (Dana Peters) app for iPhone and iPad [free]

SkyView Free – Explore the Universe (Terminal Eleven) app for iPhone and iPad [free]

Online Resources

At-Bristol Science Centre: www.at-bristol.org.uk

Core Knowledge UK Science: www.coreknowledge.org.uk/science.php

Discovery Museum, Newcastle: www.twmuseums.org.uk/discovery

Edinburgh's Camera Obscura: www.camera-obscura.co.uk

Glasgow Science Centre: www.glasgowsciencecentre.org

Museum of the History of Science, Oxford: www.mhs.ox.ac.uk

Natural History Museum London: www.nhm.ac.uk

Royal Institution Christmas Lectures: www.richannel.org/christmas-lectures

Scale of the Universe 2 by Cary and Michael Huang: htwins.net/scale2

Science Museum, London: www.sciencemuseum.org.uk

ThinkTank, Birmingham Science Museum: www.thinktank.ac

Illustration and Photo Credits

Chris Beatrice, © 2011 Chris Beatrice: **13**

Mark Beech: **3, 5, 6, 12, 42, 70, 71, 72, 76, 77, 78 (a-b), 79, 80, 81, 82 (a-b), 83 (a-b), 84, 85, 216, 217 (a-b), 218, 219, 221, 294 (a)**

Pieter Brueghel the Elder (1526/1530–1569). *Peasant Wedding*, c.1567 (oil on panel). Kunsthistorisches Museum / WikiMedia Commons: **184 (a)**

Michelangelo Merisi da Caravaggio (1573-1610). *Supper at Emmaus*, c.1601 (oil on canvas). National Gallery, London / WikiMedia Commons: 177

Alfred Barron Clay (1831-68). *The Return of Charles II (1630-85) to Whitehall in 1660*, 1867 (oil on canvas). © Bolton Museum and Art Gallery, Lancashire, UK / The Bridgeman Art Library: **164**

Paul Collicutt: **48, 49, 50, 51, 53, 54, 56 (a-b), 57, 59, 60, 62, 63, 125 (a), 305, 333, 335, 336, 338, 341 (b), 342**

Charles West Cope (1811-1890). *Speaker Lenthall Asserting the Privileges of the Commons Against Charles I when the Attempt was made to Seize the Five Members*, 1866 (waterglass painting). WOA 2894, © Palace of Westminster Collection, www.parliament.uk/art: **158**

da Cortona, Pietro (1596–1669). *Caesar Giving Cleopatra the Throne of Egypt*, c.1637. Courtesy of Musée des Beaux-Arts de Lyon / WikiMedia Commons: **133**

Ed Dovey: **90**

Dutch School (17th Century). *The Embarkation of William III, Prince of Orange, at Helvoetsluis*, c.1688-99 (oil on canvas). Supplied by Royal Collection Trust / © HM Queen Elizabeth II 2013: **168**

English School (20th Century). *The Battle of Naseby*. Private Collection, © Look and Learn / The Bridgeman Art Library: **159**

English School (20th century). *King Charles II in Hiding*, 1966 (gouache on paper). Private Collection, © Look and Learn / The Bridgeman Art Library: **161**

Kate Farrer. *Icarus* (needlework). © Kate Farrer / www.bespokeembroidery.net: **187**

A.S. Forrest, 'The Days Seemed Very Long and Dreary to the Two Little Boys' from *Our Island Story* by Henrietta Marshall (1905): **119 (a)**

Benedetto Gennari Jr (1633–1715). *Mary d'Este*, 1690s. WikiMedia Commons: **167 (a)**

Benedetto Gennari Jr (1633–1715). *Portrait of King James II, in Garter Robes, the Crown and Sceptre on a Table Beside Him*. WikiMedia Commons: **166 (c)**

Girlguiding UK: **191 (c-h)**

The Great Fire of London, with Ludgate and Old St. Paul's, c.1670 (oil on canvas). Yale Center for British Art, Paul Mellon Collection: **165**

Catherine Green: **118, 142, 143 (a)**

Sir Herbert James Gunn (1893-1964). *Queen Elizabeth II in Coronation Robes*, 1954 (oil on canvas). Supplied by Royal Collection Trust / © HM Queen Elizabeth II 2013: **190**

Norman Hartnell and the Royal School of Needlework (RSN). *Queen Elizabeth II's Coronation Robes*, 1953. © HM Queen Elizabeth II 2013: **191 (a-b)**

Jodocus Hondius (1563-1612). *Sir Francis Drake*, c.1583 (oil on panel). National Portrait Gallery: **169**

Jean-Leon Huens (1921-82). *Portrait of Sir Isaac Newton* (colour litho). National Geographic Image Collection / The Bridgeman Art Library: **355**

Luke Jefford: **268 (a-b), 269 (b)**

Justus Sustermans (1597–1681). *Portrait of Galileo Galilei*, 1636. National Maritime Museum, Greenwich / WikiMedia Commons: **353**

John Tenniel: **9**, **10 (a-b)**, **11 (a-c)**, **14 (a-c)**, **15 (a-b)**, **17**, **18**

Martin Francois Tielemans (1784-1864). *Caroline Herschel (1750-1848)*, 1829. Private Collection / The Bridgeman Art Library: **356**

J. M. W. Turner (1775-1851). *The Fighting Temeraire*, 1839 (oil on canvas). National Gallery, London / WikiMedia Commons: **179**

Johannes Vermeer (1632–1675). *The Milkmaid*, c.1658 (oil on canvas). Rijksmuseum Amsterdam / WikiMedia Commons: **176**

Edward Ward (1816-1879). *The Lords and Commons Presenting the Crown to William and Mary*, 1867. WOA 2606, (c) Palace of Westminster Collection, www.parliament.uk/art: **167**

Robert Whelan and Emma Lennard: **189 (a-c)**, **190 (a)**

WikiMedia Commons: **65**, **105 (a)** (photo by Roger Wollstadt), **113 (b)**, **117 (a)** (photo by Neil Rickards), **127**, **129 (a)**, **129 (b)** (photo by Los Angeles County Museum of Art), **134** (photo by Guido Bertolotti), **137 (b)**, **138 (a)** (photo by Walters Art Museum), **143 (b)**, **149** (photo by The York Project), **151**, **155 (a)**, **160 (b)**, **166 (a-b)**, **172** (photo by Mike Peel), **185**, **193 (a-b)** (photos by Matthias Kabel), **205 (e)** (photo by Andy Davison), **207 (d)**, **208**, **209**, **210**, **211** (photo by Edwin Evans), **212** (photo by Alexander Kenney / Kungliga Operan), **213** (photo by Herbert Lambert), **214** (photo by David Hawgood), **215**, **225** (photo by Heinz-Dirk Luckhardt), **227 (a)** (photo by Peter Gordon), **290 (b)** (photo by Dave Russ), **351**

Text Credits and Sources

Poems

'Colonel Fazackerley Butterworth-Toast' by Charles Causley from *I Had a Little Cat – Collected Poems for Children* (Macmillan). © Charles Causley Estate. Reproduced by permission of David Higham Associates.

'By Myself' by Eloise Greenfield from *Honey, I Love and Other Love Poems* (HarperCollins Publishers). © Eloise Greenfield 1978. Reproduced by permission of Eloise Greenfield.

'Dream Variations' by Langston Hughes from *Collected Poems of Langston Hughes* (Vintage). © Estate of Langston Hughes. Reproduced by permission of David Higham Associates.

Stories and Legends

'Bertie and the Lion' from *The Butterfly Lion* by Michael Morpurgo. First published by HarperCollins Children's Books © Michael Morpurgo, 1996. Reproduced by permission of Michael Morpurgo.

'Finn MacCool and the Giant's Causeway' recorded by Glen Kinch and written by E2BN. Reproduced by permission of E2BN.

'The Hunting of the Great Bear' by Joseph Bruchac. © Joseph Bruchac. Reproduced by permission of Joseph Bruchac.

While every care has been taken to trace and acknowledge copyright, the editors tender their apologies for any accidental infringement where copyright has proved untraceable. They would be pleased to insert the appropriate acknowledgement in any subsequent edition of this publication.

Index